Sebastian Blohm

Large-Scale Pattern-Based Information Extraction from the World Wide Web

Large-Scale Pattern-Based Information Extraction from the World Wide Web

by
Sebastian Blohm

KIT Scientific Publishing

Dissertation, Karlsruher Institut für Technologie
Fakultät für Wirtschaftswissenschaften,
Tag der mündlichen Prüfung: 22.01.2010
Referenten: Prof. Dr. Rudi Studer
Korreferent: Prof. Dr. Dr. Lars Schmidt-Thieme

Impressum

Karlsruher Institut für Technologie (KIT)
KIT Scientific Publishing
Straße am Forum 2
D-76131 Karlsruhe
www.ksp.kit.edu

KIT – Universität des Landes Baden-Württemberg und nationales
Forschungszentrum in der Helmholtz-Gemeinschaft

KIT Scientific Publishing 2011
Print on Demand

ISBN 978-3-86644-479-9

Abstract

Extracting information from text is the task of obtaining structured, machine-processable facts from information that is mentioned in an unstructured manner. It thus allows systems to automatically aggregate information for further analysis, efficient retrieval, automatic validation, or appropriate visualization. Information Extraction systems require a model that describes how to identify relevant target information in texts. These models need to be adapted to the exact nature of the target information and to the nature of the textual input, which is typically accomplished by means of Machine Learning techniques that generate such models based on examples. One particular type of Information Extraction models are textual patterns. Textual patterns are underspecified explicit descriptions of text fragments. The automatic induction of such patterns from example text fragments which are known to contain target information is a common way to learn this type of extraction models.

This thesis explores the potential of using textual patterns for Information Extraction from the World Wide Web. We review and discuss a large body of related work by describing it within a common framework. Then, we empirically analyze the effects of a multitude of design choices in pattern-based Information Extraction systems. In particular, we investigate how patterns can be filtered appropriately. We show how corpora of different nature can be exploited beneficially and how the nature of the patterns influences extraction quality. Finally, we present new ways of mining textual patterns by modelling pattern induction as a well-understood type of Data Mining problems.

Acknowledgements

I am indebted to many people who guided and supported me during working towards my Ph.D. and writing this thesis. Most prominently, these are my advisors Rudi Studer and Philipp Cimiano. Rudi Studer gave me the chance to do this research and the guidance, trust and freedom I needed to complete it and learn a lot. Philipp Cimiano made this work possible through invaluable discussions, ideas and optimism.

Furthermore, I would like to thank my colleagues at the AIFB institute and in the X-Media project. The friendly, focused environment and the chance to build on a large body of previous experience was a great asset to me. Most of all, I would like to thank Johanna Völker, Krisztian Buza and Frank Dengler for their commitment, trust and patience during our collaborations and Sebastian Rudolph for comments and discussions during the production of this thesis.

Additionally, I am grateful to Yunyao Li, Thomas Hampp and Shiv Vaithyanathan and their colleagues at IBM for an intense collaboration during my stay at the Unstructured Information Mining group in Almaden which taught me entirely different perspectives on my research.

Most of the text in this thesis was written during my stay at TU Delft. I would like to thank Ursula and Philipp Cimiano and the Web Information Systems group of Geert-Jan Houben for their hospitality.

I owe a lot to Kathrin Heuser, Olesya Isaenko, Maria Maleshkova, Tobias Hauth, Stefan Kittler, Pascal Kretschmann, Egon Stemle, Jürgen Umbrich and Andreas Wagner who contributed their ideas and a lot of labor to my research and project work as thesis students or assistants in our lab.

Finally, I thank my parents and my sisters for supporting and motivating me not only but more intensely during my work towards this thesis.

My Ph.D. studies were financially supported by two generous Ph.D. Fellowship Awards from IBM and a travel grant from the Karlsruhe House of Young Scientists. During my Ph.D. studies I worked in the X-Media project sponsored by the European Commission as part of the Information Society Technologies (IST) program under EC grant number IST-FP6-026978.

Contents

List of Figures

List of Tables

Chapter 1

Introduction

1.1 Motivation

Technical and economic trends have increased the need for automatic extraction of information from large bodies of text such as the World Wide Web. The amount of content available on the Web is not only rapidly increasing but is also being produced in an ever more individualized manner because a growing number of private users create and share Web content [O'Reilly, 2009]. Grasping important aspects of this content automatically has become a key requirement for many applications. Web search increasingly relies on extracted information to establish a better correspondence between the user's query and the document's content by going beyond the mere presence or absence of words. In the face of a large amount of ever-growing Web content, market analysts rely on automatically extracted information to generate an overview of trends, rumors and customer opinions (cf. Chapter 10). As a further example, scientific research faces millions of potentially relevant documents (e.g. 18 million in the Medline medical literature database) the automatic analysis of which has the potential of supporting and accelerating scientific progress. A detailed description of applications of Information Extraction is given in Section 4.1.

The task of automatically extracting information from text can be thought of as compiling a list or some other structured representation of the facts that are needed for the task at hand. As an example, market analysts may compile a list of all products in the market they are surveying along with their vendors. From reading a sentence like

"Audi's new A4 TDI features a new common-rail injection system."

they conclude among other things that Audi is the maker of the A4 TDI and may add a corresponding assertion to their list.

Structured information has several advantages over text. In particular it is *more concise*, that is, looking at an appropriate table may save us reading hundreds of pages of text. Furthermore, it is *machine interpretable*. If the structure of the information is formalized in a way that a computer can process, the computer can carry out tasks with this information. If for example, a further list exists that specifies that "TDI" models feature a diesel engine, a computer would be able to answer the question "Does Audi produce vehicles with diesel engines?"

Concluding that Audi produces the A4 TDI when reading "Audi's new A4 TDI" is an almost trivial inference for a human reader and is yet hard for a machine because machines are limited to executing previously encoded instructions. Human readers would recognize Audi as a vehicle maker and if not would know that an unfamiliar capitalized word is likely to denote a company if the context suggests this. They further know that car makers tend to release new models which have names that frequently consist of combinations of letters and numbers. Several phenomena make it difficult if not impossible to produce a computer system that approaches such a phrase with the same inferences and the same ease as human readers. The *large variability* of language requires to account for an infinite amount of possible expressions that imply the same information. The *ambiguity* of terms and phrases further makes interpretation difficult. For instance, "A4" may also refer to an ISO standard paper size or a fashion magazine. Finally, the extraction has to perform faster than human interpretation of the content in order to keep up with the *scale* of the text bodies to be processed. Information Extraction therefore relies on strongly simplifying models that encode how relevant information may be mentioned in text. For the example phrase, such a model could contain the following instructions: If the sequence "'s new" is present in a text that is about the automotive domain and is preceded by a capitalized word x and followed by a combination of letters and numbers y, assume that x stands for the maker of y. This thesis is about ways to create and apply such models for extracting information from large amounts of Web documents.

1.2 Problem Statement

This thesis investigates a paradigm of Information Extraction that can be characterized as *global relation extraction* based on *seed examples*. This means that processing starts with a pre-defined relation and a small set of examples that stand in this relation (the "seeds"). Throughout this thesis, we will use the *locatedIn* relation as an example target relation. The following is an example seed set that can define a target relation:

Amsterdam	The Netherlands
Angers	France
Camptown	Lesotho
Hollywood	California
Karpacz	Poland
Mannheim	Germany
Plymouth	Massachusetts
Salinas	Brazil

Note that this is the only information on the relation the system has. Human readers can see from this list that on the left hand side, all items are cities and on the right hand side are countries. They know that a single city can be in only one country, that there are cities that carry the same name in different countries but that country names are relatively few and in the general case unique. However, this additional information relies on human background knowledge and is therefore not available for an automated system. It thus helps to imagine the seed examples as sequences of characters in an unfamiliar alphabet. All one would be able to do is to spot mentions of the seeds and observe commonalities and differences among them. The goal is to generate many more records for this table i.e., extracting further instances of this relation. To come up with these instances, observations are made about how known instances are mentioned in the text. These observations are generalized to a model that is characteristic of the relation. The model describes those properties (*features*) of text fragments that are good indicators that the fragments mention a target relation instance. In sum, the *input* is a small list of relation instances that (by example) define a relation and the intended *output* is a larger list of instances of the same relation. The focus of this work is *global relation extraction*, that is to find and formalize knowledge that holds generally true as opposed to *local* extraction that aims at deriving the information provided by a given sentence regardless of the question if it holds generally true. Furthermore we focus on *pattern-based* Information Extraction which is the most appropriate approach for *Web-based* extraction. Patterns are descriptions of text fragments that can be read as a rule: If a given pattern is present in a text fragment (i.e. the pattern *matches* that fragment) relevant information is present. We aim at automatically deriving such patterns from seed examples.

More formally, the task can be characterized as follows: Given a specific binary relation R, find instances $(x_1, x_2) \in Domain_R \times Range_R$ that stand in the relation R. Thereby, $Domain_R$ and $Range_R$ need not be known. The approach, i.e. learning an extraction model means finding a relation-specific mapping $match_R : T \to \{0,1\}$ that decides for each fragment of text $t \in T$, whether or not a given relation is expressed and in addition, an extraction function

$extract_R : T \rightarrow N^{Domain_R \times Range_R}$[1] that determines the relation instance that is present.

$$extract_R(t) = \{(x_1, x_2) | (x_1, x_2) \text{ is expressed at some position in } t\}$$

The decision that $match_R$ and $extract_R$ stand for may or may not happen in the same processing step. Clearly, with the help of statistical methods and with limited knowledge, $match_R$ can only be approximated. The goal is to produce an approximation that is precise in the sense that it does not produce many incorrect matches and has a large coverage thus identifying many of the possible extractions.

Given that we want to learn $match_R$ using observations on known outcomes on a subset of $match_R$'s domain we need countable *features* to actually formalize these observations. In its most general sense, each feature is a partial function $f : T \rightharpoondown D_f$ which decides if a given feature is present in a given text fragment $t \in T$ and if so, to which degree $d \in D_f$. We can assume $D_f = [0, 1]$ and for most features even $\{0, 1\}$.

1.3 What is Special about Operating at Web Scale?

The special focus of this thesis is on extracting information from very large document collections. There are several reasons why the large scale of the extraction task requires a set of approaches distinct from classical Information Extraction. Most prominently, both the computational costs for the induction of the extraction models (*"learning"*) and their application (*"matching"*) heavily depend on the amount of text that is processed. Most matching mechanisms evaluate all text fragments one by one making the amount of processing time grow linear with the amount of text. When operating with the entire Web, this is no longer acceptable. It is hence required to make use of indexing techniques to access relevant text sections directly. The focus of this thesis is thus on textual patterns which can be applied to search indicators for efficient matching. In very abstract terms, learning for Information Extraction is the process of observing relevant properties that allow the system to automatically identify in the data relevant information. This process requires to compare different relevant text fragments. The amount of possible comparisons grows more than linear with the amount of training input to be mined. Due to the diverse and uncontrolled nature of Web corpora techniques for mining large amount of text become necessary.

[1] We use 2^A to denote the powerset of A and N^A to denote the set of all possible multisets of zero or more elements from A.

On the upside, large corpora like the Web are an attractive source as they are rich in up-to-date information. At the same time, most relevant information is likely to appear in several positions redundantly so that errors that occur at one position may be corrected by extractions in other positions.

1.4 Trends in the Field of Information Extraction

While the extraction of information has been studied for a long time (cf. Section 4), recent developments in various areas of Computer Science, some of which we mention below, have shifted both the goals and the methods of Information Extraction research. Research in the area of *Semantic Web Technologies* has provided standard representations for formalized knowledge. These formalisms allow systems to express information about document content in a structure with a formally defined meaning that in turn enables automatic integration and interpretation of content. Semantic Web technologies allow for presentation (e.g. browsing or searching) of documents in a way that does justice to the formalized content or to infer information that is not explicitly specified but can be inferred by means of logical reasoning. At the same time, *Machine Learning* and *Data Mining* methods have experienced trends towards processing larger amounts of data as well as modeling and exploiting structure that is present in the data (cf. Section 2.3). These developments have enabled the uptake of Machine Learning and Data Mining methods in the field of *Computational Linguistics*. Today, many linguistic analysis steps such as parsing and part-of-speech tagging are routinely done with the help of learned models. In recent years, Information Extraction also started benefiting from such models. Finally, the sheer processing power that is available for extraction tasks has increased. Apart from the development of faster processors and data transfer mechanisms as well as larger main memory and storage solutions, this increase is due to the development of methods for distributed computing. As an example, the MapReduce framework [Dean and Ghemawat, 2008], one of the key technologies in Cloud Computing has been designed particularly with document analysis tasks in mind.

In addition to the technical novelties, the nature of the available content has triggered research in Information Extraction. The most prominent example is Wikipedia, which provides millions of articles of relatively high quality organized in categories and portals and partially enriched with semi-structured information. Examples of other attractive sources that have become available and processable for Information Extraction are the above-mentioned Medline texts and online forums.

1.5 Contribution

The contribution of this thesis consists of three major aspects.

- An overview is given of pattern-based Information Extraction systems with a strong focus on methods for the automatic induction of such patterns which have evolved approximately over the last 10 years. Furthermore, the focus is put on the extraction of binary relations the meaning of which is specified by example. A variety of pattern induction systems is summarized in an abstract framework and many design and configuration options are introduced. Such a framework is necessary as there is no agreed-upon view of the problem in this field of research, let a lone an accepted evaluation standard specialized on large-scale extraction. We use the framework to illustrate key design alternatives abstracting over different target relations and output structures, input sources and supervision models as well as implementation aspects. The framework is introduced in Chapter 5 along with a plugable implementation which is used in the experiments that constitute the technical contribution of this thesis.

- This thesis presents a series of experiments that aim at deepening the understanding of important design choices within the pattern induction framework. Most contributions that have been published in the field so far discuss their work on the system level. That is, almost every new study introduces a new extraction system which typically makes assumptions with regards to many dimensions of the extraction task and alters many design choices at once. However, to understand which key variables govern the setup of a good extraction system, the impact of alternative choices of each of them has to be understood. In particular with the aim of minimal supervision and automatic adaptation to new extraction tasks in mind, understanding the impact of design choices is important. In Chapter 6, alternative choices of how to filter for appropriate patterns is analyzed. Chapter 7 shows how corpus structure and size have impact on the bootstrapping behavior and in Chapter 9, the choice of pattern language is analyzed.

- Finally, an important focus of this work is on large scale extraction. While the application of patterns to the Web is quite common, scalability problems during mining have not been addressed in the literature. Most mining algorithms explore a huge space of possible patterns either by pairwise abstraction or top-down exploration of the search space (cf. Section 5.6.2 for details). Some other approaches are scalable, but do not allow for rich feature integration [Ravichandran and Hovy, 2001;

Talukdar et al., 2006]. In Chapter 8, pattern induction is modelled as a standard Data Mining problem (frequent itemset mining) which can be tackled with highly optimized data structures. In Chapter 9, this approach is taken further to allow for more flexible modeling of pattern languages. This way, we analyze, what elements patterns should be able to contain to improve extraction results.

The techniques presented in this thesis are discussed in the context of two application scenarios. One of them is based on a use case from a marketing department in the automotive industry (Chapter 10), the other builds on the idea of supporting communities in the compilation of knowledge resources that are useful for human and machine processing (Chapter 11).

1.6 Reader's Guide

This thesis consists of four parts. *Part I: Preliminaries*, introduces the context of this work. In Chapter 2, methodological and technical foundations from the neighboring fields are presented before the major Information Extraction tasks are introduced in Chapter 3. Chapter 4 presents related work from the field of Information Extraction along with applications and an overview of the relevant tools. *Part II: Large Scale Extraction Methods* begins by presenting a framework of iterative pattern-induction for Information Extraction (Chapter 5). Related systems are described by means of this framework. Further an implementation, the *Pronto* system, is introduced. Chapter 6 presents experimental results on the application of the Pronto system to Information Extraction from the Web using a standard search engine. In Chapter 7, further experiments show results about the extraction on a smaller corpus and the added benefit of Web extraction results to reduce the required input seeds. Chapter 8 presents an efficient mining algorithm for pattern induction applied in the Pronto system before Chapter 9 investigates alternatives in the choice of pattern structures. *Part III: Applications* describes two applications of the methods presented in this thesis. One of them supports market analysts in the automotive industry (Chapter 10) and one supports online communities in collaborative generation of semi-structured documents (Chapter 11). *Part IV: Conclusion* summarizes the findings and indicates potential for future work.

1.7 Published Results

We published the analysis of pattern filtering approaches as discussed in Chapter 6 to a large extend at the AAAI conference 2007 together with Philipp Cimiano and Egon Stemle [Blohm et al., 2007]. Some further results were presented at the 3rd Web as Corpus Workshop 2007 [Blohm and Cimiano, 2007]. Furthermore, we published results on the interaction of extraction from the Web and from Wikipedia at the ECML PKDD 2007 together with Philipp Cimiano [Blohm and Cimiano, 2007]. We presented the mining algorithm for pattern induction (Chapter 8) at the Ontology-Based Information Extraction Workshop at KI 2008 [Blohm and Cimiano, 2008]. The work on pattern expressivity (Chapter 9) is joint work with Krisztian Buza, Philipp Cimiano, and Lars Schmidt-Thieme and has been submitted to Taylor and Francis as a chapter of the book "Applied Semantic Technologies: Using Semantics in Intelligent Information Processing." Concerning the applications, the system for market analysis (Chapter 10) is deployed at an industrial partner's site as part of the software from the X-Media project. A paper about the on online community support (Chapter 11) has been published at the workshop on Wikipedia and Artificial Intelligence at AAAI 2008 with Markus Krötzsch and Philipp Cimiano [Blohm et al., 2008].

Exploratory studies on Machine Learning and Information Extraction have been conducted and published with Stephan Bloehdorn [Bloehdorn and Blohm, 2006] and Jürgen Umbrich [Umbrich and Blohm, 2008].

Part I

Preliminaries

Chapter 2

Methodological and Technical Foundations

The work in this thesis makes use of concepts and methods from various fields of research. In this chapter, we give an overview of these fields in order to put the work in this thesis in a context and to facilitate understanding for readers from various disciplines. Our goal is to convey an idea of the general concepts of the fields and then give details relevant to the work presented in this thesis. Hence, the overview is not intended to be exhaustive nor to balance the depth in which different aspects of the fields are covered. Books and seminal works that cover the respective fields in more depth are referenced in the respective sections. After introducing some basic concepts and terminology in the following sections, we present foundations of the field of *Natural Language Processing* before introducing methods from *Machine Learning and Data Mining* and explaining some basics of *Information Retrieval*.

2.1 Terminology

Various fields of research are concerned with the question of how information about facts in the world can be best represented for further processing. Research areas such as Logics, Databases, Semantic Web, Computational Linguistics and Artificial Intelligence have investigated this question from various points of view and with various goals in mind. Like most works in the field of Information Extraction, we approach the question how to represent information in a task-oriented way. In the following, we introduce the corresponding notation and terminology. Most of the terms should be intuitively clear to the reader; for some of them we point out the context from which they have been adopted. To ensure a general understandability of the thesis, we give preference to terms from widely adopted

Computer Science and mathematical terminology. They are enriched and complemented by terms from Computational Linguistics as well as Semantic Web research and Description Logics as its formal foundation. An overview of the history of formal modeling in general and Semantic Web formalisms can be found in a book by Pascal Hitzler et al. [2009].

2.1.1 Concepts and Relations

Almost all knowledge representation formalisms have in common that they allow statements about *objects*. Objects, also called *individuals*, are elementary units of processing and can stand in *relations* to each other. In the context of NLP, objects are sometimes referred to as (named) entities. In addition to objects there are values (e.g. numbers, specific strings etc.) which are used to describe objects and referred to as *literals*.

Objects are grouped in *classes*. Many statements are made on the level of classes of objects rather than on individual objects. In

"Tomatoes are red,"

the class of objects that qualify as tomato and the class of objects that qualify as red are under discussion. An object (such as a given tomato) can belong to one or more classes and is then called its *instance*. A class can be thought of as a mathematical set (e.g. X) of objects; its instances are the elements in the set. The number of instances that belong to a given class is called its *cardinality*. In particular in the tradition of formal semantics, the term *concept* is used for classes of objects. The view behind the term concept is that a distinction can be made between an extensional description of the concept which enumerates all instances and an intensional description which specifies criteria for determining whether an object belongs to a given concept.

When it comes to identifying objects and concepts, words seem to be a natural choice. For reasons described in Section 2.2, this leads to ambiguity. Semantic Web formalisms hence put forward *unique identifiers* and propose *name spaces* to ensure uniqueness.

Both, objects and classes can stand in *relations*. A relation is defined among several classes (e.g X and Y). A relation associates object. The associated objects are said to "stand in" that particular relation. The most common type of relation is binary (i.e. is defined between instances of two classes). In binary relations, the two classes involved are called *domain* and *range*. If the domain is X and the range is Y the relation can be formalized as a subset of the cross-product of domain and range $R \subseteq X \times Y$. All pairs $(x, y) \in R$ stand in the given relation. They are also called *instances of the relation*. In (x, y), we speak of x as the first *argument* and y as the second argument. All instances together form the *extension* of the relation.

Relations can have several general properties that provide additional knowledge about the instances standing in such a relation.

- *Symmetry:* A relation is symmetric if for every instance (x, y) the instance (y, x) exists as well. Symmetry requires that domain and range are the same. An example for a symmetric relation that specifies that x is married to y.

- *Functionality:* Functional relations are those for which at most one instance exists for each element of the domain. i.e. if $(x, y) \in R$ we know that there is no $(x, z) \in R$ with $y \neq z$. An example of a functional relation is that between persons and their birth dates. A functional relation is also called (partial) function.

- *Injection:* Injections are relations where no two values from the domain are related to the same element of the range. i.e. if $(x, y) \in R$ we know that there is no $(w, y) \in R$ with $w \neq x$. Injectivity is thus a dual property to functionality and also referred to as *inverse functionality*. An example of an injective relation is the relation between a home and its address.

- *Transitivity:* A relation is called transitive if relatedness is "passed on" in the sense that if (x, y) stand in a given relation and so do (y, z) also (x, z) stand in this relation. An example of a transitive relation is that of a person being older than another person.

- *Reflexivity:* A relation is reflexive if for every element x in the domain the instance (x, x) is in the extension of the relation. An example is the relation of two objects having the same color.

Classes can be related as well. The relations between classes correspond essentially to classical set algebraic operations. We only consider here the sub-class relationship which corresponds to the subset operator.

2.1.2 Ontologies

If a formal framework with a formally defined meaning is used to specify a shared conceptualization of a domain of interest, this specification is called an *ontology* [Studer et al., 1998]. Ontologies are widely used to formalize knowledge in particular in topic domains where an unambiguous definition of a complex terminology is needed such as in Genomics [Ashburner et al., 2000] and Medicine

[Smith et al., 2007]. The benefit of a formally defined ontology is that inferences on the information provided can be made. If the information that Peter is older than Holger and that Holger is older than Markus is given and the ontology specifies that the relation "is older than" is transitive, a system can automatically infer that Peter is older than Markus.

A special simple type of ontologies are taxonomies in which classes are arranged in a hierarchical structure by means of a single relation. The hierarchical nature of the relation requires that the relation is transitive and anti-symmetric (i.e. does not have any cycles). The most common relation for taxonomies is the subclass relation. If a class X is a subclass of Y, all instances of X are also instances of Y. We show here a naive and incomplete biological subclass hierarchy:

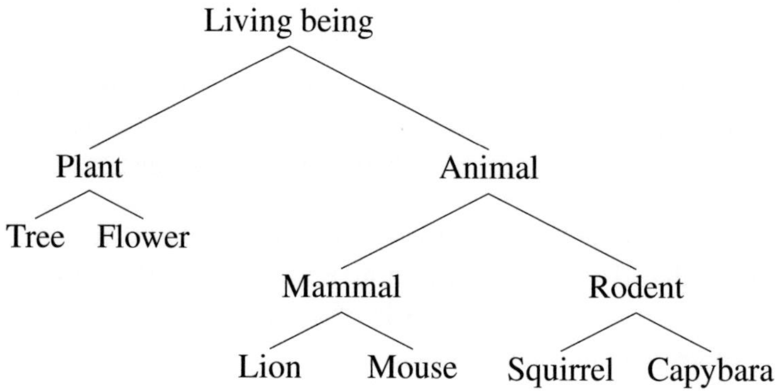

An example of an instance of the subclass relation is the class "Lion" which is a subclass of the class "Mammal." Taxonomies allow primarily one type of inference namely that of inferring relation instances by means of transitivity, thus one can infer that lions are also animals and living beings. Taxonomies are commonly described by means of a *tree* structure in which all classes are connected to their immediately related classes. Using the tree metaphor, the topmost elements are referred to as *roots*, the elements that stand in the relation to a given X and lie above X are called the *root path* of X because they constitute exactly those classes which connect X with the root. An example biological taxonomy could have "Living being" as root and the root path of "Lion" could be "Lion, Mammal, Animal, Living being." As in our example there are no further specifications of types of lions, "Lion" lion is a *leaf*. Some taxonomies are not trees but arbitrary partial orders. This would allow a class to be subclass of several classes.

2.2 Natural Language Processing

Natural Language Processing (NLP) is a subfield of Computational Linguistics that is concerned with the application of linguistic methods to the analysis and generation of natural language statements. Natural language is our primary means of communication and can be characterized as a set of symbols, which we arrange in a structure form to statements that convey a certain meaning. The structure of a language statement is referred to as its *syntax* and the meaning as its *semantics*. The field of Computational Linguistics and NLP has proposed a great variety of conceptualizations and formalisms to describe language. They differ with regard to the aspects of language they capture and the goals they have been designed for. In fact, the question of how to conceptualize language interacts heavily with research on human cognition, mathematical logic and philosophy.

When aiming at NLP, more specifically the extraction of information, the conceptualization becomes driven by what helps to computationally process language as far as that is needed to extract the target information. The methods from the field of NLP presented here are those which have been widely applied. Therefore they can typically be handled well both by human designers and administrators of NLP systems and computationally by machines. In the remainder of this section, we first discuss some NLP terms and methods to describe and model language at a word level before going into the representation and interpretation of structure.

2.2.1 Words and their Semantics

Words can be characterized in many ways which typically formalize some aspect of the meaning they convey or the syntactic role they play in the structural composition of language. A common and rather coarse conceptualization of a word is the so-called "semiotic triangle" by Ogden and Richard [1923] who distinguish the "symbol" of a word, its "referent" and the "thought of reference". The symbol is the realization of the word for the purpose of communication, i.e. in written language the *surface string* by which it is written. The referent constitutes the real world objects that are denoted by the symbol and the "thought of reference" (also *concept* [Sowa, 2000] or analogous in Section 2.3.1) is the abstract intended meaning which is denoted.

Before text can be processed automatically on a word-level basis, the individual units in a sentence have to be identified. In NLP, the notion of a *token* is used for the minimal textual elements. Most tokenizers which are used for this task separate tokens by white space and take into account punctuation. The notion of a token is distinct from that of a word as special characters may be considered tokens, too. Furthermore, there may be *multi-word expressions* which are the actual meaning-bearing units. As an example, the sentence

"I called her on the cell phone."

contains seven words, eight tokens, and one multi-word expression ("cell phone").

Lexical Semantics

One way to formalize the meaning of words is to characterize relations between word senses. As it turns out, one and the same symbol can denote various concepts, and concepts can share (part of) the objects they denote. The following are the most common lexical relations which capture limited aspects of the meaning of the involved words.

Synonymy is the relation between two words that have the same meaning in some context. They can be exchanged in that context without altering its meaning (which is why one synonym of "synonymous" is "interchangeable").

Homonymy means that the same symbol denotes distinct concepts. For example, "bow" as the front of a ship or "bow" as the weapon. A special form of homonymy is polysemy where the two polysemous concepts are different but related (e.g. "foot" as in football and "foot" as in "foot of the mountain."

Hyponymy is a relation that holds between terms and generalizations of them. A hypernym of a word x is a word that denotes the same objects as x but also denotes further ones. x is then called the hyponym of that word. An example is "car" being a hyponym of "vehicle."

Meronymy is a relation that holds between objects and their parts. For example, "wheel" is a meronym of "car." There are various types of meronymy. For example, it can be distinguished, if something is a necessary or an optional part. Also different types of objects and entities have different types of parthood. As an example, "Frankfurt" only in a very general sense stands in the same relation to "Germany" as "Queen Elizabeth II" to "The Royal Family."

Antonymy is a relation between words that have opposite meanings. Antonymy is most clear in adjectives which clearly focus on one aspect ("hot" vs. "cold") but they exist among some verbs (e.g. "accelerate" vs. "break") as well as among nouns ("student" vs. "teacher").

The freely available lexical database *WordNet* [Miller, 1995] captures the relations synonymy, hyponymy and meronymy for nouns and several others for verbs and for adjectives. Synonymy is captured in form of "synsets" which list all words that (at least in one of their meanings) share a given meaning. All other relations are defined between such synsets. Apart from that, WordNet explicitly lists coordinate terms (words with a common hypernym) and indicators of frequency of usage.

Part-of-speech

A common way to capture the roles of words in the syntactic structure or specific aspects of their meaning is to assign them to word classes. The most common type of word class is called *part of speech* or grammatical category. The most prominent parts of speech are *noun*, *verb* and *adjective*. Nouns typically refer to real world things, like "espresso", "love" or "garbage" which can be further described by means of adjectives ("hot", "desperate", "worthless"). Verbs express actions e.g. "drink", "make" or "write." To test if two words belong to the same part of speech, we can make the *substitution test* and replace one for the other in a sentence and check if it remains *syntactically* correct. The process of assigning parts of speech to words in a text is called part-of-speech *tagging*. While a part of speech is a property of an individual word, one should note that tagging them requires to look at the context in which a word is used because homonymous words may belong to different parts of speech but cannot be distinguished by their surface string. For instance, "shower" may be an verb or a noun.

Table 2.1 lists the parts of speech used in the WSJ tagset [Marcus et al., 1993], a standard tagset originally used to annotate named entities in the Wall Street Journal corpus. We use the WSJ tagset in the experiments in Chapter 9. The tagset has special classes for non-word token types like numbers, symbols and special characters. Furthermore it adds *determiners* (e.g. "the"), *prepositions* (e.g. "before"), *pronouns* (e.g. "she") and *adverbs* (e.g. "violently") as well as some smaller classes. The major parts of speech are separated according to variants that are mainly due to *inflection*. Inflections are modifications of the words to express which role a given word plays in a given sentence. Verbs can have different forms for singular (one referent) or plural (several referents) and encode temporal aspects of the statement (*past tense*, *present*, *gerund*: "loaded", "loads", "loading"). Nouns are separated in singular and plural as well and adjectives allow for *positive* (e.g. "big"), *comparative* (e.g. "bigger"), and *superlative* ("biggest").

The part-of-speech tagging performed for the experiments presented in Chapter 9 was performed with a probabilistic tagger using an HMM model [Ciaramita and Altun, 2006] which was trained on the Penn Treebank [Marcus et al., 1993].

CC	Coordinating conjunction
TO	to
CD	Cardinal number
UH	Interjection
DT	Determiner
VB	Verb, base form
EX	Existential there
VBD	Verb, past tense
FW	Foreign word
VBG	Verb, gerund/present participle
IN	Preposition/subord.
VBN	Verb, past participle
JJ	Adjective
VBP	Verb, non-3rd person singular present
JJR	Adjective, comparative
VBZ	Verb, 3rd ps. sing. present
JJS	Adjective, superlative
WDT	wh-determiner
LS	List item marker
WP	wh-pronoun
MD	Modal
WP	Possessive wh-pronoun
NN	Noun, singular or mass
WRB	wh-adverb
NNS	Noun, plural
SYM	Symbol
NNP	Proper noun, singular
RP	Particle
NNPS	Proper noun, plural
RBS	Adverb, superlative
PDT	Predeterminer
RBR	Adverb, comparative
POS	Possessive ending
RB	Adverb
PRP	Personal pronoun
PP	Possessive pronoun

Table 2.1: Parts of speech in the WSJ tagset as used in our experiments. Classes for individual special characters omitted.

Other Classes of Words

Another way to classify words is grouping them into *lexemes*. A lexeme represents a group of words that can be derived from each other by means of *morphological* operations. One type of morphological modification is inflection as described above. Another one is the addition of pre- and postfixes that modify the meaning of the word ("reload"). For processing in NLP on a lexeme-basis (i.e. to ignore morphological modifications), words are assigned a *lemma*, which is a canonical form of a word (e.g. the infinitive of a verb).

A special class of words in NLP is that of *stopwords*. This application-dependant class contains all tokens that can be excluded from further processing because they can be safely assumed not to bear any meaning important to the application. As an example, search engines filter out words that are likely to be present on all pages so that their presence in a document does not contribute to determining the relevance of a page with regard to a query. Common stopwords are articles ("the", "a"), pronouns ("he", "who", "this"), prepositions ("on", "over") and conjuncts ("and", "or"). In several experiments we exclude patterns that consist only of stopwords. We use a stopword list that consists of the (alleged) stopwords excluded by Google as presented by the Wikimedia Foundation.[1]

2.2.2 Syntactic Analysis

Whether or not a natural language sentence is intelligible and what its exact meaning is, depends on the order in which words are arranged. The following example contains a sentence which appears wrong (3) and hence potentially unintelligible to English speakers and two sentences which share the same set of words but express different meanings (1,2).

"Mary drove from Saarbrücken to Stuttgart." (1)

"Mary drove from Stuttgart to Saarbrücken." (2)

"Stuttgart Mary drove to Saarbrücken from." (3)

A set of rules defining how correct utterances of a given language are built is called *grammar*. Various kinds of grammars exist. Almost all of them have in common that they break apart sentences into phrases of different types. They are

[1] http://meta.wikimedia.org/wiki/Stop_word_list

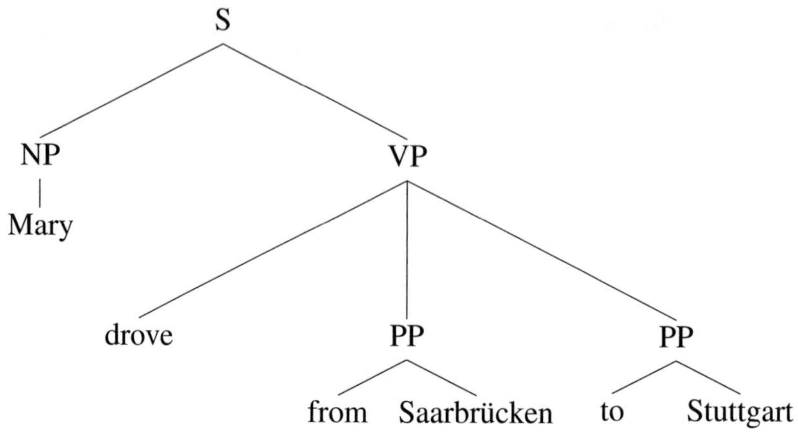

Figure 2.1: Parse tree example.

hence called *phrase structure grammars*. Sentence (1) from the above example contains the phrase "drove from Saarbrücken to Stuttgart" which has the role of describing the action that was taken (*verb phrase*). It can be further subdivided into the phrases "drove", "from Stuttgart" and "to Saarbrücken" (the latter two are examples of *prepositional phrases*). The difference in meaning between sentence (1) and sentence (2) can be explained by the different city names sharing a prepositional phrase with "to" and –likewise – sharing a prepositional phrase with "from." Another essential type of phrases are *noun phrases* which name and further describe the nouns in a sentence. Phrases of different kinds can play different *syntactic roles*. For example, "Mary" plays the role of the subject performing the action which is an argument of the verb phrase which consists of the predicate "drove" naming the action and prepositional phrases further specifying it.

Given a sentence in a language and its grammar, one can determine its phrase structure. Figure 2.1 visualizes the phrase structure of sentence (1). Such a structure allows IE systems to derive an assignment of syntactic roles which in turn may facilitate the extraction of information from the sentence.

The process of determining the phrase structure of a sentence is called syntactic parsing. Two challenges exist in parsing: ambiguity and a large hypothesis space. Consider the following example sentence:

"Mary drove Peter from Stuttgart to Saarbrücken."

The prepositional phrase "from Stuttgart" may be a part of the noun phrase "Peter from Stuttgart" or directly of "drove Peter from Stuttgart to Saarbrücken." In the former case, the phrase "from Stuttgart" names the origin of Peter in the latter the start of the journey. The parser would have to derive and output both alternative parses. The large hypothesis space is due to the fact that grammars are built up of many local rules the application of which may allow for the application of further rules. In many cases, rule applications are possible at some time during the process but do not lead to an ultimate result because at some later point, no further rule applications are possible. This can be thought of as rejecting a hypothesis of a partial parse. Due to these challenges, parsing takes a significant amount of time for each sentence processed (cf. the work of Ravichandran [2005] for a comparison of running times of different NLP techniques for Information Extraction). Full parsing is hence rarely used in Information Extraction which is why no particular natural language grammars and parsing systems are discussed here. An introduction to the currently very common probabilistic approaches to parsing is given by Manning and Schütze [1999] a detailed overview of many aspects of the syntactic structure of natural language is given in a book by Akmajian et al. [1995]. An alternative to parsing is *chunking*, a heuristic process to determine some phrases within a sentence without completely analyzing the phrase structure. Chunkers usually rely on part-of-speech tags in combination with a set of rules or with a trained statistical classifier and are able to operate much faster.

2.2.3 Summary

Information Extraction commonly makes use of many linguistic methods for text processing. The key concepts were introduced in this section. Techniques consist of classifying and labelling words along various linguistically motivated dimensions such as part-of-speech and lemmas. Further, some semantic aspects of words are established by describing relations that hold between words. Finally, the syntactic structure of text can be captured by parsing or chunking. An overview of the use of such techniques in the IE literature is given when individual extraction systems are introduced in Chapter 4 and Section 5.6. Some frameworks that integrate linguistic processing tools are presented in Section 4.1.2.

2.3 Machine Learning and Data Mining

Machine Learning is a rather interdisciplinary sub-field of computer science which is concerned with approaches to make computer programs improve by experience. The behavior of the programs thus not only depends on explicitly coded instructions but on a predefined model along with observations in the input data. Thereby, machines become able to adapt to aspects of the data they process which are not known or fully understood at the time when the machines are set up. Machine Learning can hence be considered part of the field of Artificial Intelligence and make use of concepts and methods from formal disciplines like logics, statistics and information theory but also from biology, cognitive science and other natural sciences as approaches are inspired by learning in living beings. Data Mining is a field of research that is concerned with deriving relevant information from large amounts of data. Thereby, both the model by which the obtained information is structured and the information itself can be derived during mining. Machine Learning and Data Mining have a large overlap in methods and models.[2]

Formally, Mitchell [1997] defines a Machine Learning problem as given by a *task*, a *performance measure* and *training experience*. As an example, a learning problem may be to create a named-entity tagger the task of which is to decide for a given word if it is of a specific entity type. The training experience consists of texts in which the entities of that type are labelled and the performance measure would be the number of choices correctly made by the tagger. Generally, the task is captured in form of a *target function* $f : \mathcal{X} \rightarrow \mathcal{Y}$ which constitutes the decisions that are to be learned. The decisions are just captured by mapping values from some *input space* $\mathcal{X}$ to values from the *output space* $\mathcal{Y}$. The mapping is not known in advance (otherwise learning would not be necessary) and can only be approximated. The individual dimensions of the input space are referred to as *features*. Training experience provides the learning system with *training examples* that can be used to learn to approximate the target function. The performance measure indicates the appropriateness of the approximation to some task frequently by means of verifying if the decisions the learned system makes on some *test examples* are appropriate to the task.

This overview covers methods that can be divided into *supervised* and *unsupervised* Machine Learning methods. This distinction is commonly made in the literature and affects task definition, performance measure and the nature of training experience. In supervised learning, training examples are of the form $(x, y) \in \mathcal{X} \times \mathcal{Y}$ and explicitly state values the target function should return for the training inputs. The goal is then to approximate an underlying target function $f : \mathcal{X} \rightarrow \mathcal{Y}$ which generalizes over the mapping presented during training. *Unsupervised* learning means that explicit target class values are not available. Training examples here are only values from $\mathcal{X}$. The target function learns to assign values from $\mathcal{Y}$, which in the unsupervised case is usually a set of cluster labels that is not specified in advance. The goal is to yield a target function that accounts for interesting properties of the data. Other unsupervised Data Mining methods derive some other abstract descriptions (e.g. Association Rules) of the data that do not map to individual data points.

[2] In many cases, the distinction of Machine Learning and Data Mining lies in the application. Other application-oriented bordering and overlapping fields are knowledge discovery in databases (KDD) and intelligent data analysis (IDA).

The supervised and unsupervised methods discussed here are selected to allow for an understanding of Machine Learning for Information Extraction in general and the methods applied in this thesis in particular. We leave out many alternative learning methods as well as paradigms not prominently employed for Information Extraction (e.g. reinforcement learning, most regression methods and most clustering techniques). Broader overviews and in-depth coverage of a large variety of methods can be found in the classical textbook by Mitchell on Machine Learning [1997] or in a more recent work by Kononenko and Kukar [2007] who cover both Machine Learning and Data Mining. An overview with focus on learning and Data Mining for Web-oriented applications is given by Liu [2007].

2.3.1 Supervised Methods

Supervised Machine Learning, as formalized above, aims at predicting outputs of the target function based on known training input-output pairs from the function. One distinguishes the prediction of continuous values, *regression*, and the prediction of a finite set of target values (referred to as classes or labels), *classification*. In both cases, the goal is to achieve a good generalization over the training examples that captures the important laws governing the data. Two possible types of errors should thereby be avoided: When *overfitting*, the model replicates the training data too closely and thereby includes into its decision aspects that do not belong to the interesting properties of the data (noise). On the other hand, if the approximation is too loose, overfitting is avoided, yet the error on the data may increase.

We present here several recent approaches for supervised learning. They were chosen to be those used most prominently in IE literature.

Support Vector Machines

Support vector machines (SVMs) [Boser et al., 1992; Vapnik, 1995] are a widely used method for binary classification (i.e. $|\mathcal{Y}| = 2$). They constitute an instance of the class of linear function models which aim at separating data in a vector space by means of a hyperplane. More specifically, SVMs compute the maximum margin hyperplane by iteratively selecting from the training examples so-called support vectors which along with some parameters define the separating hyperplane. In a trained SVM, the support vectors represent the training examples which are closest to the separating hyperplane. Classification consists of mapping an element from $\mathcal{X}$ to the side of the hyperplane it lies on and returning a label that corresponds to the label of the support vectors on this side of the hyperplane.

A method based on a separating hyperplane requires that most of the data points are linearly separatable, i.e. that there exists a hyperplane which correctly divides at least most of the data points into the desired classes. The so-called *Kernel trick* is employed to increase linear separatability by mapping the data from the input space $\mathcal{X}$ to a different, possibly higher-dimensional *feature space* $\mathcal{X}^*$ in which the desired separatability exists. The kernel trick is based on the observation that the only operator needed to compute a separating hyperplane in the feature space is the inner product. Conceptually, the kernel is a function $\kappa : \mathcal{X} \times \mathcal{X} \mapsto \mathbb{R}$ that given two elements $x, y \in \mathcal{X}$ from the input space, computes the inner product of the corresponding elements in the target space $\phi(x), \phi(y) \in \mathcal{X}^*$.

$$\kappa(x, y) \quad = \quad < \phi(x), \phi(y) >$$

The benefit of the kernel trick is that showing a limited set of properties for κ ensures that κ is appropriate for the use of the kernel without specifying ϕ explicitly. For example, the definitions of kernels for text processing in [Giuliano et al., 2007] are defined directly as a comparison operation on text fragments not separating the steps of embedding into the feature space and computation of an inner product. A detailed discussion of kernel-based Machine Learning methods with applications from the field of natural language processing and with the help of structured knowledge has been presented by Stephan Bloehdorn [2008].

Conditional Random Fields

Conditional Random Fields (CRF) [Sutton and Mccallum, 2006; Lafferty et al., 2001] are a class of very general discriminative probabilistic models. Probabilistic models introduce random variables $\mathbf{x}$ and $\mathbf{y}$ for the domain $\mathcal{X}$ and range $\mathcal{Y}$ of the target function. Discriminative probabilistic models are concerned with deriving the probability distribution $p(\mathbf{y}|\mathbf{x})$ which specifies the probability of a classification from $\mathcal{Y}$ given an input observation from $\mathcal{X}$. Types of models constitute a function of $\mathbf{x}$ and $\mathbf{y}$ with a set of parameters. Training is usually done by means of a maximum-likelihood estimation of parameters, that is the parameters are set in a way that maximizes the likelihood of the observed combinations of values from $\mathcal{X}$ and $\mathcal{Y}$.

CRF are very powerful because they model conditional dependance between observations of $\mathbf{X}$ and $\mathbf{Y}$. These dependencies can be arranged in graphs of arbitrary structure. Connections in the graph can encode linear order of observations or co-occurrence. Frequently, they are used to assign a sequence of labels to a sequence of observations a task which is common in computational linguistics (e.g. part-of-speech tagging), bioinformatics and speech recognition. In their most general version, they are an undirected graphical model. The graph G represents observations from $\mathcal{X}$ and $\mathcal{Y}$ as vertices V and dependencies in the model as edges

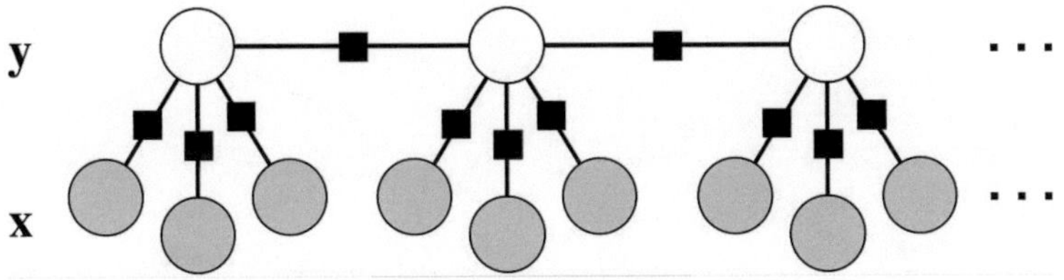

Figure 2.2: A linear-chain SVM with Markov assumption. Image due to [Sutton and Mccallum, 2006].

E. In the following, we describe the linear-chain CRF in which the structure of the graph is limited to a structure as indicated in Figure 2.2.

The model of the linear-chain CRF which additionally makes the assumptions that output labels at position t only depend on the input at t and the output label at position $t-1$ can be formalized as follows:

$$p(\mathbf{y}|\mathbf{x}) = \frac{1}{Z(\mathbf{x})} exp\left(\sum_{k=1}^{K} \lambda_k f_k\left(y_t, y_{t-1}, \mathbf{x}_t\right)\right)$$

Thereby $Z(\mathbf{x})$ is a normalization factor, $f_k(y_t, y_{t-1}, \mathbf{x}_t)$ stands for one of the K feature functions that determine if a given feature is expressed. The choice of f_k also binds the position t at which the feature is present. It indicates the probability with which a given y_t is output following a given y_{t-1} based on the distribution of inputs $\mathbf{x}_t$ at t. Note that the presence of the same feature at different positions is reflected by different feature functions. λ_k stands for the model parameter associated with the respective feature.

Practical linear-chain CRFs are likely to lift the Markov assumption by allowing for further dependencies among labels in the output sequence but at the same time tie parameters to each other assuming for example that a label that depends on a particular feature in the previous element of the sequence has the same dependency regardless of the position within the sequence. To account for more complex structures, the set of feature functions needs to be altered including their domain and range which in principle allows for the full distribution of observations.

Conditional Random Fields constitute in fact a framework that covers several other supervised probabilistic learning methods used in the literature including Naive Bayes classification and Logistic Regression.

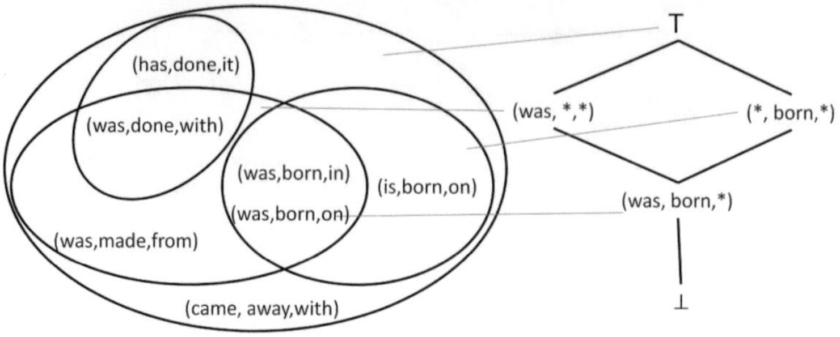

Figure 2.3: Concepts as sets of text fragments (left) and arranged in a lattice structure (right).

Concept Learning

In the following, we introduce Concept Learning, an early, non-statistical type of Machine Learning tasks [Winston, 1975; Mitchell, 1997]. While the methods from Concept Learning are not in the scope of this thesis, we use its basic notions to later give a generalized formal basis for the task of text pattern induction. Concept learning is concerned with deriving a *concept* as a Boolean function that decides for each object from a domain based on a set of *attributes* if it is an *instance of a concept*. As an example, in the domain of sportspersons, the concept of a "swimmer" may be detected based on the attribute "clothing" to have the value "swim suit" and the attribute "competition type" to be "race." Or, by the example of pattern-based Information Extraction which we will introduce later: In the domain of textual mentions, a concept may be the sentences that express the relation of a person being born at a particular date. The decision, whether a sentence belongs to this concept is based on the words of the mentions and their positions as attributes. Formally, a concept is a subset of the domain $\mathcal{X}$. c is the target function, the values of which are only known for the training examples. Concept learning is thus a supervised binary classification task ($\mathcal{Y} = \{0, 1\}$). Learning is performed by generating and testing *hypothesis functions* which are of the same type as c with the goal of deriving or approximating c. More specifically, learning is performed as a search process in the space of allowed hypotheses $X \subseteq \mathcal{X}$, which is also called the *hypothesis space* or *search space*. This space is defined by the formalization of the attributes Att. In the classical notion of concept learning, each attribute or *feature* $a \in Att$ corresponds to a function $a : \mathcal{X} \rightarrow D_a$ with a domain D_a. Each hypothesis and concept consists of a conjunction of *constraints*. In this simple formalization, each constraint γ_a on an attribute a can have three types of values $*$, $z \in D_a$ or $\emptyset$. A $*$ constraint is always true, a $\emptyset$ is always false and a constraint written as z is true for all $x \in X$ where $a(x) = z$. A concept and a hypothesis for a hypothesis space defined by the attributes $a_1, \ldots a_n$ can thus be written as a vector of constraints $\langle a_1, \ldots, a_n \rangle$.

We identify two properties of concept learning that are key to the understanding of text pattern induction:

- *Property 1:* There are several interesting properties of the hypothesis space. In particular, there exists a partial ordering $\leq$ with a single supremum $\top$ ("top") and single infimum $\bot$ ("bottom"). If for two concepts, $c_1 \leq c_2$ holds, then all instances of c_1 are also instances of c_2 . For each concept c holds $\bot \leq c \leq \top$. $\top$ and $\bot$ are abbreviations for "top" and "bottom" denoting the concepts that contain all or respectively no objects. The search for good hypothesis can start at the top, at the bottom, or proceed from both sides at a time. The corresponding traversal strategies are called "top-down" and "bottom-up" depending if they explore concepts in the space based by adding or by removing constraints. Figure 2.3 shows some concepts as sets of text fragments (left) and arranged in a lattice structure (right). The right-hand side shows all concepts that have at least two instances. The best concept in this space may be $(was, born, *)$ which could be found by starting with $(*, *, *)$ and becoming more restrictive (top-down) or by starting by concrete phrases and becoming less specific (bottom-up).

- *Property 2:* The size of the search space depends combinatorially on the number of attributes and the number of values each attribute can take. Specifically, the size of the search space corresponding to $\langle a_1, \ldots, a_n \rangle$ is $1 + \prod_{1 \ldots n} (|D_{a_n}| + 1)$. The constant 1 stands for $\bot$, the added 1 for each constraint stands for the option of setting it to $*$ (note that all options involving at least one constraint set to $\emptyset$ are equal to $\bot$).

Partial Supervision

The provision of training examples for supervised learning is one main cost factor. Approaches have been developed to reduce the number of labelled examples from $\mathcal{X}$ needed by making use of unlabelled examples. These techniques are referred to as "semi-supervised." One general approach, which plays a major role in the framework presented in Chapter 5 is *bootstrapping* which iteratively evolves a classifier by taking parts of its output as input in the next iteration. Bootstrapping is introduced in more detail and illustrated by applications from NLP in Section 4.2.2. Bootstrapping can be performed with any classifier. A special variant called *positive-only learning* requires the classifier to output some confidence score with the classification. The classifier is trained initially on positive examples only and iteratively re-trained always taking the examples which are classified negative with the highest confidence as artificial negative examples.

Also, semi-supervised variants of supervised learning algorithms exist [Liu, 2007] such as the transductive SVM or the biased SVM.

2.3.2 Unsupervised Methods

As described above, unsupervised methods derive target functions from data from an input space $\mathcal{X}$ in the absence of sample target output values from the functions domain $\mathcal{Y}$. The aim is to find some function that describes the data well for the purpose at hand. Such unsupervised methods help to produce an overview of the data without an explicit specification which distinctions are relevant. Most unsupervised methods are therefore particularly interesting for Data Mining.

Association Rule Mining

The goal of Association Rule Mining is to describe co-occurrence dependencies between Boolean attributes of objects. An example association rule is

"People who buy apples also buy bananas. This true in 85% of the apple purchase events which make up 20% of all purchase events."

Association rules formalize implications among the presence of attributes and come along with frequency indicators on how often the antecedent and the consequent rule apply. A set of association rules can constitute a target function that given an object $x \in \mathcal{X}$ and its attributes outputs associated attributes. The above textual example of an association rule could be part of a target function that associates apple shoppers with banana shoppers. However, association rule mining is not concerned with deriving an appropriate set of rules to describe the relevant underlying properties of the data but rather enumerates all those association rules that fulfill certain frequency criteria. In the simplest case, objects are characterized as a set of attributes from an alphabet A and association rules $B \rightarrow C with B, C \subseteq A$ give frequencies $\mathit{freq}(B \cup C|B)$ ("confidence") and $\mathit{freq}(B \cup C)$ ("support"). The frequency criterion is commonly defined as a frequency threshold freq_{min} as $\mathit{freq}(B \cup C) \geq \mathit{freq}_{min}$.

In the above example, "20%" corresponds to the support, "85%" is the confidence.

The challenge in association rule mining is the combinatorially many possible association rules that exist for a given alphabet A. There exist several standard algorithms for mining (cf. [Schmidt-Thieme, 2007; Liu, 2007] for overviews). The key idea of all of them is to organize co-occurrence counting in a way that avoids as far as possible counting attribute sets that will not contribute to any association rule. One such algorithm is Apriori [Agrawal and Srikant, 1994] which explores the space of possible attribute combinations in a depth-first manner and uses a Prefix tree data structure to count occurrences. Extensions of these algorithms for objects with complex structures have been proposed [Agrawal and Srikant, 1995; Srikant and Agrawal, 1997], most commonly, sequences of objects and attribute sets which are arranged in a taxonomy. In this thesis, we use techniques from association rule mining to generate textual pattern in Chapters 8 and 9. We do not use association rules themselves but exploit the algorithms to generate candidates for frequent textual patterns. The mining algorithms used are introduced in the respective chapters.

Clustering

The most common type of unsupervised learning method is *clustering* which comes in a large variety of forms. The general idea is to assign entities from the input space $\mathcal{X}$ to classes without a predefined criterion or set of examples for class membership. Clustering is done with regard to some notion of similarity. Clustering is not in the focus of the technical work presented here. However, it is used as a preliminary step in pattern induction in the Snowball system. [Agichtein and Gravano, 2000]

A popular clustering algorithm is *k-means* [Kaufman and Rousseeuw, 1990; Duda et al., 2001]. It is based on the principle of iterative relocation as it iteratively adapts the position of k elements from the input space $\mathcal{X}$ until they form good representatives of the training examples. More specifically, k-means initializes a set $R \subset \mathcal{X}, |R| = k$ of representatives and then, given a set of unlabelled training examples $X \subset \mathcal{X}$ repeats the following two steps until a stopping criterion is reached:

- for each $x \in X$ compute the closest representative $l(x)$ in R. $l(x) = \arg\min_{r \in R} |x - r|$. Thereby $|\cdot|$ is (usually) the squared Euclidean distance.
- Relocate r into the center of the cluster r defines: $newValue(r) = centroid(x \in X | l(x) = r)$.

Because of the local nature of the updates, k-means is of a hill-climbing nature and standard methods for avoiding local optima can be used such as repeated application, simulated annealing and an appropriate choice of stopping criteria. The algorithm makes the assumptions that the number k of target clusters is known beforehand and that all features of the input space are continuous so that centroids and distances can be computed. For both these assumptions there exist variants of the algorithm that circumvent the assumptions (e.g. k-medoids for arbitrary input spaces). For some applications, such as the construction of a terminological taxonomy from text [Cimiano, 2006], it is desirable to have a hierarchy of clusters.

A variant of k-means called bi-section k-means [Steinbach et al., 2000] does so by recursively partitioning (parts of) the input space using k-means with $k = 2$.

Geometric Embedding

Another form of unsupervised analysis of data is referred to by the general term *Geometric Embedding* which is a way to perform *dimension reduction* on the data by associating each data point to one representative out of a set of representatives which is arranged in some (low-dimensional) structure. The most popular instance of Geometric Embedding is the *Self-Organizing Map* (SOM) [Kohonen, 1997], which is defined by a set of representatives $m \in M$. Each m is associated with a reference element from the input space $rep_m \in \mathcal{X}$ and a position in an Euclidean space (the map) pos_m. It is necessary that there is a distance measure $|x_1, x_2|$ between any two elements x_1, x_2 from $\mathcal{X}$.

SOM training consists of adjusting the representatives such that assigning each element from $\mathcal{X}$ to its closest representative on the map renders a meaningful layout of the data from $\mathcal{X}$ on the map. This is achieved by iterating over the following steps for each x from a set of unlabelled training instances X repeatedly:

- Find a "winner" representative $w = arg\,min_m |rep_m, x|$
- Adjust rep_w towards x (such that $|rep_w, x|$) is decreased.
- Adjust the representatives which are close to w on the map towards x as well to a decreasing degree the larger the distance on the map.

After having been initialized with random elements from $\mathcal{X}$, followed by sufficient training, the SOM will develop a selectivity for similar input items in the same region of a map. This is due to the adjustment of neighbours during training. The arrangement of the map reflects interesting distributional aspects of the data. However, not necessarily all interesting aspects are taken into account due to the reduction of dimensions.

The map layout makes SOMs with a 2D space an appropriate tool for data visualization which has been used in an NLP context [Kohonen et al., 2000]. Furthermore, we experimented with using the SOM for inducing generative models of sequences [Strickert et al., 2005] and, by means of an extension, to detect prominent relation types among hyperlinked documents [Bloehdorn and Blohm, 2006].

2.4 Information Retrieval

Information Retrieval is concerned with the task of presenting for a given query the documents that are most relevant. The most prominent and extensively investigated retrieval task is that of Web Search. The characteristics of Web Search are that documents have to be chosen from a large amount of heterogeneous hyperlinked Web documents and that queries are typically posed in form of very few keywords. In this thesis, like in several other works in the field of Information Extraction, search engines are used as an interface to document collections. More specifically, we use the Google search engine the major principles of which we will present in this chapter. Introductions and overviews of research in the field of Information Retrieval can be found in books by Chakrabarti [2002], Baeza-Yates and Ribeiro-Neto [1999] as well as Liu [2007].

There are two important aspects in Web search: One is the efficiency of the processing because it is expected that in a period of less than one second the right documents are retrieved among millions of candidates. The other one is of course the quality of the search results, that is how well the search results are appropriate for the information need expressed in the query. Both efficiency and quality are achieved by developing retrieval data structures that capture the most important aspects of documents. These data structures are filled ahead of time (*indexing time*) and accessed, once a query is posed (*query time*).

The indexing time data processing in Web search can be described as the following steps:

- **Crawling:** Given that Web documents are stored distributed over servers all over the world without a central register, Web search engines need to detect and download the pages on their own. This is accomplished by recursively downloading pages and following the links on them for further downloads.

- **Document preprocessing:** Each page needs to be processed in order to make the relevant content accessible for search. Typically, this means parsing the data format (HTML, PDF, etc.) to isolate the textual content and, from there, perform normalization tasks which are typically the removal of stopwords and the replacement of words by their lemmas (see Section 2.2).

- **Static rank computation:** While the relevance of a document ultimately depends on the query, there are also indicators of relevance that only depend on the document itself. Indicators of such *static* ranking are the recency of information and the authority of a source. The PageRank measure for authority [Page et al., 1998] has been employed very successfully in the Google search engine. It recursively defines page authority via the authority of the pages linking to this page.

- **Indexing:** The resulting document representation is stored in an index. The general idea of retrieval indices is presented below.

At query time, the following is accomplished:

- **Query analysis:** Initially, the query needs to be analyzed. Special instructions like multi-word sequences (via quotes in Google) or the constraints on the target page's domain name or file type need to be separated from keywords and keywords need to undergo preprocessing analogous to the document preprocessing.

- **Index lookup:** The resulting representation of the query is used to retrieve the relevant documents from the index.

- **Relevance ranking:** For typical queries there exist more results than a user is willing to inspect. Therefore, the results need to be presented in a ranked order. The above-mentioned static ranking scores need to be integrated with query-dependant *dynamic* ranking scores. Their computation depends on the retrieval model employed (see below).

- **Presentation:** Ultimately the results need to be presented to the user. Typically, for each resulting document, a summary is generated that gives an indicator of why this document may be relevant to the query.

Several *retrieval models* exist that heuristically capture the relevance of a document to a given query. The *Boolean model* conceives each word in the language as a boolean attribute to each document which is true, if the word is present in the document and false otherwise. The query is processed as a constraint on the attributes of the documents. Queries may contain the Boolean operators and documents are considered relevant if they fulfill the constraints. The *Vector Space model* describes each document as a point in a vector space which has a dimension for each term in the language. The document's value on each dimension depends on the presence of the respective word in the document. A common function to assign such a value is the TF-IDF score which relates the number of times a word occurs in a document (term frequency) to the ratio of documents containing that word. Such vectors can be computed for both documents and queries and relevance is quantified by vector-space similarity (commonly cosine similarity). Furthermore, there exist probabilistic approaches such as the *Statistical language model* which is based on conditional probability distributions of queries and documents. The approach is to derive the distribution of a query given a document $Pr(q|d)$ based on observations in the documents and then use Bayes rule to estimate the probability of a document given a query $Pr(d|q)$.

Regardless of the retrieval model, Web search engines use a term-based index to retrieve documents. The index, sometimes referred to as "inverted index" can be thought of as an index just like those at the back of a book. It lists for each term all the documents in which the term appears (*postings list*). The process of answering a query composed of multiple terms is thus based on an intersection of the postings lists of the terms. Additionally, the position of a word within a document can be encoded to allow queries for sequences of words or to reward proximity of matches. When static ranking is employed, the postings lists are sorted by the static rank of the documents. Search engines then only intersect enough of the postings lists to display as many results as can be presented at a time. Google usually presents 10 results at a time, so that the intersection can end early. Along with the results, an estimate of the total number of results is given. Due to the partial intersection of the postings lists, this estimate can be inexact.

Chapter 3

Information Extraction Tasks

In very abstract terms, the goal of Information Extraction (IE) is to get hold of the key facts in a text in an automatic fashion. Thereby, natural language analysis is performed and the goal is to produce unambiguous output of a predefined format [Cunningham, 2005]. When confined from other subfields of Natural Language Processing (NLP), Information Extraction focuses on factual information of a simple nature and trades in-depth analysis for large coverage. It aims more at identifying important phrases and simple relations than at interpreting, summarizing or representing the content of the text as a whole. Applications of IE lie in the construction of general purpose resources like dictionaries or ontologies, advanced indexing for Information Retrieval and in areas where structured information about entities needs to be collected (some examples have been given in Section 7.2). Research in IE started with the manual generation of patterns and templates for identifying key information (cf. [Rau, 1991] and [Hearst, 1992] for early applications as well as [Cunningham, 2005] and [Grishman and Sundheim, 1996] for overviews). To reduce the manual effort required to create and maintain the patterns, techniques from the field of Machine Learning were applied to IE [Sarawagi, 2008; Nadeau and Sekine, 2007]. Today, a major goal is to scale methods up to very large document collections like Wikipedia (around 3 Million articles in English only), Medline (over 18 Million medical publications) or even the entire Web.

This chapter starts out by introducing a terminology for IE aspects as it will be used in the rest of the thesis. Then, emphasis is put on different IE tasks. To this end, a series of dimensions in which those can differ are distinguished before several prominent tasks are discussed. Finally, general challenges in the field of IE are outlined.

3.1 Terminology

Some terminology is required to describe various tasks and approaches in Information Extraction. In this thesis we will use a terminology which is close to the terminology used in the ACE 2008 task definition [NIST, 2008] and extends it where necessary while others will be introduced where they are needed.

An *entity* is something that can be referred to textually (such as a person, a real world object or a numerical value). It is to be distinguished from the text fragment (*string*) itself as an individual entity can be referred to by different strings (*synonymy*) and the same string can refer to different entities (*homonymy* or *polysemic* references).

A *relation* can hold between two or more entities. If not otherwise specified or clear from the context, we use the term relation in the sense of *semantic relation*. By semantic relation we mean that the entities which stand in the relation as well as the relation itself are grounded in some meaning outside the text. This grounding can take place by associating it to a concept in a formal ontology or a task-specific conceptualization. Sometimes, this grounding is made explicit, but most of the time, it is assumed that it can take place when the extracted information is used. The entities that are related are called its *arguments*. An individual assignment of entities to the arguments is called an *instance* of the relation, the set of all valid instances is the *extension* of the relation. Note that the term "relation" itself is used ambiguously in the literature. Sometimes authors use the term "relation" or also "relationship" when they mean what we introduced here as "relation instance." Relations can be of various *arities* that is have different numbers of arguments.

Hence, the goal of IE is to identify entities and relations in text. Depending on the task at hand, one may output entities and relation instances in a list or return with them their *mentions*, that is, the text fragments they occur in. When mentions are produced, IE can be viewed as an *annotation* process that is information about individual text fragments is derived and associated with the text. When extracting information in terms of entities and relations, several *attributes* of a given mention are of interest. For entities, this is typically a *type* that specifies what kind of entity has been found. To resolve synonymy, a unique *identifier* may be introduced. For relations, multiple identifiers need to be derived: the identifier of the target relation and one identifier for each argument.

3.2 Dimensions of Information Extraction Tasks

A great variety of IE tasks have been addressed in the literature, some of which are described here. Apart from a set of rather small publicly available standard data sets, IE is performed in many specialized setups. Because the appropriateness and potential of a given method depends on many factors, the transferability of approaches between setups is difficult to predict. Thus, each setup can be considered a separate task. We will define an IE task as the task to produce a particular *type of output* on a *corpus* of a particular nature with a certain given sort of *supervision and background knowledge*. In the following, we elaborate on several dimensions for each of these aspects.

The primary reason why automated IE is dependant on so many dimensions is the fact that it relies on regularities in the input which can be altered by many factors.

Structure of Target Output. One can distinguish the goal of *entity extraction* and *relation extraction*. In both cases, one may perform *local* or *global* extraction. While local extraction annotates entities and relations in the text, global extraction aims at identifying facts that hold generally true abstracting from their particular mention in the text. Note that global and local extraction will be covered to a large extent by the same methods as both tasks require identifying mentions of instances in the text. However, global extraction integrates over all mentions of a relation. It can thus afford to miss mentions without loosing out on performance as long as the same instances are identified elsewhere in the corpus. At the same time it can increase precision by deciding on the validity of the extraction based on several mentions. Yet, in order to be able to do so, global extraction may require greater disambiguation efforts because several mentions of the same instance can only be detected as such if the instance is identified in an unambiguous manner. In fact, these two alternative choices (entity extraction vs. relation extraction and local vs. global) account for four different tasks in the ACE 2008 evaluation (cf. Section 3.3). As a terminological note, we will use the term relations both for entities and relations when describing methods that apply to both entity and relation extraction. In these cases, entity extraction can be considered the 1-ary special case of relation extraction. Another option when it comes to extraction is to allow or disallow implicit mentions of a given relation. An implicit mention is one where the relation in question is not what the text is meant to convey at the position of the mention. As an example, the sentence "Madrid is the capital of Spain." does not say that Madrid is located in Spain, yet it is reasonable to assume so and thus allowing for implicit extraction but not for explicit.

Apart from entity and relation extraction there is the notion of *event extraction*. Events are bigger units of textual content that follow a pre-defined structure. The structure causes certain textual entities to play predefined roles in this event. The goal of event extraction is to identify role-fillers in the text. As an example, in the ACE 2007 evaluation there were events like "Life/Be-born", "Business/Merge-

Org" and "Personnel/Nominate" allowing for arguments like "Person", "Place", "Position", "Time-starting", "Org." In principle, events can be thought of as n-ary relations where individual arguments can be left empty and with emphasis on certain particular argument types (actor and recipient of an action, time, location). A special case of event extraction is *single event extraction* in which a given textual unit can be assumed to reflect exactly one event. One frequently addressed example for a single event extraction task is the Seminar Announcement extraction task [Freitag, 1998] in which 485 seminar postings have to be processed each describing one talk. The goal is to extract the speaker name, the title of the talk, as well as start and end time.

Target Output Relations. The nature of the target relations themselves have a great influence on how a given relation extraction task can be addressed. On the one hand, formally definable properties like *reflexivity*, *domain and range restrictions*, *cardinality*, *functionality/inverse functionality* (cf. Section 2.1 for a formal definition and description of these properties) can have an influence on how relation instances are extracted. Two studies [Alfonseca et al., 2006; Normand et al., 2009] have shown that knowing domain and range restrictions can increase the quality of extraction. Apart from that, the numerical distribution and linguistic properties of the mentions can have an influence on how the IE task presents itself. Intuitively, if the relation instances are mentioned more often and in an unambiguous way, they are easier to extract. The target relations are therefore an important aspect of the extraction task.

Nature of Input Text. The appropriateness of a given extraction method strongly depends on the nature of the text that it is applied to. Hence, we consider the nature of the text as part of the extraction task definition. Information Extraction has been frequently applied to news wire articles [Suchanek et al., 2009], classified advertisements [Embley et al., 1998], blog posts [Reiss et al., 2008], Wikipedia articles [Wu and Weld, 2007] or the entire Web [Brin, 1999]. For the task definition, we consider the following dimensions of text corpora as relevant:

- *Corpus size.* The size of a corpus naturally has a big impact on processing time. Most extraction mechanisms operate linear w.r.t the size of the corpus. Still, when very scarcely mentioned information is looked for in very large corpora, linearly processing the entire corpus may take too long. Some systems allow for faster extraction by using web search indexing techniques to be able to operate faster at extraction time [Cafarella et al., 2005; Cimiano and Staab, 2004; Blohm et al., 2007].

- *Lexical and syntactic variability*. Given that IE exploits regularities in the way in which instances are mentioned in the text, the rich variability that natural language allows may render extraction difficult. Depending on the text source and purpose, variability may be limited. With this observation in mind, many studies have been conducted on text corpora that can be assumed to be well structured. For example, Hearst [1992] operated on *Grolier's American Academic Encyclopedia*, Suchanek et al. [2008] specifically exploited page category names in Wikipedia and Embley et al. [1998] specialized in classified advertisements.

- *Domain terminology*. A large body of work in IE is concerned with adapting IE systems to different topic domains. The biomedical domain for example features synonyms and surface string variations that can only be recognized by experts [Saric et al., 2004] as well as topic domain specific linguistic particularities [Netzel et al., 2003]. Some domain-specific studies and applications are discussed in Section 4.1.1.

- *Confidence in content*. While the representation and aggregation of uncertain knowledge is a research area in its own right, contradictions, errata and possibly even spam have to be dealt with when aiming at global extraction (i.e. finding globally true statements). Sources for such errors are multiple. On the one hand, extraction models are usually imperfect and generate a certain amount of false extractions. On the other hand, information may change over time, may depend on the point of view on a topic or may simply be false. Most global IE systems make choices with respect to exclusion of improbable information ranging from a support threshold (suggested by Brin [1999]) to entire frameworks for knowledge integration [Iria et al., 2006; Suchanek et al., 2009].

- *Language*. Finally, the language of the input is an important factor. Most research has been done on IE from the English language which is reflected by the fact that almost all studies cited here exclusively discuss English examples (for an overview with regard to entity extraction cf. [Nadeau and Sekine, 2007]). How much a given approach depends on the language typically depends on the use of language specific linguistic resources, features and heuristics.

Available Knowledge and Supervision. Apart from text, three types of input can be provided to IE. An *extraction model* encodes knowledge on how target information occurs in text. Such models can consist of textual patterns that are intended to match relevant text fragments or formalizations of statistical knowledge about such fragments. An example pattern for the *locatedIn* relation that contains cities and the countries they are located in is:

"flights to ANY_{ARG_1} , ANY_{ARG_2} from ANY airport"

Alternatively, in Machine Learning-based IE, the extraction model is learned from examples. In such cases, *training data* is required which comes usually in form of example annotations or example relation instances. Training data for the same relation could be the following set of positive examples $\{(Karlsruhe, Germany), (Tournai, Belgium)\}$.

Finally, further information on the structure of the textual input or the target output may be available. We will refer to this as *background knowledge*. Background knowledge could consist of a lexicon of possible arguments of relation instances: $\{Karlsruhe, Tournai\}$ and $\{Belgium, Germany\}$. Background knowledge can be general linguistic knowledge or information that specifically helps at extracting information of a particular type. Among those there is no clear-cut border. Linguistic knowledge may range from simple, generally applicable models that allow for token-wise tagging to formalized semantic knowledge. The most common example of the former is part-of-speech tagging [Rozenfeld and Feldman, 2006; Pantel and Pennacchiotti, 2006; Califf and Mooney, 1997; Wu and Weld, 2007; Bunescu and Mooney, 2006; Ruiz-Casado et al., 2005; Ciravegna, 2001; Culotta et al., 2006; Snow et al., 2004]. An example of the use of specific information is SOFIE [Suchanek et al., 2009] which incorporates a large ontology for verification and integration of extracted knowledge. More detailed examples on how background knowledge is employed in practice are given in Section 4. Some general principles of the formalization of semantic knowledge are described in Section 2.1.

3.3 Prominent extraction tasks

Some text corpora have been frequently used for evaluation and thus have contributed to defining interesting IE tasks. Among them are the seminar announcement dataset by Freitag [1998] and a job postings list by Califf [1997].

Initial comparative evaluations in the field of IE have been performed in the context of the Message Understanding Conferences (MUC) which were held between 1987 and 1997. An overview of the history of MUC has been published after the completion of the sixth of seven events [Grishman and Sundheim, 1996]. The tasks at MUC focused mainly on single event extraction on military reports and newswire texts. Over time, more and more complex templates were developed. As an example, the annotation of an entity of type organization would not only feature the organization's name but also a type (e.g. company), location information and alias names.

The ACE program[1] operated by the Speech Group at the U.S. National Institute of Standards and Technology (NIST) has set some standards for IE tasks. ACE stands for Automatic Content Extraction as the program aims to facilitate the investigation of various extraction paradigms. They are classified as "Entity Detection and Tracking" (EDT), "Relation Detection and Characterization" (RDC) and "Event Detection and Characterization" (EDC, not in 2008). In the 2008 competition [NIST, 2008], entity and relation extraction were evaluated separately, each in a local and a global manner and each with texts in the English and the Arabic language. Six pairs of training and testing corpora have been made available each with a different nature of text. The text types are broadcast news, broadcast conversations, newswire, weblog, usenet, conversational telephone speech. The size of the training corpora range around 50 thousand words). Seven types of target relations are considered with 18 subtypes in total [2].

All ACE tasks implicitly assume that entity extraction is a necessary prerequisite of relation extraction as all relations consider ACE entities a the candidate arguments for the relation instances.

3.4 Challenges in IE

There are three basic ideals that govern research in IE. *Quality* of extraction is one of them. Clearly, all IE systems try to avoid extracting wrong pieces of information or missing out on important content. Secondly, it is an ideal to *minimize human supervision* in the sense that as little information (which may come in various forms) as possible needs to be formalized by humans in advance. This can be achieved by resorting to available knowledge resources and by designing extraction algorithms in a way that allows them to make optimal use of as little supervision as possible. Finally, with a growing body of available texts and with increasing computational capacities, *scale* becomes an interesting factor for IE algorithms. On a technical level, a large variety of challenges exist:

- *Cost of preprocessing*: In spite of large advancements in recent years, the high computational costs and also the brittleness of tools for linguistic analysis (part-of-speech tagging, syntactic parsing etc.) is still an issue. As an

[1] `http://www.itl.nist.gov/iad/mig/tests/ace/`

[2] Note that there has not been an ACE evaluation in 2009. The Knowledge Base Population Track at TAC 2009 is the organizational successor. `http://apl.jhu.edu/~paulmac/kbp.html`

example, a study from 2005 [Ravichandran, 2005] argues based on experiments that a corpus of the size of one Terabyte would take a syntactic parser 388 years to parse.

- *Adaptivity*: As research strives to provide general understanding and solutions, care has to be taken in an inherently goal-driven field like IE not to develop systems that are only applicable to serving one particular task. Recognizing this issue, the MUC conferences started with MUC-5 to organize their challenges in two phases [Grishman and Sundheim, 1996] limiting the amount of adaptation effort: One phase in which only the general task was known and one (short) phase in which the actual data was provided and the systems could be configured to work with this data.

- *Ambiguity*: Language is by no means unambiguous. Although Information Extraction does not translate the textual content in an unambiguous representation but merely checks for the presence of certain words or other features at certain positions, the integration of synonyms and the resolution of polysemy are of importance. On a related note, the treatment of pronouns and other cases of coreferences may be required in order to get hold of the desired information.

- *Uncertainty handling*: When performing global IE, identifying the fact conveyed at a particular position in the text is not sufficient. Whether an extraction result constitutes a fact that holds true is not easy to assess. Reasons for that may be the evolution of facts over time, the limited reliability of resources, different views or conceptualizations of the aspects covered in the text or the limited reliability of the extraction process itself. The reliability of facts needs to be assessed when information is integrated globally. One way of handling the limited reliability of extraction results is assigning each fact a confidence score. However, in the general case, the different sources of lacking reliability cannot be weighted against each other.

3.5 Focus of this Thesis

This thesis studies approaches for Information Extraction at Web scale. The goal is to facilitate the collection of facts into knowledge repositories. We will demonstrate application of such automatically extracted repositories for informing user of market developments and supporting the creation of new information sources. This thesis is hence focuses on *global* extraction. Moreover, like in most studies in the literature, the focus is set on *binary relations*. This is due to several reasons. Knowledge Representation based on binary relations have been well studied both in theory (e.g. in the field of Description Logics (DL)) and in practical applications (as the widely used and standardized Semantic Web languages rely on binary relations). The wide adaptation of the DL-based OWL standard has shown how complex states of affairs can be modelled by means of several binary relations. With global extraction in mind, it is straight-forward that no distinction will be made between explicit and implicit relation mentions because the target output are not the mentions but the relation instances.

The studies presented in this thesis will work on a set of non-taxonomic relations with varying properties. While no assumptions are made with regard to logical properties of the target relations, it turns out that most relations are one-to-many or many-to-one or violate these constraints only rarely.

The main focus of this work lies in the extraction from the Web. This has several implications with regard to the nature of the input text. Most prominently, it is large and ever-evolving. In the general case, large lexical and syntactic variances have to be assumed as there is no central control governing the generation of web content. Wikipedia has also been studied as part of this thesis work. While still a Web corpus, Wikipedia provides a more controlled terminology and content quality which makes it a much-studied text collection for Information Extraction. At the same time, Wikipedia is less redundant. The differences (and potential of mutual benefit) of Wikipedia and Web data extraction are studied in this thesis.

The supervision paradigm applied in this work relies on the provision of a small number of positive examples for relation instances. Training is thus done in the absence of negative examples or with automatically generated negative examples. This makes it a *semi-supervised* learning task. The impact of token-wise lexico-semantic background knowledge (cf. Section 3.2) is studied as part of this thesis.

Chapter 4

Approaches to Information Extraction

This chapter gives an overview of the body of research and a range of applications related to this thesis. The goal is to present the previous studies on which the technical work of this thesis is built and to explore alternative and complementary approaches. The chapter is divided into three sections. By starting the related work overview with discussing *Applications and Evaluation*, we try to do justice to the fact that the field of Information Extraction is inherently goal-driven in the sense that it is less about modeling and understanding language as a whole and also less about modeling and handling the knowledge. IE rather aims at the efficient, possibly heuristic process of spotting key information in the text. Like in this thesis, *Machine Learning for Information Extraction* is the focus of most recent studies in the field of IE. The field of Machine Learning (ML) is concerned with inducing a model of given data by means of examples. This is attractive for IE because a task-specific model of how information is mentioned in text is required for each IE process and in many cases providing examples is easier than formalizing such a model manually. Finally, an overview is given on studies that are concerned with *Information Extraction and the Semantic Web*. The Semantic Web is concerned with making Web content machine understandable describing it by means of formalisms with explicit formal semantics. The Semantic Web thereby provides both attractive sources of formalized background knowledge and interesting applications because IE can be used to generate formalized metadata for Web content.

Recent overviews of IE literature include surveys by Sarawagi [2008] as well as Nadeau and Sekine [2007]. Sarawagi discusses entity extraction and relation extraction and further divides the field into rule-based and statistical approaches. A large set of tasks and applications is reviewed. Approaches are categorized by the task they solve, the methods they employ and the features that are used to describe mentions of entities and relations. When it comes to the detailed description of IE approaches, the survey limits itself to a small set of example solutions without discussing design alternatives. Furthermore, the survey features an overview over the task of "Management of Information Extraction Systems" covering aspects of document access and information integration. Nadeau and Sekine describe research in the field of named entity extraction in detail. Starting out with an overview over the development of the field since 1991, research is described in terms of the task addressed, the learning methods employed, the features used to describe textual mentions, and the methodology of evaluation. While this survey only covers entity extraction, many techniques, especially those concerned with learning extraction models, can be carried over to the extraction of relations. In both studies, the observation is made that while historically, IE operated with manually defined rules or patterns, more recent studies feature Machine Learning methods. They find the IE tasks to differ greatly in terms of the target corpora and the intended output. Furthermore, both surveys observe that, even though statistical models are more recent, both pattern-based and statistical models co-exist and there is no clear winner among them in the general case. In an article in the "Encyclopedia of Language and Linguistics", Cunningham [2005] gives an overview of the history of the field of IE and provides an overview of applications and some current developments.

4.1 Applications and Evaluation

Given the goal-oriented nature of IE, evaluation with respect to some target application is an important aspect of IE research. Evaluation of a system cannot take place ignoring the application it was designed for and conversely, systems need to show the appropriateness for some task in order constitute a valid contribution to the field. This section explores fields of applications for IE along with the text corpora and other resources they employ before introducing relevant tools and frameworks. Finally, modes of scientific evaluation are presented and discussed.

4.1.1 Evolution of Tasks and Applications

Research and development was driven by the growing interest in consolidated information on the Web in corporate settings as well as in science and research. Specialized search and browsing tools require extracted information to be able to provide relevant documents and facts. Another driving factor was the availability of resources that on the one hand provide a lot of information for extraction and on the other hand serve as auxiliary sources of background knowledge. We describe here some prominent applications, corpora and resources.

A prominent type of application for IE are specialized Web search and browsing tools. A popular subform of this, tools for aggregating advertisements such as price comparison websites or job search engine have been a focus of research from early on [Soderland et al., 1999; Embley et al., 1998]. Recently, IE results for many domains have been integrated in the general domain Web search engine Bing.[1] Bing thereby relies on IE results provided by Powerset [Converse et al., 2008]. Powerset's results are output of IE processing involving linguistic analysis on selected Web resources including Wikipedia.

Corporate applications differ from Web settings in several ways. On the one hand, size, confidentiality and nature of the texts are different, so that the IE tasks are posed differently [Fagin et al., 2003]. On the other hand, content authors, information system providers and information system users follow a common interest because they belong to the same organization [Blohm, 2005]. The possibly smaller size, the more uniform nature of the corpus and the common interest facilitate the use of IE as compared to open Web setups. Facilitating factors are that more background resources are available, the added value for the system provider is higher and spam can be neglected. In the field of information retrieval, specialized enterprise search solutions were developed such as Ontoprise SemanticMiner [Moench et al., 2003] or IBM Omnifind which provide enhanced and flexible text analysis as features. Special setups have been developed to extract and use corporate knowledge [Dadzie et al., 2008; Iria et al., 2007]. Due to the inherently closed and confidential setting of enterprise information systems, scientific evaluation is difficult in particular when it comes to comparing work on the same dataset. An exception is the Enron dataset which comprises 400 Megabytes of corporate e-mails which have been made public in the course of a lawsuit [Klimt and Yang, 2004]. This corpus has been used for IE for example by Yunyao Li et al. [2008].

In the domain of *scientific research*, CiteSeer [Giles et al., 1998] was one of the very early specialized search tools on the Web that heavily rely on IE. It uses IE to build a citation index of research publications that are available on the Web. Its initial form relied on a rule-based extraction process with manually encoded rules. While CiteSeer aims at indexing of research papers from all subject areas, much research effort has been put into facilitating research of particular domains. These and other efforts are sometimes referred to by the term "eScience", possibly to suggest that the automated processing actually takes over some of the work of the scientists. Depending on the subject, special measures need to be taken to account for domain specific terminology [Saric et al., 2004]. For the biomedical domain there are standard datasets for evaluation along with competitive challenges available. One example is the BioCreAtIvE event [Hirschman et al., 2005] for which

[1] `http://www.bing.com/`

the set of tasks consists of entity extraction tasks like gene name identification and normalization and relation extraction like protein-protein interaction.

Most applications that are in use today are search oriented. For search, template-like metadata (e.g. bibliographic or product data) and entity detection are particularly useful. In addition there are applications that aim at summarizing and aggregating information across document borders. To this end, like in this thesis, global relation extraction is performed. For example Martin Hofmann-Apitius et al. [2008] detect entities and relations in biomedical texts and make them available for knowledge-aware browsing. Further areas of application for global relation extraction exist in fields like market analysis and in the creation of large knowledge bases as discussed in more detail in Chapters 10 and 11.

One of the most popular resources for IE is Wikipedia[2] which is a hypertextual encyclopedic reference that is continuously developed by volunteer authors following a wiki paradigm. It is available in many languages featuring 2.9 Million documents in English as of July 2009. Wikipedia is widely used for IE not only due to the broad domain coverage and the high quality of the content but also because of the rich amount of formalized or semi-formalized content in form of page categorization and attribute-value pairs presented in so-called infoboxes. This thesis comprises a set of experiments on IE on Wikipedia (Chapter 7) in the course of which related work on Wikipedia IE is discussed (Section 7.1).

An even larger and also rich information source is the Medline literature database provided by the U.S. National Library of Medicine.[3] It contains 18 million records describing publications in the life sciences domain from the 1960s on. The abstracts provided in the records are a popular source for IE (e.g. [Saric et al., 2004; McIntosh and Curran, 2009]). WordNet [Miller, 1995] is a highly structured and manually compiled lexical resource is which also has been used as background knowledge for IE (e.g. [Snow et al., 2004]). Recently, resources provided by the Open Linked Data initiative such as DBPedia [Auer et al., 2007] (e.g. [Kobilarov et al., 2009]) and YAGO [Suchanek et al., 2008] (e.g. [Suchanek et al., 2009]) have found use as resources for IE as well as the APIs of Web search engines (e.g. [Ravichandran and Hovy, 2001; Cimiano and Staab, 2004; Rosenfeld and Feldman, 2006]).

4.1.2 Tools and Frameworks

Information Extraction systems are relatively complex software artifacts. Apart from the actual decision where in the text a relevant entity or relation is men-

[2] `http://www.wikipedia.org`
[3] `http://www.nlm.nih.gov`

tioned, there are several tasks to accomplished. In particular, document input has to be processed, textual content has to be separated from markup and other non-textual document content. Furthermore, the descriptive features upon which the decision is based need to be computed which requires running NLP tools like sentence or paragraph splitters, part-of-speech taggers, chunkers, parsers and possibly supplemental IE tools. These features as well as extraction results have to be stored and represented in a way that provides convenient access for further processing. The most widely used IE frameworks are GATE [Cunningham et al., 2002] which is developed by the University of Sheffield and UIMA [Ferrucci and Lally, 2004] which was initially developed by IBM Research and is now an open source incubator project hosted by the Apache foundation. Both GATE and UIMA view feature computation and IE itself as annotation of text spans. They allow users to configure a cascade of annotators which is subsequently applied to the text on a document by document basis. Annotators access the text and previous annotations via a common data model. One of UIMA's key features is that this data model is strongly typed and can be extended programmatically. Both frameworks come with a set of basic annotators and provide a programming interface that allows developers to create annotators that execute arbitrary Java code. GATE comes with a rich and widely used pattern matcher called JAPE. From some personal experience with UIMA [Blohm, 2005; Umbrich and Blohm, 2008], we find it a convenient platform for developing lightweight annotators that enable the identification of straight-forward entities or perform relevant preprocessing steps. The developer has a lot of freedom as arbitrary code can be executed. This comes at the expense of interoperability and integratedness. Annotators can only be exchanged if they follow the same data model. Efforts exist to make use of the type system facility to increase interoperability [Hahn et al., 2007]. A further challenge for using UIMA with large scale IE is the not necessarily efficient access to annotations provided (due to specific API issues).

A recent rule-based IE system, "System Text for Information Extraction" or "System T", [4] has been released as a prototype by IBM Research. It allows pattern authors to define mentions of target instances and n-ary relations by means of a rule language called AQL. AQL has a syntax very similar to SQL but queries for text spans instead of database rows. Intuitively, user-defined types of text spans take the role of columns and co-occurrences of these spans take the role of rows. As an example, one could query for all phone numbers occurring within a maximum distance from a person name. Thereby, special AQL operators allow the user to define how phone numbers and person names are identified. The underlying view of IE taken is an algebraic one [Reiss et al., 2008] much like in database

[4] `http://www.alphaworks.ibm.com/tech/systemt/`

query processing which opens the way to matching optimizations. If in the above example, phone numbers are much cheaper to identify than person names, then System T would decide to search for numbers in the entire text and search for person names only within the relevant context window around the phone numbers.

A popular tool for Machine Learning for Information Extraction is the "Mallet" tool suite [McCallum, 2002]. It contains a set of sequence tagging tools that allow for supervised extraction by means of a user-defined set of token features. It supports learning methods like Hidden Markov Models, Maximum Entropy Markov Models, and Conditional Random Fields.

4.1.3 Evaluation

A number of evaluation initiatives and standard corpora exist for Information Extraction (cf. Section 3.3). Still evaluation is not straight-forward. Alberto Lavelli et al. [2008] give an overview of problems that may arise when evaluating and comparing IE systems. Upon these observations, they derive suggestions for improved IE evaluation. They distinguish "data problems", "problems of experimental design," and "problems of presentation." While data problems are mostly related to potential errors in annotation and formatting, problems in experimental design include varying approaches to train/test split selection, the lack of study of the impact of individual features, inconsistencies in penalization of variabilities in the text fragments extracted and incompatibilities of match count strategies. Concerning the presentation of results they observe that frequently not all interesting measures or diagrams are reported or that only an insufficient subset of standard corpora are used for evaluation. One should note that this survey has been written with a closed-corpus supervised extraction paradigm in mind. Many recent studies have varied the supervision method and aimed at extraction from the World Wide Web. This adds at least the following additional problems with regard to comparability.

- *The uncountability of negatives:* As the procedures do not actually process the entire Web, the amount of (correctly or incorrectly) not extracted information ("negatives") is not known. In the absence of false negative counts, recall cannot be given. Studies on Web-based extraction report absolute result counts [Ruiz-Casado et al., 2005; Tomita et al., 2006; Talukdar et al., 2006] or notions of relative recall [Pantel and Pennacchiotti, 2006].

- *The incomparability of corpus and corpus access:* Studies vary in the way the Web is accessed. Hardly reproducible approaches include downloading a fraction of the Web based on a set of queries beforehand

[Rosenfeld and Feldman, 2006] and crawling an undefined portion of the Web accessing it via an own search engine [Cafarella et al., 2005].

In principle, all Web-based extraction systems suffer from these problems as the content of the Web and the view search engines provide on them is changing permanently.

4.2 Machine Learning for Information Extraction

It is widely assumed in the Information Extraction community that Machine Learning techniques enable much faster and less labor intensive adaptation to tasks and domains [Sarawagi, 2008; Nadeau and Sekine, 2007; Ravichandran, 2005]. While the setup or domain adaptation of early IE systems consisted in formalizing general and task-specific linguistic knowledge, ML-based IE makes it possible to limit the human input to training examples in form of target instances or annotation of their mentions in the text. Most recent research, including this thesis, therefore focus on the automatic learning of IE models. One should note that few studies actually investigate the issue of saving labor and costs through the use of ML techniques for IE. Among the literature studied for this thesis, only one study quantifies the effort of training a system for an industrial application [Ciravegna, 2001]. To further investigate this issue one would have to contrast machine-learned versus manually created models both regarding performance and setup costs. However, a clear indicator for the trend towards ML is the large number of conference tracks and workshops at ML conferences devoted to IE [Kok et al., 2007; Blohm et al., 2008; Li et al., 2008] and conversely ML-dominated tracks and workshops at NLP conferences [Cardie and Isabelle, 2006; Carroll et al., 2007; Mooney et al., 2005].

This section focuses on three aspects in ML for IE, namely feature representation of text segments, the selection of models for learning and the training paradigm. A distinction is made between statistical ML methods and pattern-based approaches. Statistical methods are those which evolve a statistical model to decide if target information is present in a given text fragment. Pattern-based systems are often also referred to as rule-based. Their model is based on constraints on the input sequence they accept for abstraction. After presenting both types of approaches, we discuss their relative benefits and drawbacks in a separate subsection. Further closely related work is discussed when individual systems are introduced either in Sections 4.2.5 and 4.3 or in Chapter 5.

4.2.1 Features for Describing Textual Mentions

Information Extraction can take into account many different aspects of text segments to decide if a relevant piece of information is mentioned at a particular position. Those aspects have to be modelled as accessible features. In the simplest case, the features are exactly the tokens that constitute a textual mention. Those can be represented as a sequence or a set. Usually, further features improve the quality of extraction as they provide further information about the mentions. A feature d can be thought of as a function $f_d(s)$ with $f_d : S_d \mapsto R_d$ which assigns each textual segment s from the set of possible segments S_d a value from the feature's range R_d. Depending on the choice of S_d and R_d different types of features can be distinguished:

- *Token-based features* are those features in which S_d is the set of all individual minimal textual units (tokens). The most straight-forward token-based feature is the token's surface string itself. All others provide information that describe the token on a more general level or incorporate information that can be concluded from the context. Token-based features can capture lexical and semantic features of tokens like part-of-speech, number, case and synonyms as well as type information of various kinds (based on lists, taxonomies, named-entity taggers etc.) and orthographic features (capitalization, characters used etc.).

- *Mention-based features* encode information that holds for the entire mention (i.e. the text fragment which is under consideration) which is relevant for deciding whether or not the target relation is present at that position. Mention-based features can be any property that can be observed about a fragment of text.

- *Structural features* usually need to be encoded as combinations of several token-based or mention-based features. They describe the layout structure of the document or the textual or grammatical structure present in or derived from the text.

The most frequently used token-based features in IE apart from the surface string are POS [Rozenfeld and Feldman, 2006; Culotta et al., 2006; Califf and Mooney, 1997; Bunescu and Mooney, 2006; Ruiz-Casado et al., 2005; Wu and Weld, 2007; Pantel and Pennacchiotti, 2006; Alfonseca et al., 2006; Ciravegna, 2001] as well as named-entity types [Rosenfeld and Feldman, 2006; Culotta et al., 2006; Agichtein and Gravano, 2000; Bunescu and Mooney, 2006; Ruiz-Casado et al., 2005; Ciravegna, 2001]. Furthermore, regular expression matches can distinguish orthographic speciality [Brin, 1999;

Wu and Weld, 2007; Culotta et al., 2006] (e.g. those which render the presence of proper names likely). Several studies [Califf and Mooney, 1997; Yangarber, 2003] use synonym information by annotating WordNet synsets. The Yago ontology is used for the same purpose [Suchanek et al., 2009]. Morphological information for tokens is also applied [Ciravegna, 2001].

Wu and Weld [2007] as well as Wang et al. [2007] use corpus-specific mention-based features which are derived from structured information given on the page. The document URL is used as a feature by Brin [1999]. Claudio Giuliano et al. [2007] use typical word-based features (in particular the surface string and punctuation) in mention-based manner by aggregating surrounding tokens in a bag-of-words manner and combine token-based and mention-based features as a linear combination of kernels. Examples of structural features are dependency parse trees [Snow et al., 2004; Xu et al., 2007] and connecting paths in an ontology [Culotta et al., 2006].

4.2.2 Statistical Learning: Methods and Training

As introduced in Section 1.2, relation extraction (and entity extraction analogously) can be viewed as a classification task that decides if a given text fragment expresses the target relation and an additional processing step that identifies the arguments within the mention.

There are several ways in which these two steps are combined when relation extraction is modelled as a statistical learning problem.

- *Argument-driven:* First detect potential arguments of the relation in text and then decide, if they stand in the target relation. In the sentence "Sheffield is a city in England.", an argument-driven system would first spot "Sheffield" and "England" as possible relation arguments and then decide, if the textual context justifies asserting a *locatedIn* relation instance between them. Most statistical models base on a previous identification of the argument slots either by assuming named-entity tagging (possibly in coarse categories) to be performed prior to relation extraction or by employing sequence models that distinguish tokens.

- *Fragment-driven:* Alternatively, one can first identify a text fragment that is likely to hold a mention of a relation instance and then identify the arguments. In the above example, a fragment-driven approach would first spot "is a city in" as a good indicator of the *locatedIn* relation and then spot the arguments "Sheffield" and "England" in the text.

Argument-driven processing by means of named-entity tagging is almost the standard procedure [Rosenfeld and Feldman, 2006;

Rozenfeld and Feldman, 2006; Agichtein and Gravano, 2000; Yangarber, 2003; Bunescu and Mooney, 2006; Ruiz-Casado et al., 2005]. An alternative is the use of otherwise distinguished entities such as link-title pairs [Culotta et al., 2006]. Also argument-driven extractors are those relying on sequential models operating on token-based features [Culotta et al., 2006].

Details of these systems along with additional uses of classifiers for Information Extraction are discussed in Section 5.6.

A great variety of statistical classifiers have been applied to Information Extraction. The most common techniques are introduced in Chapter 2. Many approaches model the IE task as classification in a vector space using SVM [Snow et al., 2004], Naive Bayes [Etzioni et al., 2005] and classical Logistic Regression models. Due to the sequential nature of language, models that incorporate sequence structure like SVMs with sequence Kernels [Zelenko et al., 2003; Giuliano et al., 2007] and linear-chain Conditional Random Fields (CRF) are frequently employed. Finally, models that enable capturing more complex graph-like structures are frequently used [Culotta et al., 2006; Wu and Weld, 2007; Giuliano et al., 2007]. The graph structure can represent grammatical structure, hyperlinks between text segments, document metadata or similarity. Examples of the different uses for the literature are given below sorted both by the models they employ and the nature of the supervision. Furthermore unsupervised models like vector space clustering and the induction of Hidden Markov Models (HMMs) or statistics via suffix-tree computation have been used as intermediary learning steps to generate text patterns.

In Section 2.3 the distinction between *supervised and unsupervised* ML was introduced. When it comes to IE, several special forms of supervision have been proposed in the literature. This is due to the fact that the cost of supervision is one of the key cost factors of IE and some types of supervision are cheaper to come up with than others. Training of classifiers usually requires *positive and negative examples* to derive an appropriate model. There are so-called *semi-supervised* models that make use of both labelled an unlabelled data for training. For IE, those approaches which only require labelled input from positive examples, are a common variant of semi-supervision. They build on the idea of generating negative from unlabelled training data by assuming unlabelled positions to be negative.

One popular extension of supervised ML is *bootstrapping*. The general idea of bootstrapping-based IE is that models and extraction output can be co-evolved. A model can lead to new extraction output and extraction output can be used as training instances to improve the model. Bootstrapping approaches run over several iterations of training and application of the model. In terms of supervision, bootstrapping re-uses classification output as training examples to re-train the model in the next iteration. The assumption is that output is improved over the iterations. Thereby, bootstrapping can be applied to pattern-based or statistical models. The term bootstrapping is a reference to a proverb about pulling oneself out of a swamp by one's bootstraps. Initial work in applying this principle to IE has been done by Brin [1999] and Riloff and Jones [1999]. Since then, many adaptations of this paradigm have followed [Agichtein and Gravano, 2000; Etzioni et al., 2005; Pantel and Pennacchiotti, 2006; Yangarber, 2003; Culotta et al., 2006; Tomita et al., 2006; Talukdar et al., 2006; Xu et al., 2007]. Results show that hundreds and thousands of instances can be extracted with the provision of only around 10 training examples. The principle of bootstrapping is also at the heart of the framework introduced in Chapter 5 and a subject of investigation in Chapters 6 and 7.

One further variant of semi-supervised learning is *self-supervised* learning in which examples are generated from unlabelled data by means of labelling heuristics [Banko et al., 2007; Downey and Etzioni, 2008; Rozenfeld and Feldman, 2008]. Finally, Active Learning has been widely studied in the ML community and applied to Information Extraction [Thompson et al., 1999; Soderland et al., 1999].

Many ML methods for IE use methods that represent the input space as a vector space in which each dimension stands for some feature typically discarding order and structure of the text; other models use input space representations that preserve the sequential order of text or other structures. Approaches using *vector space* models include the one by Snow et al. [2004], TextRunner [Banko et al., 2007] and KnowItAll [Etzioni et al., 2005] who use Naive Bayes (or in the first case also standard Logistic Regression-based) classification to assess the quality of extracted instances. The feature sets for the Machine Learning method differ: Snow et al. and the KnowItAll system perform classification of instances based on which patterns they match. The Snowball system performs clustering based on the presence or absence of words. The clusters are then used to induce patterns which are further refined by means of bootstrapping.

In terms of *sequence models*, SVMs with appropriate Kernels are used [Suchanek et al., 2006; Bunescu and Mooney, 2006; Culotta and Sorensen, 2004; Giuliano et al., 2007]. Recently, CRF have become quite popular for this purpose [McCallum and Li, 2003; Culotta et al., 2006]. Giuliano et al. use a CRF for the entity extraction part of the study.

There are several sequence models that perform *unsupervised* learning to find relevant properties in the data, which are then used to generate textual patterns. Talukdar et al. [2006] use an algorithm for the induction of HMMs which describes words as emissions of an HMM. These emissions occur in the linear order of the words in the text. Each HMM describes a set of sequences that were aligned by so-called "trigger phrases." With appropriate techniques, HMMs on language-like sequences can be induced even from relatively noisy data [Strickert et al., 2005]. The induced transition probabilities are used to generate salient text patterns. Similarly, text sequences can be counted into a Suffix Tree data structure [Ravichandran and Hovy, 2001] which allows also to find frequent sequences that are likely to constitute good patterns.

Work on *structured input* frequently is also based on CRFs or SVMs. Zelenko et al. [2003] use Tree Kernels in combination with an SVM to represent dependency parse structure. A similar setup is presented by Culotta and Sorensen [2004] but augmented by token-wise structured features such as WordNet hypernyms. A graph-labeling model is used by Chen et al. [2006]. Known and candidate relation instances are modelled as vertices in a graph. Edges are introduced and weighted based on the similarity of the contexts they occur in. Known instances are assigned labels depending on the relation. The labels are then propagated in a way that allows for appropriate generalization over the examples.

4.2.3 Pattern Induction

Text patterns are underspecified and explicit representations of text sequences that are of the same nature as the textual content itself. Each text sequences either matches a given pattern or does not match it. Textual patterns are the most prominent form of rule-based extraction. They can be viewed as a set of constraints that each text fragment matching these patterns has to fulfill. Patterns are formalized as a sequence of text plus additional markup that essentially serves two purposes: On the one hand restricting matches with regard to additional features and on the other hand introducing underspecification by means of markup that allows for alternatives in matching. The set of markup allowed determines the expressivity of the patterns that can be written and thereby defines a *pattern class*.

An example of a pattern is:

"flights/NNP to/IN ANY_{ARG_1} ,/, ANY_{ARG_2} from/IN ANY airport/NN" (1)

Thereby, ANY_{ARG_1} is a *"wildcard"* that matches any token and the codes after the slashes specify part-of-speech constraints. The pattern thus encodes two types of token-based features: the token itself and its part-of-speech. The pattern matches at all positions where words which have the specified combinations of surface string and part-of-speech occur in the same order as in the pattern allowing for arbitrary matches at the wildcard positions. Argument wildcards distinguish position which hold the desired target information.

This section describes key developments in the automatic induction of patterns for Information Extraction and presents several dimensions in which induction approaches differ. A framework for pattern induction for relation extraction is presented in Chapter 5 which features also a more formal introduction to the notion of pattern used for the technical work presented in this thesis. A variety of approaches from the literature are then described by means of this framework. While this section provides an overview of the literature, we refer the reader to Section 5.6 for a systematic and detailed overview of pattern-based design alternatives. Furthermore, Chapter 9 presents a study on the impact of features from the pattern classes and therefore surveys related work with interesting pattern languages.

Approaches to learning textual patterns for IE differ with regard to the pattern class employed and with regard to the algorithm that is used.

All pattern induction algorithms create the patterns as generalizations over one or several textual mentions. These mentions along with the pattern class define a space of potential patterns. The algorithms differ with regard to how this space is explored. The most important requirements for pattern induction algorithms are good precision and recall as well as good runtime behavior. There are three general approaches to pattern induction.

- *Guided exploration:* Some algorithms explore the space *top-down* starting with very general patterns which tend to match too many mentions and then refine those by making them more specific i.e. adding constraints. The alternative is the *bottom-up* exploration where overly specific patterns are generalized by removing constraints. In both cases, pattern *quality assessment* plays an important role in deciding to remove or add constraints. A frequent approach to bottom-up induction is based on pairwise alignment of mentions. Based on the alignment, shared features are added as constraints and all others can take arbitrary values [Rosenfeld and Feldman, 2006; Rozenfeld and Feldman, 2006; Ruiz-Casado et al., 2005; Pantel et al., 2004]. In some cases, derived patterns are recursively fed back as candidates for further pairwise abstraction. Similarly, Brin groups mentions by common text between the arguments and then generalizes by deriving longest common substrings [Brin, 1999].

  Top-down approaches make additional assumptions to guide the exploration. Califf and Mooney [1997] operate top-down but only within the potential abstractions over two randomly selected mentions at a time. Soderland et al. operate similarly [1999] but additionally extend the patterns so that they are able to impose constraints on the content of the arguments. The $(LP)^2$ algorithm [Ciravegna, 2001] operates top-down adding constraints from one pattern only but ruling out alternatives in a greedy manner. This greediness has as a consequence that all mentions that are covered by a pattern that was induced will not take part in the induction of further patterns.

- *Frequency of mentions:* Other implementations guide the exploration of the pattern space with the help of information about the mentions, in particular their counts. Mentions are counted with the help of specialized datastructures like suffix trees [Ravichandran and Hovy, 2001; Pantel and Pennacchiotti, 2006] or automata [Talukdar et al., 2006] which are then used to determine appropriate generalizations.

- *Underspecified representation:* In the extreme case, no exploration takes place at all. Simply, the abstraction that makes text mentions to patterns takes place by discarding information when each mention is transferred to a pattern. The generalization is then implicitly done by the selection of the features that are not discarded and the quality is assured by subsequent pattern evaluation. Such approaches are taken by McIntosh and Curran [2009] using the two preceding and two following tokens as pattern, by Fabian Suchanek et al. [2009] using all tokens between the arguments as well as by Snow et al. [2004] who use dependency paths. Another approach which does not perform exploration of the pattern space is presented by Paşca et al. [2006]. Their patterns allow for underspecification because each token not only matches the exact word found at a position but all words that are distributionally similar within some corpus.

In Part II of this thesis, one algorithm is presented that finds all patterns with a certain minimum number of constraints that are the abstraction of at least two sequences in a bottom-up manner (Section 6.2.1) and two algorithms based on frequent itemset mining that exhaustively find all patterns with a certain number of mentions in the training data and certain minimum requirements on the constraints (Chapters 8 and 9).

While there exist a large amount of design alternatives for pattern-based Information Extraction, few studies actually compare the impact of design alternatives. Exceptions include a study by Tomita et al. [2006] in which setups very close to DIPRE [Brin, 1999] and Snowball [Agichtein and Gravano, 2000] are compared. Two studies investigate the use of knowledge about a relation's cardinality as additional background information in order to more precisely assess the quality of induced patterns [Alfonseca et al., 2006; Normand et al., 2009]. Alfonseca et al. develop a relatively task-specific filtering mechanism for patterns in a question answering scenario. Normand et al. show for one relation in a very simple but statistically nicely modelled extraction framework that precision and recall can be increased if it is known that a target relation is functional.

The PORE [Wang et al., 2007] system learns link-title relations in Wikipedia articles. While no text-based extraction in the stricter sense is performed because most features used exploit the particular structure of Wikipedia (categories, infoboxes etc.) rather than its textual context, an interesting extension of the bootstrapping approach is presented. PORE extends an algorithm for positive-only learning. Positive-only learning iteratively improves an initially weak classifier which is trained knowing a set of positive examples P. In each iteration, those examples which are classified as negative are added as negative training examples for the next iteration. PORE extends this procedure by evolving the positive examples also in a bootstrapping manner. Results show that this bootstrapping procedure performs better than extraction with one iteration of positive only learning alone.

In a recent study by McIntosh and Curran [2009], several aspects with regard to the choice of examples for bootstrapping of a Named-Entity-Categorizer are investigated in detail. They base on the observation that the choice of the seed instances is of crucial importance for the quality of the output. Even when starting out with 10 seeds and extracting 100 instances, precision can vary by up to 30%. The paper proposes to account for this phenomenon by taking an unsupervised bagging approach to extend the seeds: The instances extracted in the first iteration are distributed into many overlapping seed sets (the bags). Those then serve as seeds for the next iteration which is run once for each bag separately. The instances extracted starting with each of these bags is combined after one iteration and serves as a more stable and high-quality set of instances. Furthermore, McIntosh and Curran use *distributional similarity* as a measure for instance filtering: Newly derived instances are only accepted if they are more similar to the seeds than to other candidates. This is meant to prevent "semantic drift" i.e. the change of the semantics of the target relations by the introduction of more and more instances from a different relation.

4.2.4 Patterns vs. Statistical Models

The distinction in pattern-based approaches and approaches based on statistical ML is fairly commonly done [Sarawagi, 2008; Nadeau and Sekine, 2007]. While early work almost exclusively focused on patterns and fundamental methods in the field of ML continue to evolve, one cannot say that patterns are about to be replaced by learned methods. We present here the benefits of both types of approaches before discussing several studies that use both, patterns and statistical ML.

The strengths of pattern-based approaches stem from their explicit nature. On the one hand, the explicit nature allows human interpretation and verification. On the other hand, explicit patterns can be mined and matched with methods that use the explicit nature for optimization. For example, we present studies of this aspect in Chapters 8 and 9 in which optimized mining takes place by means of Frequent Itemset Mining. A similar approach is the one taken by Jindal and Liu [2006]. They use Sequential Pattern Mining – a modification of Frequent Itemset Mining – to derive textual patterns for classifying comparative sentences in product descriptions. While, like our approach, encoding sequence information, their model is not able to account for several constraints per word. Additionally, the scalability aspect has not been a focus of their study as mining has only been performed on a corpus of 2684 sentences with a very limited alphabet. For optimized matching, information retrieval indices have been used [Cimiano and Staab, 2004; Etzioni et al., 2005]. A notable variant of this approach is presented by Michael Cafarella et al. [2005] who use a specialized search engine that allows them to encode additional features (in particular part-of-speech tags) into the query. The study presented in Chapter 6 uses the Google Web search engine for pattern matching. Even in the absence of such an index, patterns can be matched efficiently using finite-state automata [Jurafsky and Martin, 2000]. A further advantage of patterns is that by using distinguished tokens as argument slots, the identification of arguments is straight-forward while statistical methods in most cases require previous identification of the arguments by means of named-entity-taggers or other markup [Bunescu and Mooney, 2006; Culotta et al., 2006].

Statistical models numerically compare descriptions of present candidate mentions to the model. During the process, a value is computed that quantifies how well the candidate fits the model. Thereby, each feature contributes to this score to a certain extent. This makes statistical models more robust to noise or variability in the data as a deviation in one feature can be compensated for by others. In the literature, statistical models are commonly used when a large number of features is integrated. For example, Culotta et al. [2006] integrate surrounding words, presence on type lexicons, matches of regular expressions for orthographic specialities, part-of-speech, frequent prefixes and suffixes and conjunctions of theses features. Yet, the pattern-based algorithm presented in Chapter 8 also allows us to integrate arbitrarily many finite-domain token-based features.

Because both patterns and statistical models have their advantages, they have been combined in various ways. Talukdar et al. [2006] induce a probabilistic model (an HMM) which is then used to generate patterns. The Snowball system [Agichtein and Gravano, 2000] employs a mixture model which uses vector space clustering to group relation mentions and then generates from each cluster patterns which also allow for inexact weighted matches. In several studies [Snow et al., 2004; Etzioni et al., 2005; Suchanek et al., 2009], pattern matches serve as features for a statistical model which decides which relation instances to keep and thereby integrates individual mentions of relation instances into global extraction results.

4.2.5 Systems and Tools

This section describes some learning IE tools that have been presented in the literature. The descriptions are meant to provide an overview of the systems. Implementation details that are relevant to the scope of this thesis are presented in more detail in Section 5.6.

The first system that combined pattern-based IE, a bootstrapping-based learning algorithm and the use of data from the Web was *DIPRE* by Brin [1999]. DIPRE was shown to learn instances of the *authorOf* relation starting from five positive examples. It takes an iterative induction approach which bootstraps a set of textual patterns. The induction algorithm is simple but effective as far as the evaluation on 20 output instances goes. DIPRE provides simple examples of a lot of design choices that were later refined. Patterns were filtered by "specificity" as measured by the number of tokens they contain. Arguments are filtered by regular expression patterns to ensure that they matched the format in which author names and their works are usually presented.

The *Snowball* relation extraction system [Agichtein and Gravano, 2000] is an early successor of DIPRE which comprises many refinements that have been influential on later developments. While Snowball like DIPRE builds on iterative pattern induction trained with a few seed examples, it presents a new view on patterns which allows for partial matches and it assumes that the arguments are identified prior to matching by a named-entity tagger. Also, the evaluation of extracted instances is introduced which builds on the degree of match and on the assumption that the extracted relation is many-to-one. The degree of match is essentially the Euclidean distance between bag-of-words vectors. Snowball's pattern induction algorithm which is introduced in Section 5.6.2 makes use of vector space clustering to group mentions which should be combined to a pattern. Snowball has been evaluated on a relatively large corpus of 180,000 news articles for extraction of instances of the *headquarteredIn* relation, i.e. companies and the location of their headquarters. The evaluation reports that for this relation, precision and recall of Snowball range at about 85%. It is compared against a baseline which simply counts co-occurrences of named entities which is aroung 5 percentage points worse in precision and has approximately the same recall.

The $(LP)^2$ single event extraction system [Ciravegna, 2001] somewhat stands in the tradition of wrapper induction. It takes a new perspective on the extraction task by viewing it as the insertion for start and end tags before and after the argument. Thereby, separate patterns are induced for start and end tags. $(LP)^2$ makes use of relatively many token-based features (part-of-speech, case, lemma, type-specific lexicons). Patterns (called rules in $(LP)^2$) are induced with a greedy bottom-up algorithm (cf. Section 5.6.2). As a novelty, $(LP)^2$ makes use of "contextual rules" to make sure that opening and closing tags are present in combination and of "correction rules" that eliminate small errors if the argument borders are misplaced by a small number of tokens. $(LP)^2$ has been evaluated on two standard datasets, the CMU seminar announcements and the job postings dataset (cf. Section 3.3) showing precision between 75% and 99% depending on the event slot.

The *KnowItAll* system [Etzioni et al., 2005] is an entity and relation extraction system that aims at global extraction. It takes a bootstrapping approach but features new ways in which supervision is provided. KnowItAll is among the first systems that access the Web via a search engine for IE. Instead of requiring seed examples as input, KnowItAll generates examples by means of generic text patterns (similar to Hearst patterns [1992]). A further novelty presented by KnowItAll is the use of distributional features, so-called "discriminators" for instance evaluation. Discriminators are simple generic patterns that have been designed for the purpose of searching for them on the Web in combination with newly extracted instances. The match counts in combination with various discriminators serve as features of an instance which are provided to a Naive Bayes classifier in order to decide if the instance is actually correct. KnowItAll has been evaluated on Web extraction of city and country entities as well as the relation between movies and the actors starring in them. Precision of between 60% and 80% has been reported for lists of between 100 and 1000 instances.

As an example of a fairly recent line of work which aims at IE from Wikipedia, we discuss here the *Kylin* system [Wu and Weld, 2007] which performs single event extraction on Wikipedia pages with the goal to enrich Wikipedia's semi-structured content presented in so-called "infoboxes." A study on IE from Wikipedia along with the discussion of further related work can be found in Chapter 7. Kylin learns to identify missing attribute values for infoboxes by training a cascade of statistical classifiers for three decisions: "Document classification" decides if a given infobox is appropriate for a given document. "Sentence classification" decides if a given sentence contains a target attribute value and an "extractor" finally extracts the argument. While document classification is done by a heuristic, sentence classification is done using a Maximum Entropy model with tokens and part-of-speech as features. The extractor then uses CRFs with a very large feature set most of which are token-based in nature. Kylin has been evaluated on four types of infoboxes reporting between 75% and 98% precision and around 60% recall.

A fairly generic and recent implementation of a system for closed-corpus relation extraction by means of statistical Machine Learning has been presented by Claudio Giuliano et al. [2007]. Relation extraction is done as a two step process featuring named-entity classification followed by relation classification. Named-entities are identified with a CRF model with a set of token-based features (surface string, part-of-speech, orthographic features such as capitalization, gazetter matches and n-gram context). Relations are extracted by means of classifying co-occurrences of identified named entities. For this purpose, an SVM with two different types of kernel is used: a bag-of words kernels that features the greater context and a sequence kernel for the local surroundings with a larger set of features (similar to the above). The system has mainly been built to study the impact of these kernels showing that the combination indeed leads to an improvement. Precision and recall are reported to be around 70%-80% on a TREC information retrieval evaluation corpus.

4.3 Information Extraction and the Semantic Web

The general idea of the Semantic Web vision [Berners-Lee et al., 2001] is to make Web data available for automatic inference. In particular, this requires the data to be structured according to a given schema. The Semantic Web community advocates formal ontologies as schemata. Both the creation of ontologies and the structuring of information are highly labour-intensive but can be partially performed or assisted by IE technology. In the following, we present work from the field of Ontology Learning as well as work that extracts data particularly with a Web scenario in mind.

4.3.1 Ontology Learning and Population

Ontology Learning aims at acquiring a domain model from data [Mädche and Staab, 2004] and is thus – if it is done from text – akin to Information Extraction. If it is done with the aim of finding new concepts and properties, Ontology Learning complements IE by providing the schema that extracted information can be formalized in.

Philipp Cimiano [2006] presents a topology of Ontology Learning tasks called "Ontology Learning Layer Cake" which organizes tasks belonging to Ontology Learning by increasing complexity meaning that more complex tasks rely on the output of less complex tasks. At the lower end of the layer cake, terminology-based tasks like "acquisition of the relevant terminology" and "acquisition of synonym terms / linguistic variants" can be found followed by the identification and organization of concepts and relations. "Instantiation of axiom schemata" and "definition of arbitrary axioms" form the upper end with regard to complexity.

Cimiano gives an overview of a large body of work in Ontology Learning before presenting approaches which among other things advance organization of concepts by means of agglomerative clustering and Formal Concept Analysis (FCA), a technique which is based on deriving a concept lattice (a partially ordered set with a distinguished supremum and infimum) that orders concepts by their properties. On a higher level in the layer cake, possible properties for concepts are learned by means of a set of predefined patterns and statistical correlation. Finally, among others, the PANKOW system is presented that performs global entity extraction for the purpose of adding instances to an ontology ("Ontology Population"). It matches a set of predefined patterns by means of a Web search engine. Match count estimates provided by the search engine are used to statistically assess the correctness of candidate entities.

Starting from the observation that most Ontology Learning systems do not exploit the expressivity that ontology formalisms like OWL provide, Johanna Völker [2008] focuses on learning "expressive ontologies", i.e. ontologies that formally give rich descriptions of their concepts and relations. The LExO and RELExO systems she presents are able to acquire class description in a semi-automatic manner. Sentences that describe a class are parsed using a dependency parser. With a set of hand-coded rules, the resulting dependency parse trees are translated into class descriptions. For example, one rule states that the application of an intersective adjective Adj (i.e. an adjective that further restricts the meaning of the noun it refers to) to a noun phrase NP defines a class consisting of the intersection of all entities for which NP applies with those for which Adj applies. e.g. "foul apples" is the intersection of the class of all apples with the class of all foul objects. In RELExO, the so-derived class descriptions are refined by asking questions to a user. Furthermore, the RoLExO system is able to learn restrictions for domain and range of relations (e.g. that the author of a publication needs to be a person) based on user answers on carefully chosen questions plus optional empirical observations (i.e. that the authors of all publications in the KB happen to be persons). To add more expressivity to learned ontologies, an algorithm called LeDA was presented that decides if two classes A and B are disjoint (e.g. by definition are not allowed to share any instance). For this purpose, a decision tree classifier was trained with a large set of features including comparison of the surface string, differences in distributional features of the class labels in several corpora and distance measures of associated texts (e.g. Wikipedia articles).

A recently published system by McDowell and Cafarella [2008] integrates several ideas from previous systems for extending existing ontologies. Their system, called OntoSyphon relies on both Hearst patterns for extraction (as in PANKOW [Cimiano et al., 2004]) and match counts for discrimination (as in KnowItAll [Etzioni et al., 2005]). It uses the Bindings Engine [Cafarella et al., 2005] for efficient annotation-aware matching.

4.3.2 Bringing Semantics to the World Wide Web

In the following, we present several pieces of related work that address the task of deriving knowledge from Web pages. These fall into two categories. Those, which focus on a rich schema [Suchanek et al., 2007; Suchanek et al., 2009; Culotta et al., 2006] and those which focus on operating at the scale of the Web but with lighter or undefined schema [Ravichandran, 2005; Banko et al., 2007;

Davidov et al., 2007]. The technical work of this thesis can also be viewed as part of the category with large scale and light-weight schema.

A widely used and large ontology that has been constructed by (heuristic) large scale IE from Web data is the YAGO ontology [Suchanek et al., 2008]. It has been constructed by bringing semi-structured data in Wikipedia into a structured form and has been used to integrate various data sources in the course of the Linked Data initiative [Bizer et al., 2009]. The construction of Yago makes use of the observation that authors assign articles to "Conceptual Categories" and "Relational Categories." Conceptual categories like "American physicists" allow the system to conclude by means of linguistic processing (among other things an alignment with WordNet) that the entity described on a page in this category is in fact a physicist. Similarly, relational categories like "1879 births" or "rivers in Germany" are translated to ontological facts. Furthermore, manually written patterns for the translation of Wikipedia infoboxes to ontological facts are employed as well as redirecting pages, which are used to conclude synonymy.

The authors of YAGO also present an innovative approach of integrating ontology T-box and A-box knowledge (from Yago) into the extraction process [Suchanek et al., 2009] by modeling the decision whether a given pattern match actually expresses a target relation instance in logical formulae. Ontological facts, pattern matches, the ontology T-box and some general rules on how a new relation instance can be deduced from them are modeled as formulae in propositional logic with associated weights. A good choice of patterns and instances is identified simultaneously by solving a maximum satisfiability problem (MAX-SAT). Solving a MAX-SAT problem is done by determining a variable assignment that maximises the number of satisfied clauses. Using the weights of the formulae solution of the MAX-SAT problem assigns weights to the variable assignments which indicate if they can be added to the knowledge base while keeping it as consistent as possible. The advantage of such a model is that three steps that frequently occur separately in Information Extraction can be treated by solving one maximum satisfiability problem: pattern selection, entity disambiguation and consistency checking. The system is evaluated on small text corpora of up to 2000 Wikipedia articles, 150 newspaper texts and 3440 Web documents. It produces results with very high precision ($\geq 90\%$ for most relations) which beats state-of-the-art systems while maintaining the same level of recall. From the performance figures provided, the generation of the probabilistic logical formulae presents itself as a computational bottleneck while the satisfyability problem is solved rather quickly.

Another work that aims at integrating an ontology in the extraction process is presented by Culotta et al. [2006]. They learn what they call *relational patterns* which constitute paths of length > 1 in ontologies represented as networks of relations between instances. These relational patterns serve as features to a

CRF model that performs the identification of mentions in the text. As an example a $father \rightarrow wife$ could support the $mother$ relation, i.e. the confidence of a $mother(m, s)$ increases if we know that s has a father of which m is the wife. In the study by Culotta et al. the relational patterns and the extraction result are co-evolved by training an SVM which uses both relational patterns (initially a large set of candidate paths) and textual features. This framework straightforwardly also allows integrating background knowledge by adding relational paths or individual relation instances from external sources (e.g. an ontology). The approach has been evaluated on 271 Wikipedia articles. Relations have been assumed to be expressed in hyperlinks which have been manually labelled for training. An increase in precision from 65% to 72% can be observed whith the help of relational patterns while recall is also slightly improved.

While the above studies focus on the integration of an ontology with Web documents, the following work focuses on scale. The work of Ravichandran [2005] explicitly focuses on IE from large "terascale" corpora with the aim of extracting the taxonomic is-a relation. Evaluation is done one 70 million page Web corpus (116 GB) and a smaller newspaper corpus. The work integrates a pattern-based approach using patterns that are automatically learned and evaluated and a clustering-based approach using standard token-based features as well as pattern matches and co-occurrence counts. This combination reaches a precision of around 70% and yields around 1 million instances.

Recently Banko et al. [2007] introduced the idea of "Open Information Extraction", aiming to extract all relations contained in a large Web corpus (9 million Web pages). To this end, a CRF classifier is trained that identifies subject, predicate, and object of a relation in a sentence. Training of this classifier is done in a semi-supervised manner by providing unlabelled but parsed text along with heuristics that allow the system to identify relation instances in parse trees. While the output of Open IE may be useful for search applications, it differs from other IE results in that it does not adhere to a predefined schema. Concretely, predicates are derived on a by sentence basis which leads to the fact that the same relation expressed by sentences with different predicates will not be integrated. Recently, it has been shown that the output of Open IE can be used as features for classical IE to increase precision [Banko and Etzioni, 2008]. A similar, schema-less approach is taken by Davidov et al. [2007] operating on a smaller scale but attempting to integrate relation instances expressed with different predicates.

Part II

Large-Scale Extraction Methods

Chapter 5

The Iterative Pattern Induction Framework

This chapter presents a framework that abstracts over various approaches to large-scale global relation extraction found in the literature. Critical points in this framework are identified and a series of experimental investigations is presented that shed light on these critical points.

As outlined in Chapter 4, key challenges in large scale global Information Extraction are on the one hand to minimize the amount of expensive human knowledge that has to be put into the process in form of training examples or other form of supervision and on the other hand to cope with massive amounts of input texts. For this reasons, iterative *bootstrapping* approaches are widely used on the task in combination with textual *patterns*. The framework used here is a general version of bootstrapping for pattern induction. The general idea of bootstrapping and related work on the subject have been introduced in Section 4.2.2.

Patterns can be thought of as simple crisp binary classifiers which have an explicit and intuitive interpretation. Initial successes with (manually specified) textual patterns for relation extraction date back to the work of Hearst [1992]. When aiming at operating at large scale, they are frequently used due to the following advantages over learned statistical models:

- In particular with the goal of global relation extraction in mind, one important problem is identifying the actual relation instance within a sentence. That is, it is one thing to decide, if the sentence "The Hague is the seat of the government of The Netherlands" expresses the *locatedIn* relation and another one to actually spot $(TheHague, TheNetherlands)$ as the instance. With patterns, this can be done easily by distinguishing certain elements of the patterns as "argument slots." Otherwise additional measures are necessary. In many works that apply other types of classifiers to the task, this is either done by using a named-entity tagger [Snow et al., 2004] or with two cascaded classifiers [Wu and Weld, 2007].

- A pattern-based representation enables the use of techniques from the field of of Data Mining that efficiently and exhaustively find patterns. These algorithms, as discussed in Section 2.3, are optimized for high volumes of data that are analyzed in near-linear time. They integrate interesting types of structure and background knowledge into the mining process as required for mining.

- Patterns as opposed to discriminative models have a more or less direct textual interpretation which allows using Information Retrieval techniques for efficient matching [Cafarella et al., 2005; Blohm et al., 2007]. Information Retrieval techniques as described in Section 2.4 separate processing into indexing-time processing and query-time processing. The expensive data-linear processes can be done once as preprocessing (or existing indices can be used) while the extraction itself can be considered a query-time process that makes use of efficiently structured data.

5.1 Framework Overview

Intuitively the idea of iterative induction of extraction patterns can be described as follows:

The process starts out with a set of relation instances that are known to be correct:

$$\{(Hollywood, U.S.), (Osnabruck, Germany), (Nice, France)\}$$

It then looks, how they are mentioned in the corpus, which could be:

- “The richest people in the U.S. live in Hollywood”
- “The happiest people in Germany live in Osnabrück”
- “The luckiest people in France work in Nice”

It then looks what else is mentioned in the same way in the corpus and conclude that those are also instances of the relation. e.g. conclude $(Sheffield, UK)$ from

“The hardest-working researchers in the UK live in Sheffield”

With those new instances, repeat the process if more instances are needed. In this example, the complexity of the task is hidden in the step of looking for “what

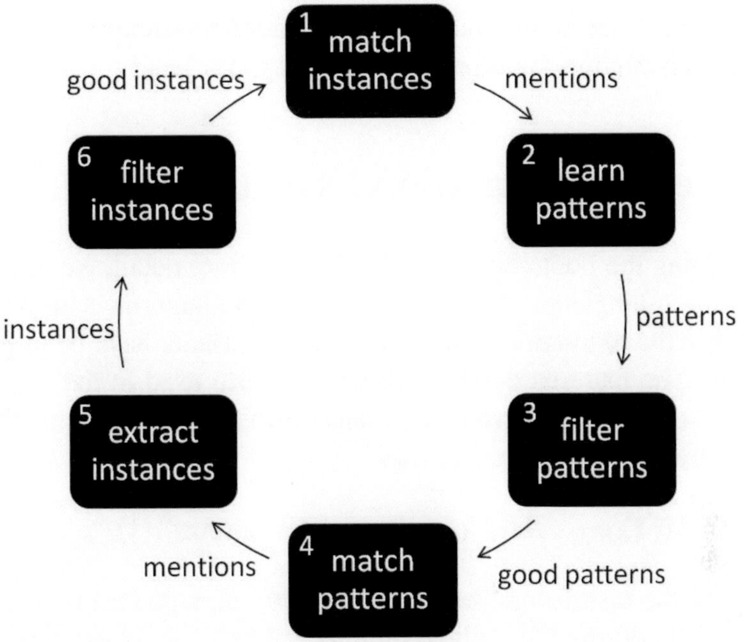

Figure 5.1: Illustration of the sequence of steps in the induction cycle.

else is mentioned in the same way." It comprises representing relation mentions in a way that makes their key features computationally accessible, identifying general patterns in those mentions and identifying mentions of these patterns. How these tasks are accomplished is the focus of much research some of which is summarized in this chapter.

The diagram in Figure 5.1 gives an overview of this process which can be divided into six steps. First, the instances are matched in the corpus (1) which generates a set of instance mentions. Pattern learning then takes place (2). Patterns, i.e. underspecified generalized descriptions of the mentions are generated. These are then filtered (3) to yield only those patterns that are likely to produce good results when they are subsequently matched (4). The thus produced mentions are processed to extract new relation instances (5) which are in turn filtered. In the following, a more formal description of the processing will be given.

Note the symmetry in the cycle: For both patterns and instances there is one step where they are matched, another one where they are generated from mentions and for both a filtering step exists. In fact, the set of patterns and instances co-evolve. This state of affairs was called *Pattern-relation duality* by Brin [1999].

It may seem unnecessary to list filtering of patterns and instances as a separate step. It could be considered the task of the pattern learner and the instance extractor to produce high-quality output. Yet, in the literature, these steps are usually separate in the sense that they build on different assumptions or input. The separation thus facilitates the discussion of the approaches.

5.2 Patterns for Relation Extraction

Before describing the bootstrapping algorithm in more detail, we define here the extraction pattern language. The exact nature of the patterns is an important design choice for the extraction system and many variants have been proposed in the literature. The patterns described here are those used in the experiments in Chapters 6, 7 and 8. Alternative pattern languages are presented and discussed in Chapter 9. Patterns may look as follows.

"flights to ANY_{ARG_1} , ANY_{ARG_2} from ANY airport" (1)

In terms of the task formalization in Section 1.2, a pattern is a function $m : M \rightarrow \{0, 1\}$ that returns 1 if a given fragment of text $t \in M$ expresses the target relation and 0 otherwise. Furthermore, if required, it also constitutes a function $e : 2^{M \rightarrow Domain_r \times Range_r}$ that returns the relation instances that are present. We use an r subscript to indicate sets that are assumed to be constant over the run of the algorithm but which depend on the relation in question.

Patterns are usually strongly limited subsets of regular expressions. They thus represent languages that can be described with regular grammars and accepted by non-deterministic Finite State Automata (NFA). NFAs are finite state machines which can have a finite set of states and which accept input sequences if they lead from a specified start state via permitted transitions to an accepting end state. A transition is only possible if the transition label matches the next element of the input sequence (cf. [Jurafsky and Martin, 2000] for a discussion of regular expression and NFAs in the context of Natural Language Processing). Regular expressions consist of the following symbols and operators: Terminal tokens from an alphabet A, the empty string ε, the concatenation operator (represented by whitespace here), the alternation operator | and the Kleene star repetition operator $*$, and $\emptyset$ representing the empty language. While approaches to learn (almost) the full expressivity of regular expressions exist [Li et al., 2008], the full expressivity is hardly ever used when operating with automatically matched patterns.

Figure 5.2 shows regular expression operators and their interpretation as portions of an NFA in the standard graph-based visualization. States are visualized as graph nodes displayed as circles containing the state's label. Transitions are visualized as labelled directed edges. Figure 5.3 shows the example pattern (1) as a NFA. Note that the token alphabet is the lexicon of words. We use an abbreviation for large alternations in writing $||(B)$ for the alternation of all elements in

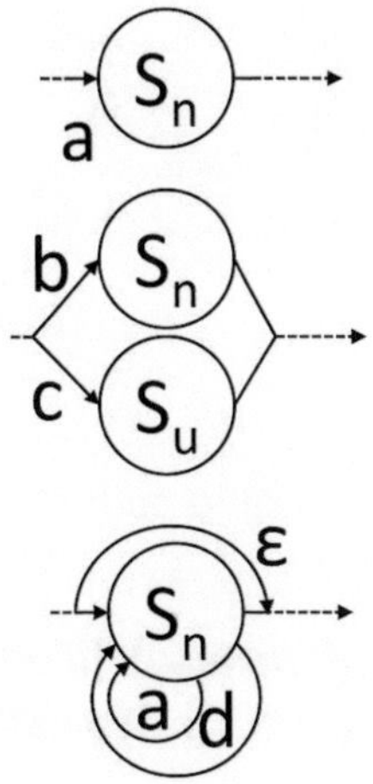

Figure 5.2: NFA representation of pattern elements. $A = a, b, c, d, T = b, c$.

B and ANY denotes all words from the alphabet A, i.e. $||(A)$. Note that we will interprete patterns such that they are allowed to start and end anywhere in the text.

As the full expressivity of regular expressions is not used in Information Extraction from large scale text collections, this thesis uses a simplified representation that allows us to describe all pattern languages discussed. It consists of the following elements:

- *Token*: a. A token from the input text represented by its surface string.
- *(Typed) Wildcards*: ANY/$||(T)$. An element of the pattern that matches an arbitrary single token in the input sequence. In the typed case, matching only occurs for tokens of a certain type T (with respect to POS, NE-tag or another type of background knowledge available).
- *Skips*: $ANY*$. An element of the pattern that matches zero to many tokens in the input sequence regardless of their type.
- *(Restricted) Skips*: $||(A\backslash T)*$. A token in the pattern that matches zero to many tokens in the input sequence regardless of their type unless it is of the type it has been restricted to.

Any of the above pattern element types can be marked as *argument slot*. Most commonly, typed wildcards are used for this purpose. We distinguish arguments slots by adding an arg_n subscript. Note that patterns formalized in this manner do not make use of the Kleene star (except implicitly by allowing starts and ends anywhere in the text). Not all systems make use of all possible pattern elements.

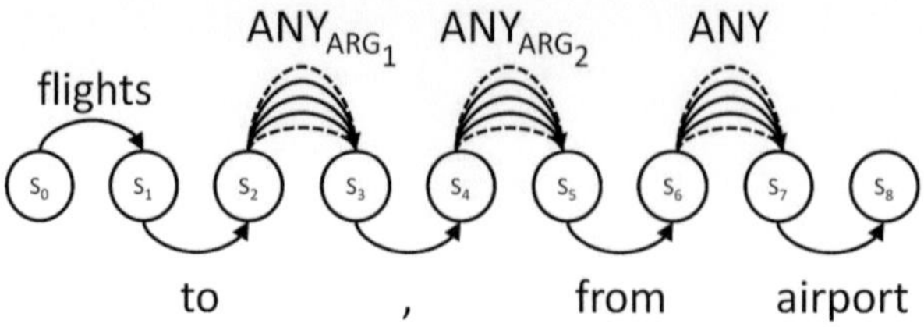

Figure 5.3: Example pattern (1) as NFA.

The choice of allowable pattern elements defines the set of possible patterns and hence their expressivity (cf. Chapter 9). We call such a configuration a *pattern class*.

5.3 The Algorithmic Framework

Figure 5.4 describes the generic pattern learning algorithm as it is used in our experiments. It subsumes many of the approaches from the literature, the most prominent of which are discussed in Section 5.6. For most of the experiments presented here, the *Pronto* system has been developed as a generic implementation of this algorithm. An overview of Pronto's functionality is given in Section 5.5. Implementation and configuration details are discussed along with the respective studies in the following chapters.

The types of entities are handled by the algorithm are relation instances, patterns and textual mentions. As introduced above, relation instances are of type $Domain_r \times Range_r$. The algorithm receives a seed set of instances $Inst'$ as input and maintains during its processing a set $Inst$ of instances which will contain the desired output when the algorithm terminates. Patterns are composed of the elements described in Section 5.2. At the level of abstraction discussed here, patterns are primitive objects from the set of all possible patterns P_{pc} which is defined by the pattern class pc that is used. During the execution of the algorithm a set P_{pool} of patterns is maintained that constitutes the currently learned model for relation extraction. An initial set of patterns P_{init} may be provided at starting time of the algorithm [Yangarber, 2003]. Textual mentions can be any fragment of text in the corpus. T constitutes the set of all text fragments (i.e. all possible mentions. When the focus is pattern mining and matching the composition of patterns and textual mentions will be discussed. Mentions are temporarily generated by pattern and instance matching. The sets M_p and M_i contain them.

The algorithm starts with a set of initial instances $Inst'$ of the relation in question – so called *seeds* – and loops over a procedure which starts by acquiring mentions of the instances currently in $Inst$. For the *locatedIn* relation the seed set may be $\{(Vancouver, Canada), (Karlsruhe, Germany), ...\}$ Further, patterns are learned by abstracting over the text mentions of the instances. The new patterns are then evaluated and filtered before they are matched. From these matches, new instances are extracted, evaluated and filtered. The process is stopped when the termination condition DONE is fulfilled (typically, a fixed number of iterations is set). In detail, the function calls have the following effect.

- The matching functions MATCH-INSTANCES: $2^{(Domain_r \times Range_r)} \rightarrow N^T$ and MATCH-PATTERNS: $2^{P_{pc}} \rightarrow 2^T$ take as input a set of instances or patterns respectively. They produce a set of mentions by matching the relation instances or the patterns to the corpus. A match of a relation instance is a co-occurrence of its arguments within a defined context. For patterns, all their matches in the corpus are returned. How exactly a match is defined and how the access to the corpus takes place are design choices for the implementation.

- The function LEARN-PATTERNS: $N^T \rightarrow 2^{P_{pc}}$ represents the actual pattern induction process which abstracts over a set of instance mentions M_i and returns patterns that are likely to match correct relation instances and not irrelevant mentions. Several alternative induction algorithms will be discussed in the following chapters.

Patterns and instances are then evaluated and filtered. These steps are listed separately for conceptual clarity. They may consist of a scoring and ranking process followed by the application of a percentile or threshold cut-off. Note that several evaluation processes or conditions may be combined. EVALUATE-PATTERNS: $N^{P_{pc}} \rightarrow \mathbb{R}^{P_{pc}}$ and EVALUATE-INSTANCES: $N^{(Domain_r \times Range_r)} \rightarrow \mathbb{R}^{Domain_r \times Range_r}$ thus reflect the traversal over P or $Inst$ respectively while PATTERN-FILTER-CONDITION: $P_{pc} \times \mathbb{R}^{P_{pc}} \rightarrow \{true, false\}$ and INSTANCE-FILTER-CONDITION: $(Domain_r \times Range_r) \times \mathbb{R}^{Domain_r \times Range_r} \rightarrow \{true, false\}$ stand for the application of a filtering criterion. When for a given pattern p or an instance i the corresponding filter condition function maps to true, it is kept, otherwise it is removed. Note that by this formalization, the patterns are kept in P_{pool} over iterations. P_{pool} is thus an evolving collection of rule-based knowledge about how relation instances are mentioned in text. In this sense, the pattern induction process as presented here can be considered a simple instance of Genetic Programming: A population of patterns is kept that reproduces by means of producing instances which lead to new patterns. Fitness is measured by pattern quality measures and filtering performs the corresponding selection.

In the system presented by Riloff and Jones [1999] patterns are not taken over in next iteration. The only gained information after each iteration is a (carefully

ITERATIVE PATTERN INDUCTION$(Patterns\ P_{init}, Instances\ Inst')$
$Inst \leftarrow Inst'$
$P_{pool} \leftarrow P_{init}$
while not DONE
do $M_i \leftarrow$ MATCH-INSTANCES$(Inst)$
  $P_{pool} \leftarrow P_{pool} \cup$ LEARN-PATTERNS(M_i)
  $Eval_P \leftarrow$ EVALUATE-PATTERNS(P_{pool})
  $P_{pool} \leftarrow \{p \in P_{pool} \mid$ PATTERN-FILTER-CONDITION$(p, Eval_P)\}$
  $M_p \leftarrow$ MATCH-PATTERNS(P_{pool})
  $Inst \leftarrow Inst +$ EXTRACT-INSTANCES(M_p)
  $Eval_I \leftarrow$ EVALUATE-INSTANCES$(Inst)$
  $Inst \leftarrow \{i \in Inst \mid$ INSTANCE-FILTER-CONDITION$(i, Eval_I)\}$

Figure 5.4: Iterative pattern induction algorithm starting with initial patterns P_{init} and instances $Inst'$

filtered) set of new instances. They refer to this variation as "mutual bootstrapping."

The function EXTRACT-INSTANCES: $N^T \rightarrow 2^{Domain_r \times Range_r}$ reflects the previously mentioned tasks of identifying the relation instances present in the relation mentions identified and then integrating the extracted instances into one set.

5.4 Assumptions and Challenges in Iterative Pattern Induction

The above algorithm makes several assumptions which are important to be kept in mind as they determine limits of the approach. We mention the major assumptions here in a very abstract manner before deriving challenges that arise from a more practical point of view.

Assumption 1: Uniform Mentions There are one or more uniform ways in which instances of a target relation are mentioned in text that distinguishes them from non-mentions. This uniformity can be observed by looking at the contexts of a limited set of mentions.

Assumption 2: Redundant Instances In order for the iterative nature of the algorithm to be beneficial , instances that are derived during one iteration should improve the model for the next iteration. Thus, relation instances are supposed to be mentioned in multiple contexts. An example, probably explains this best. Consider the inference made in Section 5.1 where it is concluded that $(Sheffield, UK)$

is an appropriate instance because it occurs in the sentence “The hardest-working researchers in the UK live in Sheffield.” The benefit of bootstrapping is that in the next iteration, all matches of $(Sheffield, UK)$ can be used as candidates for patterns. If this is the only time, Sheffield is mentioned, $(Sheffield, UK)$ is not very valuable in the next iteration. So, bootstrapping can only work if the same facts are entailed from several mentions, which we refer to as redundancy here.

Assumption 3: Explicit Model When operating with patterns as opposed to arbitrary (statistical) discriminative models, one makes the assumption that the uniformity assumed under (1) can be represented as a reasonably compact set of constraints.

Assumption (1) and (2) together can be paraphrased with “observing mentions of instances can lead to new instances.” Thereby (1) requires that mentions of several instances share some aspects that can be identified and (2) requires that sufficiently many instances occur in several contexts. The practical impact of this assumption is discussed in Chapter 7. (3) requires that it is beneficial to write the model down as a pattern. Patterns mostly consist of conjunctions of non-negated constraints. Please refer to Section 4.2.4 for a discussion of benefits of pattern representation and other representations.

Bootstrapping-based systems have been developed to achieve relatively large output with very little input by re-using previous output as training input. However, one needs to keep in mind that output quality during bootstrapping underlies complex dynamics: Both, precision and recall need to be kept under control while other side conditions like time efficiency need to be considered. In the following, a set of fundamental challenges for Information Extraction by means of iterative pattern induction are identified.

Challenge 1: Cost of Supervision. The vision behind this research is developing a system that is relatively autonomously able to inform itself from Web sources. Costly human intervention is to be avoided. Such intervention may occur in two forms. On the one hand, it occurs in the form of example instances. On the other hand, an important, less obvious way of providing knowledge to the extraction system is intelligently choosing extraction parameters, appropriate filtering strategies and the level of pattern representation according to the task at hand.

Challenge 2: Generalization Complexity. Patterns are underspecified representations of text fragments that aim at describing a salient subset of the set of available fragments. They are induced in the LEARN-PATTERNS step of the algorithm by abstracting over textual mentions. This requires to detect commonalities between textual mentions. Depending on the notion of commonality applied, this may quickly become computationally complex. If for example, pairwise comparison of the mentions in M_i is required, this would amount to $O(|M_i|^2)$ comparisons. This for example becomes necessary in the algorithm presented by Rosenfeld and Feldmann [2006], where sequences are aligned in a pairwise manner and pattern are generated if the alignment fulfills certain criteria.

Challenge 3: Pattern Quality Prediction Dilemma. The quality of a pattern – like of any other crisp binary classifier – can be assessed by counting the two types of errors possible (erroneous positive and negative classifications). However, assessing those would require full knowledge of the target relation. PATTERN-FILTER-CONDITION thus needs to make an uninformed estimate of the quality of a pattern.

Challenge 4: Dependance on Redundancy. Pattern-based Information Extraction relies on the fact that relation instances are mentioned in the corpus in a way that makes it possible to detect and exploit commonalities in these mentions. Primarily this requires that relevant commonalities exist. If no interesting commonalities are present, neither pattern-based nor statistical IE can be performed. Additionally however the bootstrapping nature of the algorithm requires that a critical mass of relation instances is mentioned in more than one context. As an illustration consider the state a system is in after one iteration of the loop in Figure 5.4. $Inst$ contains all relation instances that can be found by patterns that can be derived from abstracting over the contents of $Inst'$. In the second iteration, new patterns can only be derived if $Inst \setminus Inst'$ are mentioned in a way that allows to derive new interesting contexts which usually requires that M_i of the second iteration contains more than M_p from the first iteration.

Challenge 5: Error Proliferation. Finally, if wrong instances are accepted into $Inst$, they contribute in the next iteration to the generation of patterns. It may thus happen that patterns are induced that are trained to generate wrong instances.

These challenges will be tackled in the following chapters. Chapter 6 puts a particular focus on the problem of quality prediction (3) which also has implications for Challenge (5). In Chapter 7, the notion of redundancy (4) is in the focus which is addressed in a way that relates also to the cost of supervision (1). The generalization complexity is a particular focus in Chapter 8.

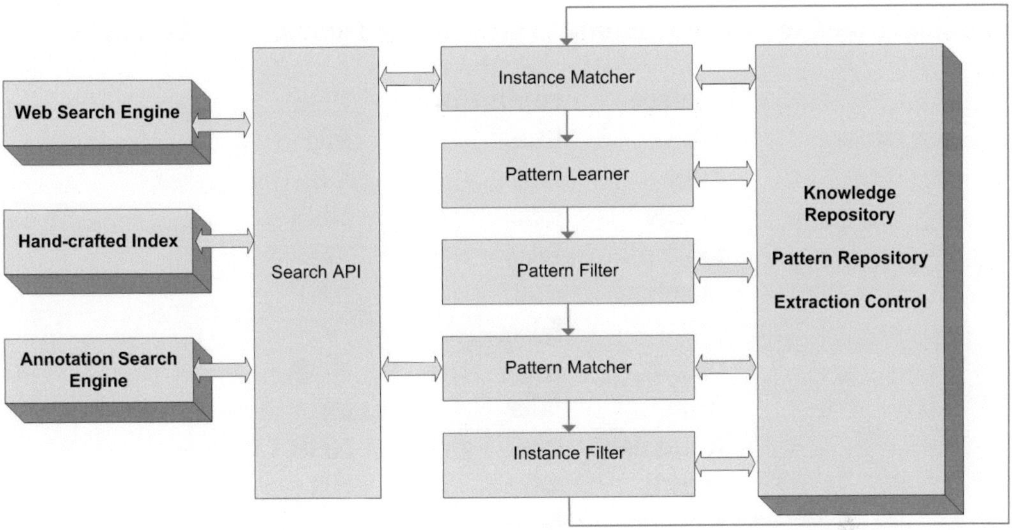

Figure 5.5: Key components of the Pronto System.

5.5 The Pronto System

An Information Extraction system called Pronto has been developed for the studies presented in this thesis. Its major purpose is to serve as a workbench to enable experiments that allow us to further understand the dynamics behind large-scale Information Extraction with little supervision. To this end, the system has been developed to show a great degree of plugability and configurabilty. A general overview of the system is given here while the design and configuration of individual components are discussed in more detail along with the experiments they are applied with in Chapters 6, 7, 11 and 10.

5.5.1 Key components of Pronto

The Pronto system reflects the above formalization of the iterative pattern induction cycle. The structure of the algorithm is captured in an extensible manner by means of interfaces that define the individual processing units as well as the data structures for patterns, instances and textual mentions.

The data structures for patterns and mentions have an analogous structure. For each token, a set of feature expressions can be specified. In a Mention, the features describe the text in the mention, in a Pattern, these features serve as constraints for matching. A pattern matches if all its constraints are fulfilled. Tokens can be distinguished as argument slots. The following is a feature-based representation of a mention of the example pattern from Section 5.2. The constraint-based view on patterns used in Pronto is similar to that used by Fabio Ciravegna [2001].

surface	**capitalization**	**POS**
We	true	PRP
offer	false	VB
flights	false	NNS
to	false	TO
Hamburg	true	NNP
,	false	,
Germany	true	NNP
from	false	IN
Rotterdam	true	NNP
airport	false	NN
.	false	.

Relation instances are stored by implementations of the Instance interface which allows specifying possibly n-ary instances (although all experiments and the current implementation operate with binary relations only). For flexible evaluation, pointers are kept between patterns, instances and mentions. In particular for a pattern, all its previously matched mentions can be retrieved as well as all instances extracted. Analogously, all matching patterns for an instance or a mention can be retrieved.

The composition and configuration of iterations in the induction framework can be configured in an XML-based file format depending on the task at hand. WorkflowItem interfaces are available for the steps presented in the algorithm in Figure 5.4 (InstanceMatcher, PatternLearner, PatternEvaluatior, PatternMatcher, InstanceGenerator, InstanceEvaluator). The configuration is loaded by a runtime environment which then executes the individual workflow items. The runtime environment loads the individual workflow items, provides them with the data environment and controls iterations and termination.

Pronto is being used in the X-Media research project (cf. Chapter 10). A brief user guide for Pronto is available in a report we published within the X-Media research project [Iria et al., 2009]. Pronto can be downloaded as open source software from `https://sourceforge.net/projects/prontoie/`.

5.5.2 Pronto Matching with Google Search

Pronto is able to use the Web as a corpus and access it via Web search. In particular, the Google API has been implemented. In the following, pattern and instance matching by means of the Google API is described. In order to identify mentions of instances in $Inst$ on the Web, the search index is accessed via Google's Java API querying for pages on which all words present in both arguments of the instance can be found. The arguments themselves are quoted. A fixed number $num_{matchInstances}$ of results is retrieved. From those, only the result headers and text snippets are kept which contain all arguments within a distance of at most $max_{argDist}$. As an example, the instance $(\text{SanJose}, \text{California})$ would be translated to the query `"San Jose" "California"`.

A fictional Google result for this query is:

Cheap flights in California - San Jose departures
We offer flights to San Jose, California airport from all major destinations on the West Coast of the U.S. and Canada ...

From this, with $max_{argDist} = 10$ and $t_{prefix} = t_{suffix} = 2$, the following mentions will be processed further (white space indicates token borders):

```
flights in California - San Jose departures
flights to San Jose, California airport from
```

From these and other mentions, pattern induction may produce the pattern:

"flights to ANY_{ARG_1} , ANY_{ARG_2} from ANY airport"

MATCH-PATTERNS(P) matches each pattern in P by running a set of queries to the Google API. For each query, a fixed number of search results $num_{matchPatterns}$ is retrieved. The queries are generated by taking the surface string constraint for each token in a blank-separated manner. Tokens with empty surface string constraints (above marked by ANY) are represented by a $*$ wildcard, which - when used in quotes - will be replaced with any word or very few words in this position in the Google results. This sequence is stripped from leading and closing $*$ wildcards and surrounded by quotes. For instance, the above pattern example would be translated into a Google-query as follows:

```
"flights to * *  * from "
```

The comma in the pattern is represented as an individual token with the comma surface string. During querying, however, it is omitted as Google discards punctuation characters in queries.

In a subsequent analysis step, properties of the pattern that cannot be established by Google matching are checked. In particular, Google ignores punctuation and only matches lemmas thus discarding word morphology (e.g. "live" vs. "lived") and capitalization. For this purpose, the individual text fragments (title and snippets) returned by the Google API are tokenized and the respective features are computed for each token. The resulting sequence in the Mention format is then matched to the patterns. Matching mentions are then fed to the InstanceGenerator which identifies the argument slot fillers and thereby generates new instances.

5.6 Related Extraction Systems

In the following, the most important related work on iterative pattern induction is discussed. In line with the scope of this thesis we put an emphasis on the aspects of a large scale (or at least implementations with a potential to scale to large text collections) and on the task of global relation extraction. After giving a brief overview of the systems, we organize the presentation of the related work by the algorithmic steps presented in this framework. In doing so, we intend to shed light on the design alternatives that exist at each step which would otherwise be difficult as almost each major contribution to the field has been made based on a new system which makes new assumptions on the task at hand.

With a few exceptions, the approaches discussed in this chapter are based on a set of rigid patterns in the line of Hearst [1992], which are matched on corpora of varying size or the Web via a search engine. The seminal work of Brin [1999] introduced the basic bootstrapping algorithm, and thereby the automatic generation of patterns, for relation extraction while Riloff and Jones [1999] proposed an almost identical method for entity extraction.

Another early system is that of Ravichandran and colleagues [2001] which has been applied and evaluated in question answering scenarios. An interesting feature of Ravichandran's system is the automatic detection of reasonable pattern borders with suffix trees as a data structure that allows retrieving occurrence counts for all sub-strings of the mention in linear time.

Several systems have addressed the task of learning instances of concepts, among them KnowItAll [Etzioni et al., 2005], PANKOW [Cimiano et al., 2004] and Espresso [Pantel and Pennacchiotti, 2006]. The KnowItAll system has even been extended with pattern learning capabilities to discover new patterns [Downey et al., 2004]. Other recent works vary in pattern structure, induction algorithm and the extraction task [Rosenfeld and Feldman, 2006; Rozenfeld and Feldman, 2006; Pantel et al., 2004]. A similar system is that of Snow et al. [2004] which integrates syntactic dependency structure into pattern representation but has been only applied to the task of learning instance-of relations or isa-relations. Similarly, Roman Yangarber [2003] operates on rather abstract syntactic representations. Xu and Uszkoreit [2007] also use dependency structures but focus on extracting n-ary relations.

A different form of pattern representation was introduced in the Snowball system [Agichtein and Gravano, 2000] which relies on annotation of named entities with their category which can be used in formulating the patterns. Parts of the pattern are represented as bag-of-words vectors and not plain strings, thus capturing the frequency of the words occurring around the arguments in diverse mentions. Other pattern-based system are discussed here for particularities of their induction algorithms [Ciravegna, 2001; Soderland et al., 1999; Califf and Mooney, 1997] which induce pattern in a top-down or bottom-up manner taking a generate-and-test approach. This is analogous to concept learning as introduced in Section 2.3.1. These works rather stand in the tradition of wrapper induction and event detection. In the work of Ruiz-Casado et al. [2005], Information Extraction from Wikipedia text is done using hyperlinks as indicators.

5.6.1 Matching Instances and Identifying Contexts

In DIRPE [Brin, 1999] mentions are viewed as a seven-tuple:

$$(\mathrm{arg}_1, \mathrm{arg}_2, \mathrm{order}, \mathrm{url}, \mathrm{prefix}, \mathrm{middle}, \mathrm{suffix})$$

where the arguments arg_1 and arg_2 are restricted to match relation-specific regular expressions. prefix, middle and suffix constitute the text before, between and after the arguments. *order* encodes which argument occurs first. url encodes the address of the document the mention has been found in. Prefix, suffix (and most likely also the middle part) have a specified maximum length. With appropriate settings, the phrase

"flights to Schiphol, The Netherlands from Heathrow airport"

would be represented as:

$$(\mathrm{Schiphol}, \mathrm{TheNetherlands}, 1, \texttt{url}, \text{“flights to”}, \text{“, ”}, \text{“from Heathrow airport”})$$

Similarly, mentions are formalized in the Snowball system [Agichtein and Gravano, 2000] in terms of prefix, infix and suffix the difference being that those positions are represented as weighted bags of words, thus discarding word order. Furthermore, named-entity tags are stored for the argument positions which apparently also serve for identifying the order.

$$(\mathrm{arg}_1\mathrm{type}, \mathrm{arg}_2\mathrm{type}, \mathrm{prefix}, \mathrm{middle}, \mathrm{suffix})$$

For example:

$$(\mathbf{City}, \mathbf{Country}, \{\text{“flights”}, \text{“to”}\}, \{\text{“, ”}\}, \{\text{“airport”}, \text{“from”}, \text{“Heathrow”}\})$$

An alternative approach to representing context is replacing the arguments with a uniform slot marker and then representing them as one string [Ravichandran and Hovy, 2001; Pantel and Pennacchiotti, 2006; Rosenfeld and Feldman, 2006; Rozenfeld and Feldman, 2006]. The mechanism for instance matching used by the mentioned systems is by querying a web search engine followed by argument identification on the returned results. It results in text with highlighted arguments:

"flights to $\underline{\text{Schiphol}_1}$, $\underline{\text{The Netherlands}_2}$ from Heathrow airport"

A similar view on mentions is taken by Ciravegna [2001] where start and end markers of an annotated sequence (like XML tags) are noted as separate tokens. This slightly different view is taken to allow for separate rules for the introduction of start and end tags. In addition, for each token, linguistic information (lemma, lexical category, semantic category) is kept in a table.

"flights to <arg1>Schiphol</arg1> , <arg2>The Netherlands</arg2> from Heathrow airport"

The different ways of representing mentions (except from a few additional features) all hold the same information as they constitute different ways to highlight arguments. The details in which these representations differ come into play when it comes to pattern induction and pattern matching.

5.6.2 Pattern Induction

The task of pattern induction is that of abstracting over the instance mentions in a way that generates a set of patterns which are likely to describe instances of the target relation. Thereby the induction process faces two challenges. First of all, it is important that the patterns optimize the quality of future extractions. To do so, the algorithms must identify the *distinguishing features* of relation instances while successfully handling two types of noise that may arise: overly specific features (preventing relevant instances to be matched) and too general features (which when not accompanied by distinguishing features lead to spurious extractions). Secondly, induction algorithms need to cope with the extremely large set of possible abstractions. There must be a way to *guide pattern search* properly. Both problems are by no means particular to Information Extraction which is why a few systems base their induction algorithms on Machine Learning algorithms which have also been applied in other fields. We present very abstract and possibly simplifying pseudo code for the algorithms which is meant to convey an intuition of the alternative approaches. A more detailed account can be found in the referenced publications.

A very simple algorithm for induction has been presented by Brin [1999]. Recall that, in their system, the pattern structure is a tuple (arg_1, arg_2, order, url, prefix, middle, suffix). The algorithm used mines for a set of patterns with equal middle string and order flag. Both, the selection of distinguishing features and the search for appropriate abstraction are quite heuristically by grouping together all mentions which share the same text between the arguments. The algorithm can be formalized as follows:

INDUCTION [BRIN, 1999]($Mentions\ M$)

$Groups \leftarrow$ groups of mentions with equal order and prefix
while $Groups \neq \emptyset$
  do
    remove $G \in Groups$ from $Groups$
    if PATTERN(G) is not too general
      then
        OUTPUT(PATTERN(G))
      else
        split G into $G'_1 \ldots G'_n$ by the first char their urls differ
        if $G'_1 \neq G$
          then $Groups \leftarrow Groups \cup G'_1 \ldots G'_n$

Where OUTPUT(G) generates a pattern from a set of mentions G of the form (order, url, prefix, middle, suffix) where order and middle are the common values for those positions, url and suffix are the longest common prefix of those values and, prefix are the longest common suffix of all prefix values of the group. Specificity is assessed by the product of the character count in prefix, middle, url, and suffix.

The pattern induction algorithm used by Rosenfeld and Feldmann [2006; 2006] as well as in a very similar manner by Ruiz-Casado et al. [2005] and Pantel et al. [2004] finds pairwise generalizations by aligning strings in an inexact manner. The patterns are then filtered by several criteria.

INDUCTION [ROSENFELD AND FELDMAN, 2006]($Mentions\ M$)

for $(m_1, m_2) \in M \times M$
  do
    $p \leftarrow$ ALIGN(m_1, m_2)
    if (COST(p) $< max_{cost}$ $\wedge$ HASRELEVANTWORD(p)
      $\wedge$HASANCHOREDSLOTS(p))
      then OUTPUT(REMOVESTOPWORDS(p))

Thereby ALIGN(m_1, m_2) finds an optimal alignment of two mentions with respect to a cost function COST(p) where omissions at both sides are allowed (at a given cost) and result in skip-markers in the alignment. HASRELEVANTWORD(p) checks that a the patterns contain at least one out of a list of "relevant words" (an unconventional way of additional supervision added to the learning) and HASANCHOREDSLOTS(p) requires that no skip markers are found around the argument slots. REMOVESTOPWORDS(p) removes stop words when found in certain positions. Skip markers match arbitrary sequences (including an empty sequence) during matching. One should note that pairwise abstraction if it is done like in this algorithm limits the reach of pattern induction. For example there may be three sentences:

"We offer *cheap one-way* flights from X to Y." (1)

"We *regularly* offer *one-way* flights from X to Y." (2)

"We *regularly* offer *cheap* flights from X to Y." (3)

Three patterns would be generated:

"offer *cheap* flights from X to Y." (1 & 3)

"... *regularly* offer ... flights from X to Y.." (2 & 3)

"We ... offer ... *one-way* flights from X to Y" (1 & 2)

The obvious pattern (eliminating "regularly", "one-way", and "cheap") is not found because pairwise combination does not make the elimination necessary.

Pantel et al. [2004] and Ruiz-Casado et al. [2005] implement abstraction in the same manner: Abstractions are generated as abstractions of pairs of mentions under the condition that they are similar enough. Ruiz-Casado et al. are much more explicit on how ALIGN(m_1, m_2) and COST(p) are implemented. The costs are based on the notion of *edit distance* implemented on a token by token basis. Abstraction is based on the alignment that minimizes the edit distance between the mentions. For each position, in which both mentions share the same token, this token will be present at that position in the pattern. A disjunction is generated at positions where both mentions differ and a skip marker is added when a token in one mention has no correspondence in the other one. While the algorithm presented by Pantel et al. is also based on edit distance, fewer details on the generation of patterns are given.

Given the model of instances as three bag-of-words vectors, Snowball [Agichtein and Gravano, 2000] is able to guide the search for appropriate abstraction by means of vector space clustering. The clusters are then turned into patterns by aggregating the bags of words of each cluster. Thereby terms are weighted by their frequency in the assumption that frequent terms also are reasonably distinguishing.

```
INDUCTION [AGICHTEIN AND GRAVANO, 2000](Mentions M)
Groups ← CLUSTER(M)
for G ∈ Groups
    do
        OUTPUT(CENTROID(G))
```

Thereby, a standard word-vector clustering algorithm is used by CLUSTER(M) and the groups are enforced to have a certain minimum mutual similarity (by a cross-product-based "degree of matched"). CENTROID(G) computes the centroids for the prefix, infix and postfix vector separately and norms them to 1.

For pattern representations that are based on one string with slot markers at argument positions, one way of identifying relevant abstractions is using suffix trees [Ravichandran and Hovy, 2001]. Suffix trees contain a node for each substring existing in a set of strings along with frequency counts of this substring. While frequency can be used as a (recall-oriented) quality indicator, this approach does not provide a straight-forward way to guide the search for patterns to prevent having too many (possibly very similar) patterns. An appropriate choice of the frequency threshold however may be determined from the suffix tree. This algorithm is an example of the technique of generating patterns from a *summarizing data structure*, much like the Frequent Itemset Mining techniques presented in Chapter 8 and 9. As opposed to the modeling presented in Chapter 8, the suffix-tree technique discussed here does not allow for an efficient integration of wildcards or tags on a token basis.

```
INDUCTION [RAVICHANDRAN AND HOVY, 2001](Mentions M)
T ← SUFFIXTREE(M)
for node ∈ T
    do
        if CONTAINSARGUMENTS(node) ∧ COUNT(node) > threshold
          then OUTPUT(t)
```

A further approach also counts string sequences in an appropriate data structure: Talukdar et al. [2006] induce automata that represent the observed mentions. Each state transition is labelled with a token that is observed. A set of relevant start-tokens ("trigger words") is determined heuristically. For each such start-token an automaton along with transition probabilities is induced using Markov-Model induction techniques. The transition probabilities are used to guide the search for relevant patterns while maintaining quality.

```
INDUCTION [TALUKDAR ET AL., 2006](Mentions M)
W ← TRIGGERWORDS(M)
for w ∈ W
    do
        C ← all maximal subsequences of all m ∈ M starting with w
        A ← INDUCEAUTOMATON(C)
        PRUNE(A)
        OUTPUT(A)
```

Where INDUCEAUTOMATON(C) counts the sequences in C into the automaton data structure, PRUNE(A) removes all transitions which do not contribute to paths that lie over a certain probability.

Several authors have presented approaches to pattern induction that stand in the tradition of Inductive Logic Programming (ILP). The goal of ILP is to induce rules (in the sense of logic programs) which entail the positive examples provided and do not entail negative examples provided. Information Extraction patterns can be considered rules that decide on the presence of an instance in a given piece of text. Relation mentions thereby serve as positive examples.

In the work by Califf and Mooney [1997], rules are conjuncts of constraints that require a certain surface string or POS tag to be present at a given position. Patterns are derived by repeatedly generalizing over pairs of mentions or other patterns by eliminating constraints or allowing the disjunction over individual constraints. The scope of Califf and Mooney is entity extraction. Mentions are represented as a triple of token lists $(prefix, argument, postfix)$. Constraints are allowed on each of these lists. There are three types of constraints: the surface string of a token, the part of speech of a token and the length of a list.

```
INDUCTION [CALIFF AND MOONEY, 1997](Mentions M)
Rules ← TORULES(M)
fails ← 0
while fails < maxFail
    do
        take (r1, r2) ∈ (Rules × Rules) randomly
        RuleList ← GENERALIZE(r1.argument, r2.argument)
        n ← 0
        while BEST(RuleList) accepts negatives
        ∧BEST(RuleList) is improving
            do
                n ← n + 1
                RuleList+ = NGENERALIZEPRE(n, r1.prefix, r2.prefix)
                RuleList+ = NGENERALIZEPOST(n, r1.postfix, r2.postfix)
                if BEST(RuleList) accepts negatives
                  then fails ← fails + 1
                  else OUTPUT(BEST(RuleList))
```

Note that GENERALIZE can produce multiple generalizations. In particular, for each constraint in which r_1 and r_2 differ, either their disjunction or the elimination of the constraint are added as two variants. NGENERALIZEPRE produces a sub-pattern with generalizations of the last n constraints left. NGENERALIZEPOST generalizes the postfix keeping generalizations of the last n constraints respectively. The algorithm constitutes an interesting combination of bottom-up and top-down processing. Because the set of patterns is initialized with the exact mentions (thus the most restrictive possible) and later generalizes patterns more and more it is bottom-up in nature. Yet, for a given pair of patterns to be generalized, generalization takes place in a top-down manner.

The algorithm employed by Soderland [1999] works in much the same way. Except that there argument patterns are learned analogously to the prefix and postfix patterns. Thus, for each pair of patterns, the algorithm starts with an empty pattern which is gradually made more and more specific. Some special treatment takes place at the argument borders to ensure that the position of the argument borders is not underspecified. These algorithms generate a lot of candidate patterns and check their quality in order to guide the further exploration of the space of possible patterns. Hence, a larger amount of supervision is required than in other scenarios. In particular – as opposed to all other algorithms presented here –

negative examples (i.e. mentions that should not be matched) are required. Califf and Mooney [1997] generated negative examples from annotated documents (in which the absence of an annotation can be considered a negative example) and Soderland enables interactive annotation.

In Ciravegna's system [2001], the task of relation extraction is viewed as that of introducing HTML-like tags into the text. The insertion is triggered by patterns (called rules by Ciravegna) that constrain the surface string or some other features of a sequence of tokens. Even though each argument that is identified consists of a start and an end tag, both of them are induced by separate patterns. Two types of patterns exist: Stronger tag patterns and weaker contextual patterns. Contextual patterns only match if the match of a tag pattern has been found in the vicinity.[1] For a given mention, all possible abstractions are considered (GENERALIZE(m)), evaluated (BESTK) and depending on the quality taken up as pattern. The quality of extraction is ensured by evaluating the candidate patterns by multiple criteria on training annotations. Patterns not belonging to the best k patterns are taken as contextual patterns if their quality fulfills some minimal standards (FILTER). The amount of inserted abstractions is controlled by a covering criterion which ensures that if a pattern is induced that matches a positive instance, this instance will no longer count towards the evaluation of future patterns (this is known as sequential covering [Mitchell, 1997]). Hence, the abstraction takes place in a bottom-up manner. The search-space for good patterns is nondeterministically controlled by the order in which mentions are processed for rule induction.

INDUCTION [CIRAVEGNA, 2001]($Mentions\ M$)

$tagPatterns \leftarrow \emptyset$
$contextPatterns \leftarrow \emptyset$
while $M \neq \emptyset$
  do $take\ m \in M$
    $bestPatterns \leftarrow$ BESTK(GENERALIZE(m))
    $M \leftarrow M \setminus$ MATCHES($bestPatterns$)
    $tagPatterns \leftarrow tagPatterns \cup bestPatterns$
    $contextPatterns \leftarrow contextPatterns$
      $\cup$ FILTER(GENERALIZE(m) $\setminus$ $bestPatterns$)

Some work has been done in inducing patterns not on the textual form but on the grammatical structure of the mentions. For this purpose, paths within dependency parse trees [Snow et al., 2004; Xu et al., 2007] as well as very abstract

[1] In fact, there is a third type of patterns that take care of the correction of slightly misplaced tags.

subject-verb-object structures [Yangarber, 2003] were used. Probably due to the large number of degrees of freedom along which these structures can be abstracted over, the three works cited here do not use structured mining approaches but rather generate a set of only slightly abstracted patterns and then leave the quality assurance to a filtering step. More specifically, Xu and Uszkoreit use all minimal subtrees that span all arguments, Snow et al. all paths that connect two arguments and Yangarber replaces either subject, verb or object by a wildcard.

Overall, there is a large variety of approaches to induce patterns that exist in parallel. All of them aim at identifying good combinations of relevant features. Due to the large amount of possible combinations, various approaches are taken to guide the exploration. Most of them can be conceptualized as a concept learning task as introduced in Section 2.3.1 because a pattern defining a set of relation instances is in the same way a conjunction of constraints as a formal concept. We described here approaches that explore the space of patterns top-down [Ciravegna, 2001] and bottom-up [Brin, 1999; Rosenfeld and Feldman, 2006; Califf and Mooney, 1997]. Other approaches use a mapping to a vector space [Agichtein and Gravano, 2000] or supporting data structures [Ravichandran and Hovy, 2001; Talukdar et al., 2006].

5.6.3 Estimating Pattern Performance

After inducing patterns, it is important to exclude patterns that are likely to generate an unacceptable amount of wrong instances. The quality of patterns is estimated in the literature in many different ways. Most approaches to pattern evaluation can be described in terms of a pattern-instance incidence matrix

$$O_c = \overset{\textbf{instances}}{\begin{pmatrix} c(1,1) & c(1,2) & \dots \\ c(2,2) & c(2,2) & \dots \\ \vdots & \vdots & \ddots \end{pmatrix}} \ \textbf{patterns}$$

where each cell stands for the incidence of pattern $p \in P_{pool}$ and instance i. Different values $c : P_{pool} \times I \rightarrow \mathbb{R}$ numerically describe each incidence.

The approaches can be characterized by different choices of the incidence function c, the choice of instances that are considered for the incidence matrix $EvalInst$ and the way, these values are aggregated to a *score*. We denote the set of mentions of a pattern p extracting with an instance (i_1, i_2) with $< i_1, p, i_2 >$ and use $|i_1, p, i_2|$ as a shorthand for $| < i_1, p, i_2 > |$.

The most common choice of c are incidence counts c_{count} and a Boolean indicator $c_{bool}(p, i)$ which is 1 if there is at least one incidence of p and i and 0 otherwise.

$$
\begin{aligned}
c_{count}(p, i) &= |i_1, p, i_2| \\
c_{bool}(p, i) &= sgn(|i_1, p, i_2|)
\end{aligned}
$$

Thereby, $|i_1, p, i_2|$ gives the count of mentions where the instance $i = (i_1, i_2)$ with the arguments i_1 and i_2 coincides with the pattern p. Note that we use p both for a pattern $p \in P_{pool}$ itself and for its numeric index $p \in [1, |P_{pool}|]$ in the matrix and respectively i for $i \in I \subseteq Domain \times Range$ and $i \in EvalInst$. While evaluation approaches all use the same set P_{pool} for the rows of the incidence matrix, the set of instances $EvalInst$ that is used for evaluation and that determines the columns differs between the approaches. $EvalInst$ contains at least a subset of the instances previously accepted as correct $Inst$ and may contain others (e.g. negative examples).

Apart from the choice of c, pattern evaluation mechanisms differ in the calculation of the evaluation measure $score : P_{pool} \to \mathbb{R}$. In the following, we present the most common measures adopted in the literature.

One common measure is the support of a pattern. Support means the count of instances in the training set a pattern occurs with. It is based on adding up each pattern's row in the incidence matrix:

$$
\begin{aligned}
score_{support}(p) &= \sum_{i \in EvalInst} c(p, i) \\
EvalInst &= Inst
\end{aligned}
$$

As for the choice of $c(p, i)$, one can opt for counting distinct supporting instances by setting $c(p, i) = c_{bool}(p, i)$ (as proposed by Brin [1999] and evaluated in Chapter 6) or all individual matches of each instance by setting $c = c_{count}$ as used by McIntosh and Curran [2009]. We illstruate the computation of $score_{support}$ by means of the following example:

$$
\begin{aligned}
P_{pool} &= \{p_1, p_2, p_3\} \\
Inst &= \{(\text{(Paris, France)}, \text{(Chicago, U.S.)}, \text{(Moscow, Russia)}\} \\
M &= \{m_1, \ldots, m_{355}\}
\end{aligned}
$$

We can assume for example:

$$\begin{aligned}
< \text{Paris}, p_1, \text{France} > &= \{m_{17}, m_{56}, m_{95}, m_{183}, m_{236}\} \\
< \text{Paris}, p_2, \text{France} > &= \{m_{55}, m_{65}, m_{88}, m_{184}\} \\
< \text{Paris}, p_3, \text{France} > &= \emptyset \\
< \text{Chicago}, p_1, \text{U.S.} > &= \{m_2, m_{58}, m_{87}, m_{185}\} \\
< \text{Chicago}, p_2, \text{U.S.} > &= \{m_{23}, m_{64}, m_{99}, m_{113}, m_{335}\} \\
< \text{Chicago}, p_3, \text{U.S.} > &= \{m_{173}\} \\
< \text{Moscow}, p_1, \text{Russia} > &= \{m_{88}, m_{126}, m_{263}, m_{299}\} \\
< \text{Moscow}, p_2, \text{Russia} > &= \emptyset \\
< \text{Moscow}, p_3, \text{Russia} > &= \emptyset
\end{aligned}$$

In the support-based case, the set $EvalInst$, which corresponds to the columns is exactly $Inst$, i.e. the set the three accepted instances. Depending on the choice of $c(p,i)$, O_c looks as follows.

$$O_{c_{bool}} = \begin{pmatrix} 1 & 1 & 1 \\ 1 & 1 & 0 \\ 0 & 1 & 0 \end{pmatrix} \qquad O_{c_{count}} = \begin{pmatrix} 5 & 4 & 4 \\ 4 & 5 & 0 \\ 0 & 1 & 0 \end{pmatrix}$$

The scores can then be computed as follows (using the non-boolean version):

$$\begin{aligned}
score_{support}(p_1) &= 5+4+4 = 13 \\
score_{support}(p_2) &= 4+5+0 = 9 \\
score_{support}(p_3) &= 0+1+0 = 1
\end{aligned}$$

The scores presented in the following are computed in an analogous manner.

The most common measures are estimates of precision which differ in the way false positive matches are determined. They share the choice of:

$$\begin{aligned}
EvalInst &= Inst \cup NegInst \\
c(p,i) &= c_{bool}(p,i) \\
score_{precision}(p) &= \frac{\sum_{i \in Inst \setminus NegInst} c(p,i)}{\sum_{i \in Inst} c(p,i)}
\end{aligned}$$

Here, the computation of false positives is based on a set $NegInst$ of known wrong matches. The score penalizes the presence of elements from $NegInst$ in $Inst$.

When no explicit negative examples are given there are several ways of creating an (inherently incomplete) $NegInst$. One way is to make a *functionality assumption* that is, assuming that if x is related to y in a given relation, it cannot also be related to z by this relation. This assumption is true for many relations (dates of one-time events, geographic location of non-movable objects etc.). When making this assumption, $NegInst$ can be computed as follows:

$$NegInst = \{(i_1, i_2) | ((i_1, i_x) \in Inst \wedge i_2 < i_x)\}$$

Thereby, $<$ is some order that ensures for each two i_x and i_2 that violate the functionality assumption for some i_1, the inclusion of the less plausible pair (i_1, i_2) into the set of negative instances.

Various systems [Tomita et al., 2006; Agichtein and Gravano, 2000; Ravichandran and Hovy, 2001] use the functionality assumption. There is even an empirical analysis of a generalization of the functionality approach [Alfonseca et al., 2006]. The generalization consisting in allowing arbitrary cardinality constraints for the relation and giving partial credit for unknown instances fulfilling the constraints. It is compared against a setup where only seeds are counted as $Inst$ members and seeds from other relations are used as $NegInst$. The functionality assumption is shown to be beneficial. Similarly, the added value of the functionality assumption is shown in [Normand et al., 2009], showing that for an appropriate relation, the so-generated negatives increase precision and recall of the extraction in particular if few examples are given.

The second source for negative instances are seed-sets of other relations that are to be learned and of which can be assumed that the relations are disjoint with the target relation. In that case, $NegInst$ will be set to the union of those seed sets excluding the relation which is currently worked on. This approach is taken by Etzioni et al. [2005] and Talukdar et al. [2006]. With both approaches, which can also be combined, $score_{precision}(p)$ is bound to overestimate the actual precision of p as it only penalizes a subset of all possible negative instances. Finally, there are some systems which base their induction process on an annotated training corpus [Ciravegna, 2001] or a very large training set assuming all relation instance not in the training set to be false (e.g. WordNet [Snow et al., 2004]).

The scores used in the WHISK [Soderland et al., 1999] and URES [Rosenfeld and Feldman, 2006] systems also build on error estimates using training data. WHISK uses a simple form of the Laplacian expected error estimate $\frac{e+1}{n+1}$ when observing e errors on n extractions. This amounts to:

$$\begin{aligned} EvalInst &= Inst \\ c(p,i) &= c_{count}(p,i) \\ score_{laplace}(p) &= \frac{\sum_{i \in Inst \setminus PosInst} c(p,i) + 1}{\sum_{i \in Inst} c(p,i) + 1} \end{aligned}$$

WHISK evolves an annotated training corpus so that all instances are considered an error which have not been annotated. While $score_{laplace}(p)$ is close to $1 - precision$ for large set of extractions, it penalizes less productive patterns because for small $Inst$ sets the impact of the added 1 in the denominator plays a big role. For example, a pattern which only extracts one correct instances will score 0.5, a pattern extracting 9 positive instances and no negatives will score 0.1.

For URES, the ratio of positive to negative instances $NegInst$ is used where negative instances are derived based on a variant of the functionality assumption that also assumes that a sentence only contains one positive instance.

$$\begin{aligned} EvalInst &= Inst \cup NegInst \\ c(p,i) &= c_{bool}(p,i) \\ score_{URES}(p) &= \frac{\sum_{i \in Inst \setminus NegInst} c(p,i)}{\sum_{i \in NegInst} c(p,i) + 1} \end{aligned}$$

The Espresso system [Pantel and Pennacchiotti, 2006] takes an innovative approach to pattern (and instance) evaluation operating recursively. Espresso estimates pattern quality with the help of instance quality and vice versa. At the same time, it uses pointwise mutual information (PMI) as a measure of association between patterns and instances.

$$pmi(p,i) = log \frac{|i_1, p, i_2|}{|i_1, *, i_2| \; |*, p, *|}$$

The above count notation is extended to allow for arbitrary matches when marked with $*$. By means of an instance confidence measure $score(i)$, Espresso's measure can be described as:

$$\begin{aligned} c(p,i) &= score(i) \cdot c_{bool}(p,i) \\ EvalInst &= Inst \\ score_{Espresso}(p) &= \frac{\sum^{i \in Inst} \left(\frac{pmi(p,i)}{max_{pmi}} \cdot c(p,i) \right)}{|Inst|} \end{aligned}$$

Thereby max_{pmi} is the maximum PMI between all patterns and all instances in the matrix.

In the LPPL system [Tomita et al., 2006] the evaluation of patterns and instances is modelled as a maximum-likelihood parameter estimation problem that is solved using the Expectation Maximization (EM) algorithm. The goal is to estimate a confidence distribution of patterns which maximizes the likelihood of the observed patterns. The instance confidence scores serve as parameters to this model. Starting out with known values for the seed instances only, the EM algorithm approximates the other instance confidences. The version of the EM algorithm used by Tomita et al. [2006] co-evolves pattern confidences $conf(p)$ and instance confidences $conf(i)$. The modeling used does not fit the above notation because a pattern-instance incidence matrix as evaluation is done on the level of the mention and matching is not a binary decision but each pattern p matches each mention $m \in M$ to a certain degree of match $dm(p, m)$. Thereby the best-matching pattern for a mention $p^*(i)$ is distinguished. The instance extracted from a mention m is denoted $i_{ex}(m)$

$$conf(p) = \frac{\sum_{m \in M | p = p^*(m)} conf(i_{ex}(m)) + 1}{|*, p, *| + \beta}$$

$$conf(i) = 1 - \prod_{m \in M | i_{ex}(m) = i} (1 - conf(p^*(m)) dm(p^*(m), m))$$

In terms of the EM algorithm, the computation of $conf(p)$ constitutes the *expectation* step and the computation of $conf(i)$ corresponds to the *maximization* step. After the algorithm terminates, the output is

$$score_{LPPL}(p) = conf(p)$$

$$score_{LPPL}(i) = conf(i)$$

In sum, all measures are computed on the basis of co-occurrence information of patterns and instances while the measures vary in the choice of the set of instances used and aggregate this information in various ways. While most measures constitute relative frequencies or make otherwise use of a probabilistic measure, they are not based on a sound probabilistic modeling of pattern quality. It is therefore understandable that the measures are employed in rather crude ranking and cut-off mechanisms. In Chapter 6, the aspect of pattern quality assessment will be investigated empirically. A selection of scoring mechanisms will be compared when applied to the same task.

5.6.4 Matching Patterns

The matching of patterns is typically a straight-forward process the implementation details of which depend on the nature of the patterns and the size and representation of the text corpus. As soon as the pattern structure strongly differs from the text, the text has to be preprocessed prior to matching (e.g. providing required linguistic markup or transforming text to a bag-of-words representation). In general, the cost of such preprocessing is at least linear with the corpus size which makes it expensive for very large corpora (which otherwise may be accessed much faster than linear-time with the help of Information Retrieval techniques, cf. Section 2.4).

This issue can be improved in two ways. Firstly, the Snowball system matches *inexpensive markup first* (the entity tags) and does further preprocessing (conversion to bag-of-words, distance calculation to patterns) only when appropriate markup combinations have been found. Secondly, the KnowItNow system [Cafarella et al., 2005] *incorporates linguistic information into the search index* by extending the index structure accordingly.

5.6.5 Evaluating Instances

Various approaches exist to assessing the quality of instances. They build on a score that is assigned to each instance which is subsequently filtered based on a threshold. In most cases, the score is based on the matches of the existing patterns while some take co-occurrence counts with other contexts into account. Most scores estimate the probability of an extraction being correct while some are based on proximity in the space of possible co-occurrences. The focus here lies on evaluation scores for global Information Extraction tasks with automatically induced patterns.

The evaluation scores for instances can be described by means of the same incidence matrix notation as above. Yet, the set of instances in question $EvalInst$ remains the set of derived instances $Inst$ in all cases.

The most straight-forward way of computing instance score is that of simply counting the matching patterns (support). This has been proposed (although not systematically evaluated) by Brin [1999].

$$\begin{aligned} c(p,i) &= c_{bool}(p,i) \\ score_{support}(i) &= \sum_{p \in P_{pool}} c(p,i) \end{aligned}$$

Assuming that pattern scores have an interpretation as a precision estimate, i.e. reflecting the probability that a given instance extracted by the scored pattern is correct, the probability of an instance being correct can be estimated as the inverse of the joint probability that all patterns mistakenly extract the instance. This model has been proposed in Snowball [Agichtein and Gravano, 2000] and adopted in DARE [Xu et al., 2007].

$$\begin{aligned} c(p,i) &= c_{bool}(p,i) \cdot score_{precision}(p) \\ score_{precision}(i) &= 1 - \prod_{p \in P_{pool}} 1 - c(p,i) \end{aligned}$$

Agichtein and Gravano [2000] additionally proposes to weight patterns from earlier iterations higher to adopt the "learning rate" over iterations.

While this probabilistic interpretation is appealing, one needs to keep in mind that the precision scores proposed in these systems are crude upper estimates and that this model makes an independence assumption among the pattern matches which disregards that the patterns have been derived using the same mining process and are therefore likely not to be independent.

Like for the patterns, Espresso [Pantel and Pennacchiotti, 2006] uses a correlation-based approach for instance assessment. In fact, in line with the pattern-relation duality, the measure is symmetric with the pattern score (with the same definitions of $pmi(p,i)$ and max_{pmi}):

$$\begin{aligned} c(p,i) &= score(p) * c_{bool}(p,i) \\ EvalInst &= Inst \\ score_{Espresso}(i) &= \frac{\sum p \in P_{pool} \left(\frac{pmi(p,i)}{max_{pmi}}\right) \cdot c(p,i)}{|P_{pool}|} \end{aligned}$$

Another recursive approach is that by Tomita et al. [2006] as presented in Section 5.6.3. Similarly, URES [Rosenfeld and Feldman, 2006] uses pattern scores and a notion of degree of match to score instances, the details of which are not published. The above-mentioned systems (as far as they describe the actual filtering step) use a threshold to filter instances although it is not mentioned how this threshold has been actually computed.

An alternative approach to instance evaluation is to assess their appearances in other contexts than the present pattern sets. We will call these approaches *distributional*. Etzioni et al. [2005] propose the use of so-called "discriminators". Discriminators are generic patterns that are indicative for whether or not two terms stand in a specific relation. Extracted instances are combined with the discriminator patterns and matched in the corpus. The match counts are used as a feature to compare instances. This principle is a way of assessing distributional similarity (compare [Paşca et al., 2006]). Examples for discriminators are "city ANY_{city}" for the unary relation of being a city or "ANY_{ceo} CEO of $ANY_{company}$" for the relation between a company and its CEO. The distribution of counts of instances co-occurring with these discriminators is used to assess instance quality. More specifically, given a set of discriminator patterns $Disc$ for each instance $i \in Inst$ a vector is generated

$$d(i) = (\ldots, pmi'(d,i), \ldots)$$

Where $pmi'(d,i)$ is according to Etzioni et al. [2005] a (strongly simplified) version of Pointwise Mutual Information.

$$pmi'(d,i) = \frac{|i_1, d, i_2|}{|i_1, *, i_2|}$$

The decision whether a given i is in fact an instance of the target relation is then made by a Naive Bayes classifier which is trained on a set of previously accepted instances as positive examples and instances of known disjoint classes (seeds of other target relations) as negative examples. The set of discriminators which has to be produced for each target relation separately constitutes additional supervision. A heuristic and a bootstrapping-based method are presented to come up with discriminator patterns automatically.

A different way of distributional instance evaluation is presented by McIntosh and Curran [2009] and Paşca et al. [2006]. They use vector space similarities between bag-of-words vectors of words occurring around the instances. Distributionally more similar instances are considered better. McIntosh and Curran use this distance to quantify the "semantic drift" for a given instance. This is done by relating the distributional similarity of the seeds to newly extracted instance to the distributional similarity among the newly extracted instances. If an instance is closer to the newly extracted instances than to the seeds, it is considered likely that the new extraction does not capture the original semantics of the target relation as described by the seed set.

The hyponymy extraction system presented by Snow et al. [2004] uses a Naive Bayes classifier Θ directly on the pattern-instance incidence matrix O_c where c is chosen to represent co-occurrence counts:

$$\begin{aligned} EvalInst &= Inst \\ c(p,i) &= c_{count}(p,i) \\ score_{classifier}(i) &= \Theta((c(1,i),\ldots,c(|P_{pool}|,i))) \end{aligned}$$

where $(c(1,i),\ldots,c(|P_{pool}|,i))$ is the projection of $O_c(i)$ on its ith column. Θ is trained on a set of positive and negative seeds. Aiming at extending WordNet, Snow et al. make a good approximation of negative examples by allowing all noun pairs not standing in a hyponymy relation in WordNet as negatives.

A thorough probabilistic model which estimates the correctness of instances in a probabilistic manner is enabled by the URNS model [Downey et al., 2005] which estimates the probability that a given mention is an instance of a given class C (which may be a relation) based on the frequency of observed extractions. In particular, it produces a probability estimate $P(i \in C | i \text{ matches } k \text{ times in } n \text{ draws})$. URNS models the extraction process as repeated draws from an urn. Each draw corresponds to one match of a pattern (or set of patterns) and can either produce an error ball or a correct ball. In both cases, the ball has a label i belonging to the instance that is being extracted. Apart from a precision estimate of the pattern(s) that caused the given count of extractions it only takes as input counts (or estimates) for the frequency of the target class and of errors. The URNS model was applied in several systems [Cafarella et al., 2005; McDowell and Cafarella, 2008]

5.7 Evaluation Paradigms

In the following chapters technical work with implementations of the framework introduced in this chapter will be presented. While the exact experimental setup is dependant on the study, common datasets and common evaluation measures have been used.

5.7.1 Datasets

Training and test data of global relation extraction consists of relation instances. While for training, a small set of seed examples is sufficient, the full extension of the target relation needs to be known for evaluation purposes.

We obtained large relation sets using (i) a DAML version of the CIA World Factbook (for currency), (ii) lineup data from 50 years of FIFA soccer games provided by the SmartWeb project[2] and (iii) exploiting Wikipedia categories in a semi-automatic manner using the CatScan tool by Daniel Kinzler.[3] The latter allowed us to retrieve all members of a category. CatScan was applied recursively to also obtain members of sub-categories.

The data sets have been chosen to differ according to various dimensions, most notably in size. The *currencyOf* dataset, for example, is relatively small and constitutes a relation with clear boundaries with almost no changes over time. The other relations are likely not be reflected fully in the data sets.

- *albumBy*: 19852 titles of music albums and their artists generated from the Wikipedia category "Albums by Artist."
- *bornInYear*: 172696 persons and their year of birth generated from the Wikipedia category "Births by Year."
- *currencyOf*: 221 countries and their official currency according to DAML export of the CIA World Fact Book.

[2] `http://www.smartweb-project.de`

[3] `http://tools.wikimedia.de/~daniel/WikiSense`

http://www.daml.org/2001/12/factbook/ Manual modifications were done to reflect the introduction of the Euro as official currency in many European countries.

- *headquarteredIn*: 14762 names of companies and the country they are based in generated from the Wikipedia category "Companies by Country." http://en.wikipedia.org/wiki/Category:Companies_by_country

- *locatedIn*: 34047 names of cities and the state and federal states they are located in generated from the Wikipedia category "Cities by Countries." http://en.wikipedia.org/wiki/Category:Cities_by_country Note that a considerable number of cities are contained in this data set with both their state and their federal state.

- *productOf*: 2650 vehicle product names and the brand names of their makers generated from the Wikipedia category "Vehicles by Brand." http://en.wikipedia.org/wiki/Category:Vehicles_by_brand

- *teamOf*: 8307 soccer players and the national teams they were playing for between 1950 and 2006.[4]

It is important to note that also the Wikipedia collections have been compiled manually by authors who assigned the documents to the respective categories and have been checked by further community members. Thus, the datasets can be regarded to be of high quality. Further, due to the vast coverage of Wikipedia, the extensions of the relations can be assumed to be relatively complete.

In the experiments, small samples (size 10, 50 and 100) of the datasets were taken as input seeds. Initial tests showed that taking prominent instances as seeds strongly increases the system's output quality over random seeds. It can be expected that in most real scenarios prominent seeds are available as they should be those best known to the users. With two exceptions,[5] we took the number of in-links to the Wikipedia articles mentioned in each instance as an indicator for their significance in the corpus and selected the top n samples with respect to the harmonic mean of these counts.

[4]This data set is a courtesy of the SmartWeb consortium (see http://www.smartweb-project.de/).

[5]For cities we took the average living costs as an indicator to ensure that Athens Greece was ranked higher than Athens, New York. Population would have skewed the sample towards Asian cities not prominently mentioned in the English Wikipedia. For Albums we required titles to be at least 10 characters in length to discourage highly ambiguous titles like "Heart" or "Friends"

5.7.2 Evaluation measures

In our experiments, we relied on the widely used precision and recall measures to evaluate extraction output. These measures compute the ratio of correctly found instances to overall instances extracted (precision) or all instances to be found (recall). They are appropriate to evaluate any binary statistical classifier and have the benefit of having a probabilistic interpretation.

Both measures are computed based on the observed output *Inst*, the intended positive instances (the extension Ext of the relation) and the set (hypothetical) of all items to be classified *All*. By that two types of correct judgements and two types of errors can be distinguished:

- *True Positives*(TP): Correct positive classifications. $Inst \cap Ext$.
- *True Negatives*(TN): Correct negative classifications. $All \setminus (Inst \cup Ext)$.
- *False Positives*(FP): Erroneous positive classification. $Inst \setminus Ext$.
- *False Negatives*(FN): Erroneous negative classification. $Ext \setminus Inst$.

Precision is defined as the relative frequency of correct positive classification among all classifications:

$$precision = \frac{|Inst \cap Ext|}{|Inst|} = \frac{|TP|}{|TP \cup FP|}$$

Recall is the relative frequency of correct positive classifications among all instances that should have been classified positively:

$$recall = \frac{|Inst \cap Ext|}{|Ext|} = \frac{|TP|}{|TP \cup FN|}$$

Precision and recall are convenient quality measures for Information Extraction as they have an intuitive probabilistic interpretation: Given an instance extracted by an Information Extraction system with precision p, we know that this instance is correct with the probability p. Given a relation instance of which we know that it can be extracted from a corpus, we know that it will be extracted with probability r by a system that has recall r on that corpus.

Sometimes it is convenient to compare extraction results on one dimension of quality. To this end, the F-measure is widely used in the literature. It consists in the combination of precision and recall by the weighted harmonic mean.

$$F_\beta = (1 + \beta^2) \cdot \frac{2\ precision\ recall}{\beta^2 \cdot precision + recall}$$

The intuition behind this measure is that the overall quality lies in the balance between precision and recall and that if one of the measures is much lower than the other, this is to be penalized over-proportionally. Thereby, β weights precision vs. recall. The most commonly used β value is 1. The choice of this measure is somewhat arbitrary. How much false positives and false negative should be accepted strongly depends on the application and it is unlikely that both affect the effective quality of the system in the same manner.

As the fixed number of iterations in our experiments poses a technical limit on the number of possible extractions (e.g. Google only returns 1000 results for a query even if there are more) we use a notion of *(r)elative (r)ecall* assuming maximally extracted number of instances by any configuration in any iteration with the given relation. With $y_r(i, m)$ being the yield, i.e. number of extractions (correct and incorrect) at iteration i for relation r with method m and $p_r(i, m)$ the precision respectively, we can formalize relative recall as

$$rr_r(i, m) = \frac{y_r(i, m) * p_r(i, m)}{\max_{i,m} y_r(i, m)}$$

5.7.3 Automatic Evaluation

The extraction output has been evaluated automatically based on the data sets described above. Approximate matches are admitted by allowing the omission of words and respecting WordNet synonyms. Both automatic and manual evaluation lead to inexact assessment. The automatic assessment is inexact because an automatic evaluation system is likely to miss the intended meaning of the output (e.g. by not knowing all synonyms of a target instance). The manual evaluation is usually done only on a sample of the data and is furthermore prone to human errors. In order to investigate, the effects of manual vs. automatic evaluation, both types of evaluation were compared on the basis of the experiments presented in the following chapter. The results show that automatic evaluation underestimates precision because it misses correct instance that the system is not aware of. Refer to Section 6.3 for the comparison and a discussion on the possible causes.

5.8 Performance of Systems in the Literature

Information Extraction is a sub-field of NLP that is clearly driven by the goal of obtaining the desired information rather than modelling or analyzing linguistic properties. The evaluation of extraction output with respect to precision and recall is hence at the center of scientific arguments. Most studies focusing on large-scale and or Web-oriented IE, consider special scenarios, so that systems

System	corpus	seeds	relations	precision
Culotta et al.[2006]	1127 Wikipedia p.	annotated text	60	65% - 72%
Espresso[Pantel and Pennacchiotti, 2006]	5M words	"few"	5	49%-85%
SOFIE[Suchanek et al., 2009]	3400 Web pages	Yago ontology	13	>90%
KnowItNow[Cafarella et al., 2005]	60M Web pages	seed patterns	5	>70%
Pasca et al.[2006]	100 M Web pages	10 seeds	1	>90%
Pronto (Ch. 6)	Web	10 seeds	7	10 - 80%
URES[Rosenfeld and Feldman, 2006]	some Web pages	10-15 seeds	5	70-90%
Snowball[Agichtein and Gravano, 2000]	180k news posts	5 seeds	1	85%

Table 5.1: Performance results reported in the literature and experimental conditions.

in the literature differ with respect to many degrees of freedom. In this section, we present results reported in key studies that are discussed in this thesis. In Table 5.1, we show precision, type and size of the text collection as well as the supervision provided.

Due to the many different degrees of freedom, a conclusive statement on the superiority of one approach over another cannot be made. One can observe as a general tendency that results in the range of above 80% are not obtained by systems operating at the scale of milions of pages. Several authors observe strong variations of output quality depending on the target relations. This is in line with our observations reported in the following chapters.

No comparable way of reporting recall has been established. Several studies report absolute result counts [Brin, 1999; Rosenfeld and Feldman, 2006; Cafarella et al., 2005]. Others report results relative to other systems [Pantel and Pennacchiotti, 2006] or the full extension of the relation [Paşca et al., 2006; Agichtein and Gravano, 2000]. Our approach to take the full extension of the relation as a reference for precision and recall assessment and perform automated quality assessment is a novelty.

Chapter 6

Controlling the Quality of Induced Patterns

As indicated in Section 5.4, minimizing supervision of Information Extraction systems is an important goal (referred to as *Challenge 1* in Section 5.4). One essential subtask to achieve is to control the quality of the set of patterns so that they have the appropriate levels of precision and recall. Obviously this has to be done without knowing precision and recall of the patterns because these measures require knowledge about the intended output (the *Pattern Quality Prediction Dilemma, Challenge 3*). Pattern-based Information Extraction systems in the literature therefore use a large variety of pattern evaluation mechanisms usually computing scores that approximate precision and/or recall.

Good pattern quality measures enable the system to estimate output quality and thus to adjust other parameters of the system as required. They hence play an important role with regard to the autonomy of an extraction system. In order to investigate these aspects, we present here an empirical comparison of various evaluation strategies. We use a completely uninformed baseline and a fully informed "gold standard" evaluation strategy as natural upper and lower bounds on precision, recall and F-measure with regard to the choice of strategy. The approaches compared differ in the way they assign a utility score to each pattern which is then used to filter out inappropriate patterns. These scoring functions are called *filtering functions* throughout this chapter.

This study has been done in the Pronto system on several non-taxonomic relations. In the following, the different filtering functions that are the subject of analysis are introduced and discussed. Then, in Section 6.2 the experimental setup is described before results are presented and discussed in Section 6.3 and put into relation with related work in Section 6.1.1. A brief summary is given in Section 6.4. We have published most of the empirical results of this study at the AAAI conference 2007 together with Philipp Cimiano and Egon Stemle [Blohm et al., 2007].

Some further results were presented at the 3rd Web as Corpus Workshop 2007 [Blohm and Cimiano, 2007]. To the best of our knowledge, this is the first systematic comparison of different evaluation techniques.

6.1 Filtering Functions

As outlined in Section 5.3, the key idea of the iterative pattern induction framework is to evolve a set of patterns P_{pool} which constitutes the learned model. Before being applied, patterns are evaluated in each iteration and then filtered based on this evaluation. In the following, we discuss prominent pattern evaluation strategies from various pattern-based Information Extraction systems. They can all be described in terms of a two-step process: First, a score $score : P \rightarrow \mathbb{R}$ is assigned and then, potentially weakly performing patterns are filtered out by imposing a threshold or cut-off percentile on these scores.

From the literature we can identify five general types of pattern quality assessment.

- *Syntactic assessment.* Filtering purely based on syntactic criteria like for example a pattern's length.

- *Inter-pattern comparison.* If there is a set of patterns that is known to be good, it may be beneficial to rate a new pattern based on how similar its output is to the output of those patterns.

- *Support-based assessment.* The iterative nature of the extraction allows the system to estimate quality of patterns based on the number of mentions that contributed to the generation of this pattern. We call this number *support* like in association rule mining (cf. Section 2.3). An analogous filtering step was suggested in by Brin [1999].

- *Performance-based assessment.* The most straightforward way to assess a pattern's quality is to judge the rate of correctly produced output. Because an exhaustive assessment would require full knowledge of the target relation, heuristic performance-based assessment is typically by comparing the output of new patterns to output of previous iterations.

- *Instance-Pattern correlation.* A further indicator for the quality of a pattern is whether its presence correlates strongly with the presence of instances of the target relation. Estimating this by counting mentions of patterns, seed instances and patterns instantiated with seed instances allows controlling both precision and potential recall of a pattern within one value.

6.1.1 Pattern Filtering in Related Work

Given the focus of the study, all the systems introduced in Section 5.6 constitute related work. In particular the varying approaches to pattern evaluation as presented in Section 5.6.3 are of interest. For the present study, the focus is on filtering functions of systems which operate on Web scale or are designed with scalability in mind.

Syntactic assessment has been proposed and applied by Brin [1999], where the length of a pattern is used to predict its specificity. Inter-pattern comparison is particularly useful when patterns are induced as abstractions over individual mentions or over more specific patterns. This is done in [Ruiz-Casado et al., 2005] where all pairwise abstractions below a given edit-distance threshold are used and as a pre-evaluation filter in $(LP)^2$ [Ciravegna, 2001] which uses inductive logic programming (ILP) for abstraction. While support-based assessment is quite common for instances [Agichtein and Gravano, 2000; Etzioni et al., 2005] it has not been applied to pattern evaluation. Performance-based assessment for patterns is performed by Agichtein and Gravano [2000] and Ciravegna [2001] with a precision estimate that is also contestant in this study. A similar score is used by the URES and URIES systems [Rosenfeld and Feldman, 2006; Rozenfeld and Feldman, 2006]. Another variant called Laplacian expected error is applied by Soderland [1999]. A comparision of two rather task-specific performance-based measures in a question-answering environment is presented by Alfonseca et al. [2006]. Instance-pattern correlation is used in the Espresso [Pantel and Pennacchiotti, 2006] and the KnowItAll [Etzioni et al., 2005] systems. Both correlation scores are reproduced in this study. An innovation of Espresso is that pattern scores are used as weights in instance scores and vice-versa which captures the recursive notion of the induction process during scoring. Such a recursive evaluation can be also found in ExDisco [Yangarber, 2003]) with the difference that documents are assigned a confidence value instead of instances. The assumption is that a good set of patterns defines a good set of relevant documents which in turn contain these patterns more freuently.

In the following, we present here the filtering functions compared in the experiments, which are partly taken from the literature of state-of-the-art pattern induction systems. Note that for comparing the approaches which stem from very heterogeneous systems in the literature, only the scoring of the patterns is varied between the experimental conditions. The cut-off criterion is kept constant by working with a pre-defined number of patterns that are kept for matching whereby $|P_{pool}|$ remains constant. An individual pattern can be kept over several iterations but is re-evaluated against all patterns in each iteration. Thus, while the set of extracted instances $Inst$ is grown incrementally, the evolution of P_{pool} is non-monotonic. Discarding patterns in each iteration is common practice in most pattern induction systems from the literature and in line with the idea of mutual bootstrapping [Riloff and Jones, 1999]. Intuitively, it prevents the double induction of noise both in the set of patterns and in the set of instances.

6.1.2 Performance-Based Filtering

Agichtein and Gravano [2000] use the output of previous iterations to approximate a *performance-based* precision measure for each pattern. Recall from Section 5.7.2 that precision can be defined as:

$$precision = \frac{|TP|}{|TP \cup FP|}$$

with TP and FP being the set of correctly and erroneously extracted instances, respectively. Agichtein and Gravano define FP as the set of instances violating the assumption that the target relation is many-to-one. For this study, we slightly generalize this notion of precision no longer distinguishing incorrect and unclassified extractions to overcome Snowball's restriction of only operating on many-to-one relations by defining FP as the set of all instances not previously extracted. Following Agichtein and Gravano we use the output of previous iterations to approximate a *performance-based* precision.

Definition 1 $score_{prec}(p)$: *Let* $m(p)$ *be the instances matched by pattern* p*, and* $Inst$ *to be the seeds of the current iteration. Approximating the precision amounts to relating the number of instances a pattern extracts that have been accepted as correct in previous iteration to all instances it extracts:*

$$score_{prec}(p) = \frac{|m(p) \cap Inst|}{|m(p)|}$$

This measure may heavily underestimate the actual output quality of a pattern if that pattern is able to generate many previously unseen – but correct – relation instances. The following strategies have been adopted to overcome this limitation.

6.1.3 Instance-Pattern Correlation for Filtering

Several systems from the literature use a measure called Pointwise Mutual Information (PMI) as an *instance-pattern correlation* measure. Mutual Information is a correlation measure with information theoretic interpretation that measures the mutual dependence of two random variables. Pointwise mutual information focuses on a specific pair of outcomes. We evaluate here two different approaches of pattern assessment via mutual information which use relative corpus frequencies of instances and patterns to measure correlation.

Definition 2 $score_{pmi}(p)$: *PMI measures the strength of association between two discrete random variables A and B and is defined as:*

$$pmi(A,B) = log\frac{P(A,B)}{P(A)P(B)}$$

In the PMI-based correlation, the events of a pattern occurring in a given fragment of text and that of an instance occurring in a given fragment are correlated ($pmi(p,i)$). Pattern confidence values can be computed by averaging over a random subset of the currently accepted instances $Inst$ (whereby sampling is done for efficiency reasons).

$$score_{pmi}(p) = \frac{1}{|Inst|}\sum_{i \in Inst} pmi(p,i)$$

The $pmi(p,i)$ is defined in different ways two of which are given below.

The notation for pattern and instance match counts is adopted from Pantel and Pennachiotti [2006]. We write $|arg_1, p, arg_2|$ to denote the number of corpus matches of a query generated by filling the arguments of instance $i = (arg_1, arg_2)$ into the argument slots of pattern p. At any position $*$ means allowing arbitrary values for the pattern or the argument replaced. If for example the passage "... flights to London, England" appears 12 times in the text, it would hold that

$$|\text{London, flightsto..., England}| = 12$$

Definition 3 $pmi_{KnowItAll}(p,i)$: *The KnowItAll [Etzioni et al., 2005] Information Extraction system uses PMI in the following way to assess coherence of a pattern-instance pair (p,i) in:*

$$pmi_{KnowItAll}(p,i) = \frac{|i_1, p, i_2|}{|i_1, *, i_2|}$$

Note that the logarithm of the fraction is not used in the computations in KnowItAll which however does not affect the ranking of the results for which the score is used. The same is true for the fact that both PMI-based formulae operate on absolute counts instead of probabilities.

In KnowItAll, this measure is used to generate a feature vector for classification of patterns. In the present work, we use an average of pmi values over a subset of $Inst$ of size 15 to quantify the patterns output quality.

Definition 4 $pmi_{Espresso}(p,i)$: *In the Espresso system [Pantel and Pennacchiotti, 2006], PMI is used in a different way aiming at* *relating the event of the pattern occurring in the corpus and the event of the instance occurring in the corpus: The intuition behind this is that a pattern is good if it occurs preferably in association with instances from $Inst$ and conversely instances from $Inst$ have a strong association with the pattern.*

$$pmi_{Espresso}(p, i) = log\frac{|i_1, p, i_2|}{|*, p, *|\ |i_1, *, i_2|}$$

For the experimental comparison of the PMI-based filtering functions, Google's result count estimates were used to estimate probabilities. A discussion on how these are created can be found in Section 2.4.

The multitude of different probabilistic modelings for pattern filtering available suggests that arguments from probability theory can merely serve as a motivation for a certain measure but not guarantee success. It is likely that there is no universally appropriate modeling due to the unpredictable underlying distributions.

6.1.4 Support-Based Filtering

In addition to the above filtering functions, we further present a simple filtering function based on the count of distinct instances from which a pattern was generated:

Definition 5 $score_{support}(p)$: *Given the number of distinct instances present in the mentions from which a pattern was generated, i.e.* $distinct\_generators(p)$, *we define*

$$score_{support}(p) = |distinct\_generators(p)|$$

Thus, $score_{support}$ evaluates patterns by the number of different seed instances from which they have been produced, hence favoring more general patterns and penalizing patterns which just hold for a few examples.

6.1.5 Base Line and Gold Standard

Definition 6 $score_{random}(p)$: *As a baseline condition, a pattern evaluator has been implemented that assigns random confidence values* $score_{random}(p)$ *to all patterns. The choice of patterns for the instance generation hence does not depend on their output quality nor on further syntactic criteria.*

Note that the Pronto system applies some syntactic heuristics to filter out pattern candidates that are far too general or too specific (cf. Section 6.2.1). Hence, all patterns that are put into the filtering are of some minimum quality. This explains why even the baseline system with random selection performs relatively well (see the results in Section 6.3).

Definition 7 $score_{gold}(p)$: *In order to estimate the upper limit of the potential of performance-based pattern evaluation, we introduce a scoring function that is based on the full knowledge of the extension G of the target relation. This extension is made available externally from large datasets we produced for that purpose (compare Section Experiments):*

$$score_{gold}(p) = \frac{|m(p) \cap G|}{|m(p)|}$$

We use the term gold standard for this measure even though the measure may still be out-performed for two reasons. Firstly, the extensions of the relations used are not necessarily complete in the dataset. Secondly, the measure regards only precision not coverage or syntactic properties. Yet, this measure can provide a good indicator of how well a perfectly informed filtering function would perform and thus serves to study limitations of the approach.

6.2 Experimental Setup

In order to assess the potential of various filtering functions, we have performed experiments with various target relations and filtering functions. The goal of our experiments is to explore the strengths and weaknesses of different filtering functions from the literature, comparing these results to the baseline $score_{random}(p)$ as well as an approximation of an informed upper bound $score_{gold}(p)$. In the following, the setup of the Pronto system is described in detail before the remaining experimental details are presented.

6.2.1 Configuration of the Pronto system

This section gives implementation details of the Pronto system for the experiments on pattern quality. The system configuration was kept constant over the experiments varying only the filtering functions for the patterns and operating with several target relations. The World Wide Web was accessed through the Google API as described in Section 5.5.2.

To ensure the generality of the results, we have refrained from integrating specific additional knowledge in our implementation. Common forms of background knowledge applied in the literature are thesauri, filters for part-of-speech or syntactic criteria and knowledge about the type of relation in question (e.g.

part-of-speech tags [Pantel and Pennacchiotti, 2006] or named entity classification [Agichtein and Gravano, 2000]).

Note that all parameters chosen for the experiments have been determined experimentally to ensure stable extraction quality across typical configurations and target relations.

Matching Instances

In order to identify mentions of the current seed set on the Web, the search index is accessed via Google's Java API querying for pages on which all words present in both arguments of the instance can be found. A fixed number $num_{matchInstances}$ of results is retrieved. From those, only the result headers and text snippets are kept which contain all arguments within a distance of at most $max_{argDist}$. For the experiments presented in this chapter we set $max_{argDist} = 4$ and decrease $num_{matchInstances}$ from 200 to 20 in steps of 45 over 5 iterations.

Learning Patterns

Learning patterns aims at finding representative abstractions of as many valid mentions of relation instances as possible. Patterns are expressed as a set of constraints on the tokens. There are two types of constraints: the *surface string* of individual words and their corresponding *capitalization.*

The learning algorithm essentially merges groups of mentions on a token by token basis. Constraints that are shared by all mentions within a group are kept while the others are eliminated. An unoptimized version of the algorithm for merging is given in Figure 6.1 for illustration purposes. Basically, it ensures that all subsets of the set of found mentions M are merged, if they share a certain minimum number of constraints. The pattern

"flights to ANY_{ARG_1} , ANY_{ARG_2} from ANY airport" (1)

may have been generated by the following example mentions:

"... flights to Athens , Greece from Heathrow airport..."
"... flights to Paris , France from JFK airport..."

Thus, the generalization effectively corresponds to computing the least general generalization (LGG) of two patterns as typically done in bottom-up ILP approaches (compare [Muggleton and Feng, 1990]).

The procedure MERGE(p, p') takes the patterns p and p', aligns them by their arguments and generates a pattern containing only the constraints that p and p' share for any of their token positions. The function CONSTRAINTS(p) counts

```
LEARN-PATTERNS(M)
Queue ← M
P_new ← ∅
while NON-EMPTY(Queue)
do
   o = FIRST(Queue)
   for o' ∈ M ∪ P_new
   do
      p ← MERGE(o, o')
      if CONSTRAINTS(p) ≥ min_common
        then
           P_new ← P_new ∪ p
           ADD(Queue, p)
OUTPUT(P_new)
```

Figure 6.1: The algorithm that learns patterns from a set M of mentions.

the number of non-empty constraints in p. Thereby it is ensured that at least min_{common} constraints are shared. To reduce the algorithm's time complexity, an index data structure is used to avoid the $|M|^2$ comparisons required otherwise. In particular, for the surface string constraint, a separate index is generated for each token position allowing to query for the set of mentions with a given surface string at a given position. Generating all groups of mentions that share a given set of surface strings in the same positions thus becomes a matter of intersecting sets returned from the index.

Prior to merging, the mentions are stripped off the text more than t_{prefix} words before the first and t_{suffix} words after the last argument. When comparing the mentions in which the arguments stand at different distances, only the first t tokens are considered, where t is the minimum distance encountered between arguments. For the present experiments we chose $t_{prefix} = t_{suffix} = 2$ and $min_{common} = 2$. This relatively small context is due to the fact that initial experiments revealed that the two preceding and following words are most indicative. Taking more words into account significantly increases the pattern induction time required. For example, the phrase

"cheap flights to Athens , Greece from Heathrow airport."

Would be trimmed to

"flights to Athens , Greece from Heathrow"

And due to $max_{argDist} = 4$ phrases like

"Athens is my favorite city in Greece."

would not be considered at all.

In its pure form, the algorithm generates much more candidate patterns than could reasonably be processed further. Therefore heuristic filters are applied to exclude potentially worthless patterns. In particular, the following steps are undertaken:

- For each pattern, the number of mentions from which it was generated is considered, and all patterns originating from less that t_{merge} distinct instances are discarded.
- Patterns with less than min_{common} constraints other than punctuation or stop words[1] are eliminated.

Initial experiments have shown (in line with results by Agichtein and Gravano [2000]) that punctuation contains important information for extraction patterns. Therefore, punctuation characters are treated as individual tokens. As punctuation is disregarded by Google, the presence of punctuation characters is established in an additional matching step as described in Section 5.5.

Filtering Patterns

In each experimental setup, one of the filtering function described in Section 6.1 is applied to all patterns. PATTERN-FILTER-CONDITION(p) is defined to always retain the top 100 best-scoring patterns according to filtering functions, i.e. $|P_{pool}| = 100$. Thus, newly learned patterns compete against those kept from previous iterations and may replace them. Filtering is important to exclude too specific (e.g. " the Acropolis in ANY_{ARG_1} , ANY_{ARG_2}" which would only extract the instance $(Athens, Greece)$) or too general patterns (e.g. "... ANY_{ARG_1} is in ANY_{ARG_2}..." which would also match "My birthday is in March."). The number of 100 has shown to be an appropriate pattern pool size in preliminary experiments.

Matching Patterns

MATCH-PATTERNS(P) matches each pattern in P by running a set of queries to the Google API. For this purpose, patterns are translated to queries as described in

[1] as available at `http://meta.wikimedia.org/wiki/Stop_word_list`

Section 5.5.2 and then matched. The resulting set of pattern matches is then fed to EXTRACT-INSTANCES(M_p) which identifies the argument slot fillers and thereby generates new instances. The number of results considered for each pattern is $num_{matchPatterns} = 60$. Note that for multiple mentions of the same instance, only one instance is generated. However, the set of patterns $generators(i)$ which extracted the instance i is kept for confidence computation.

Filtering Instances

The overall goal of evaluating instances it to estimate the confidence that they belong to the target relation. For the purpose of the experiments we compute the confidence of an instance by averaging over the confidence that Pronto assigns to the patterns that extracted the instance.

$$score(i) = \frac{\sum_{p \in generators(i)} score(p)}{|generators(i)|}$$

INSTANCE-FILTER-CONDITION(i) is implemented to be true for the top $p_{filterInstances}$ per cent of the newly generated instances. We chose $p_{filterInstances} = 50\%$ that means, the top 50% of the newly extracted instances are kept for the next iteration, *in addition* to those which have been accepted in earlier iterations. That is, while the patten set is kept at a constant size, the output is grown monotonically.

Iterating

The choice of the termination condition DONE greatly depends on the target application and its requirements with respect to coverage and precision. In the experiments presented here extraction terminates after a fixed number $t_{iterations}$ of cycles.

Table 6.1 summarizes the parameters discussed in this section and how they are set for the present experiments. Note that these parameters have been optimized systematically in previous experiments but are kept general enough to work well with all target relations under investigation.

6.3 Analysis of Results

The empirical analysis of filtering functions is based on the assessment of precision and recall as defined based on the evaluation data described in Section 5.7. The results of the experiments are based on both an automatic verification of the results with respect to the seven data sets and a human validation of these results.

Size of the seed set	$\|Inst'\|$	10
Size of pattern set	$\|P\|$	100
Results retrieved for each instance	$num_{matchInstances}$	200 – 20
Maximum tokens between arguments	$max_{argDist}$	4
Windows around arguments	$t_{prefix} = t_{suffix}$	2
Minimum support for pattern	t_{merge}	2
Minimum number of constraints per pattern	min_{common}	2
Results retrieved for each pattern	$num_{matchPatterns}$	60
Ratio of instances kept after filtering	$p_{filterInstances}$	50%
Number of iterations	$t_{iterations}$	5

Table 6.1: Parameter values as used during the experiments.

While the automatic evaluation has the advantages that no sampling effects occur and that it can be obtained quickly for all experimental conditions, this comes at the expense of two problems. First, the data sets do not necessarily reflect the entire extension of the relation (e.g. *teamOf* only contains data for international soccer players not for other sports or national leagues and the *bornInYear* dataset is incomplete for even more obvious reasons). Second, name ambiguities may not be fully resolved in automatic evaluation. To address this, two students at our university not involved in the development of the system were given random samples of 100 instances of the output for each relation and each type of filtering function. Evaluation was done for all filtering functions for three relations and for two filtering functions ($score_{support}$ and $score_{gold}$) for all relations. The evaluators were asked to verify each fact using the Web as a resource. The results suggest that automatic evaluation strongly underestimates the system precision (on average by factor 1.81). In fact, in almost all cases with exception of the *headquarteredIn* relation, which in general is quite spurious, the precision of the system is significantly better with respect to the manual evaluation, such that we can conclude that the precision of the system is indeed close to state-of-the-art systems such as Espresso, which achieves precision rates of 49% - 85% on a text corpus.

In the following, several aspects of the extraction process are investigated in detail. Primarily, the differences in output quality of the filtering functions is discussed. A focus is put on what can be derived from the comparison with an informed upper bound and a random baseline and on how precision and recall interact.

6.3.1 Relative Comparison of Filtering Functions

The impact of the choice of the filtering function on the precision of the output can be observed in Figure 6.2. The precision of the output of the last iteration has been plotted over the relations examined and the filtering function chosen. The results of a two-sided paired Student's t-test given in Table 6.2 show the significance of the observed differences (on the automatic evaluation results). The null hypothesis is that the results for all relations of the two filtering functions compared originate from the same distribution. A '$<$' or '$>$' indicates that the null hypothesis could be rejected at an α-level of 0.10 and a '$<<$' or '$>>$' indicates rejection at an α-level of 0.05.

The significance tests show that our informed upper baseline $score_{gold}$ outperforms all other strategies and that $score_{support}$ and $score_{prec}$ are superior to $score_{random}$. However, the PMI-based evaluation measures implemented in KnowItAll and Espresso do not perform significantly better than the baseline, while at the same time no significant difference could be in fact observed between the filtering functions $score_{support}$, $score_{pmi_{Espresso}}$, $score_{pmi_{KnowItAll}}$ and $score_{prec}$.

Figure 6.2 suggests that the lack of a clear winner is due to different output quality for different relations.

	gold	support	Espr.	Prec.	Rand.	Know.
gold	-	>>	>>	>>	>>	>>
support	<<	-	-	-	>	-
Espresso	<<	-	-	-	-	-
Precision	<<	-	-	-	>>	-
Random	<<	<	-	<<	-	-
KnowItAll	<<	-	-	-	-	-

Table 6.2: Results of a significance test on the difference of output distributions of the filtering functions over all relations. $>$ indicates significantly higher results of the approach of that row over that in the column with an α level of 0.10 and $<<$ of 0.05. $<$ and $<<$ stand for lower performance respectively.

Upper and Lower Bounds of Performance

In this section, the results are discussed in the light of the baseline provided by $score_{random}$ as well as an upper bound provided by the informed $score_{gold}$ filtering function. While $score_{random}$ incorporates no information whatsoever into its selection, $score_{gold}$ incorporates complete information about the extension of the

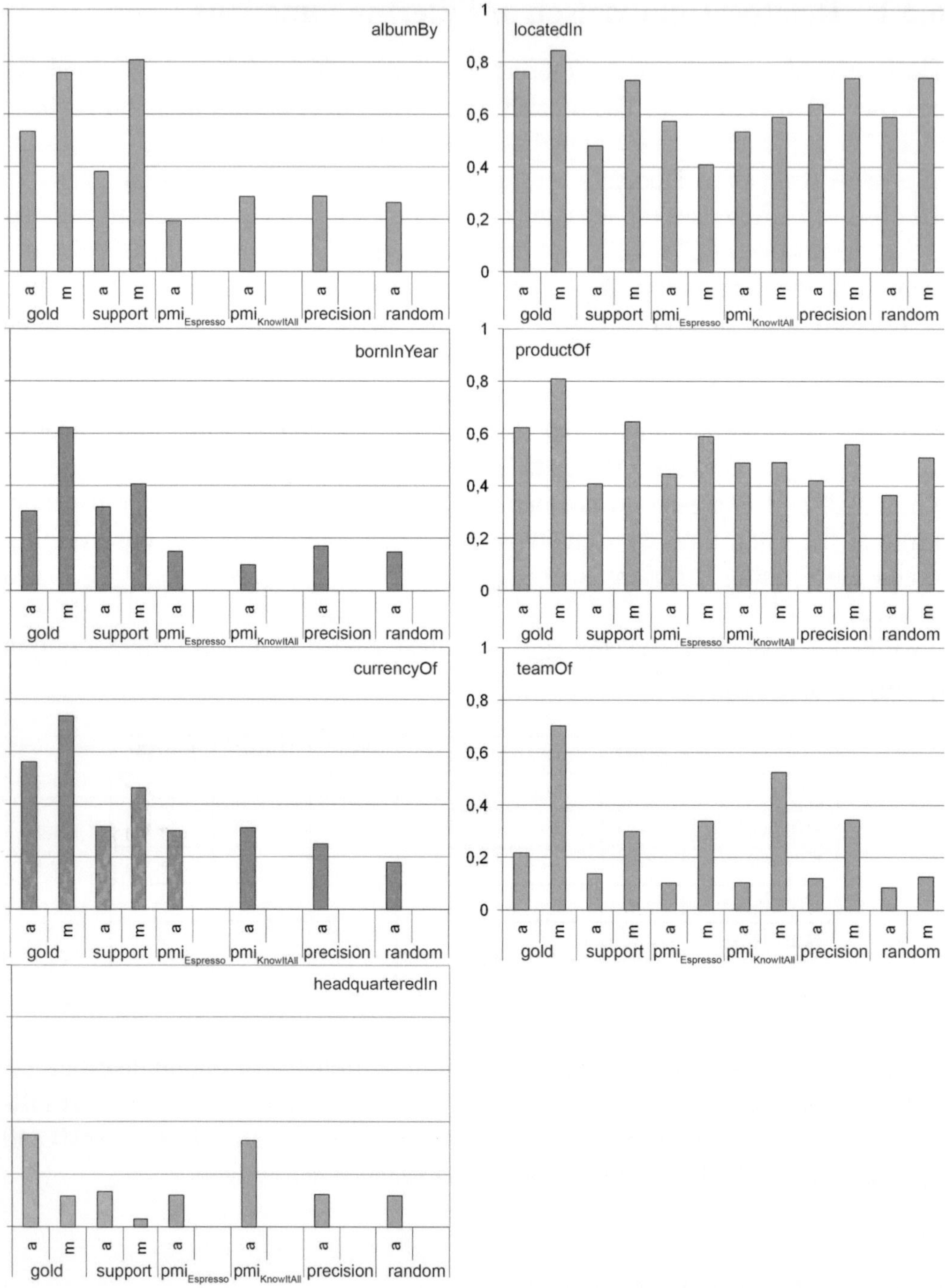

Figure 6.2: Overall output precision after 5 iterations for the 7 different relations and evaluation strategies based on automatic evaluation. Results for exhaustive automatic evaluation (a) and sampled manual evaluation (m).

relation and thus represents a 'fully informed' evaluation strategy. Such complete information would actually never be available, such that it is important to stress that this evaluation strategy has to be regarded merely to assess the impact of pattern filtering.

As can be observed in Figure 6.2 and has been shown with the significance tests in Table 6.2, most filtering functions presented here perform better in terms of precision than $score_{random}$ and worse than the informed filter $score_{gold}$, which is an expected result. Although the evaluation strategies based on performance and instance-pattern correlation, as implemented in Espresso and KnowItAll do not perform significantly better than the baseline, the small differences of 1 to 7 percentage points should not be underestimated. In fact, for comparability reasons, the baseline – like all other filters – comes with a pre-filter which excludes all patterns with only one supporting instance. It is important to emphasize that the random selection baseline in combination with this pre-filter provides already a non-trivial baseline difficult to outperform.

Figure 6.4 indicates that while $score_{gold}$ is clearly superior, no other strategy is a clear winner (e.g. the statistically significantly better precision of $score_{support}$ comes at the expense of recall).

Trading Pattern Precision and Recall

Figure 6.3 shows precision, recall, and F_1-measure values for different filtering functions averaged over runs on different relations. In Figure 6.4, precision is plotted against recall. The informed baseline, $score_{gold}$ is circled. The best-performing uninformed strategy, $score_{support}$ is marked in red. There is a clear superiority of $score_{gold}$ and $score_{support}$ in terms of precision. In terms of recall, however, the other filtering functions $score_{random}$, $score_{pmi_{Espresso}}$ and $score_{prec}$ are slightly superior. This negative correlation between recall and precision can be observed in the output for all individual relations but is particularly apparent for the *productOf* relation which is the relation for which all scoring functions achieve highest overall precision. The reasons for the lower recall with $score_{gold}$ and $score_{support}$ lie in the fact that many of the patterns they generate contain individual tokens that make them too specific. Manual inspection of the patterns extracted for the *locatedIn* relation with $score_{gold}$ mention a city, person name or date in a position that should have been a wildcard in 48% of the cases (as opposed to 19% with $score_{random}$). Apparently these patterns do not harm extraction precision but reduce recall.

Patterns of this degree of specificity are not valuable for extraction. In contrast, the $score_{random}$ strategy leads to overly specific patterns in only 19% of the cases and is hence more productive. The problem of $score_{support}$ becomes apparent when considering what we call "*trigger phrases*" in patterns, i.e. phrases that are

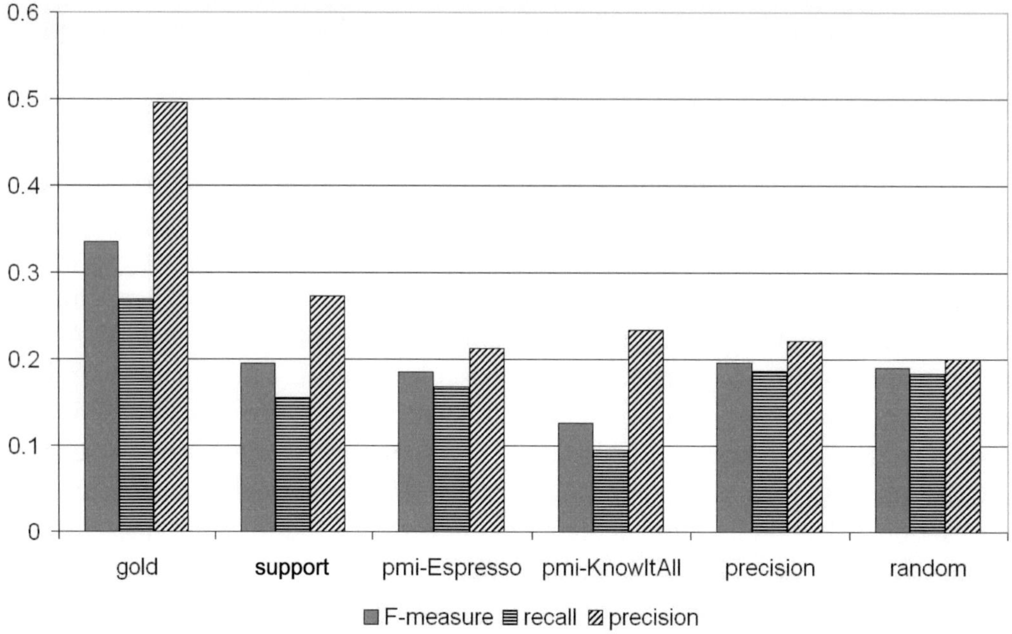

Figure 6.3: Precision, relative recall and F_1-measure by filtering strategy averaged over the 7 relations.

frequently associated with the mention of relation instances. For $score_{gold}$, nearly all trigger phrases are related to flight reservations, law firm advertising and hotel offers. The output of $score_{support}$ features many more trigger words such as advertisements for different types of local medical services, schools, restaurants and weather forecasts. Thus, $score_{gold}$ and $score_{support}$ constitute two different ways in which a set of patterns can be too specific. $score_{gold}$ prefers patterns that are too specific in the sense that they match only one or very few instances. $score_{support}$ overcomes this problem by preferring patterns generated from different instances, but there tend to be many patterns in the pattern set that are similar among each other and thus extract the same instances.

To explore the possibility of trading precision against recall, we also investigate the influence of the $p_{filterInstances}$ parameter that determines instance filtering as described in Section 6.2.1. The value was varied from 10 % (keeping very few instances) to 90 % (keeping nearly all instances). Figure 6.5 gives the precision, recall, and F_1-measure values for the *locatedIn* relation as extracted with the $score_{gold}$ filtering function and shows that changing $p_{filterInstances}$ has the desired effect of trading precision against recall while the highest F-measure is obtained with a very permissive instance filtering, which is most likely due to the fact that $score_{gold}$ typically generates relatively precise patterns. Overall, while the pre-

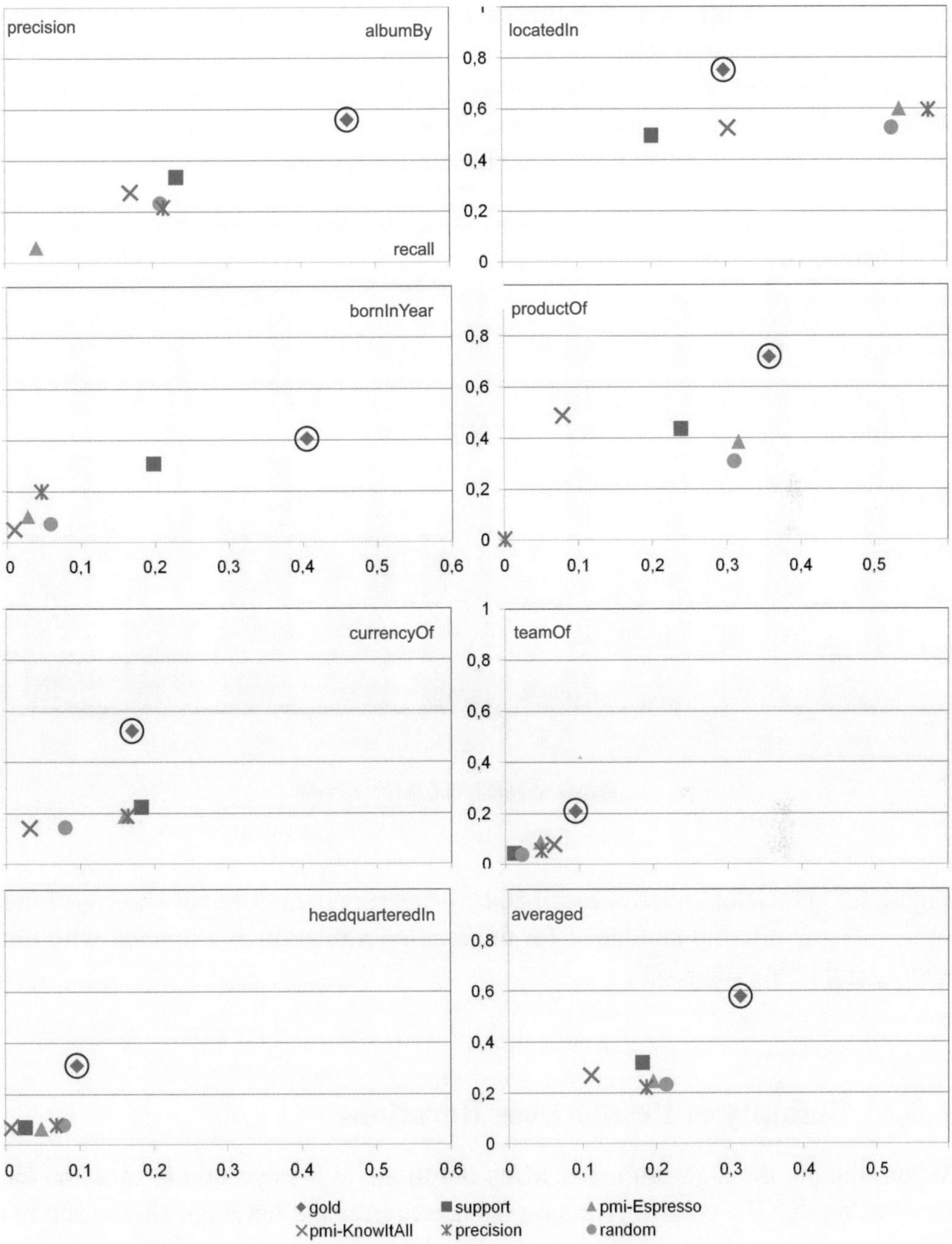

Figure 6.4: Precision over relative recall and by filtering strategy for the 7 relations and averaged. The informed baseline, $score_{gold}$ is circled. The best-performing uninformed strategy, $score_{support}$ is marked with squares. In the lower right corner, precision is plotted over recall averaged over all relations (automatic evaluation).

cision decreases with increasing percentage of instances accepted, the recall and F-Measure steadily increase.

The *locatedIn* relation and the $score_{gold}$ filter were chosen for this experiment as this is the setup with the highest precision scores achieved and also with the greatest variability in recall among the filtering functions.

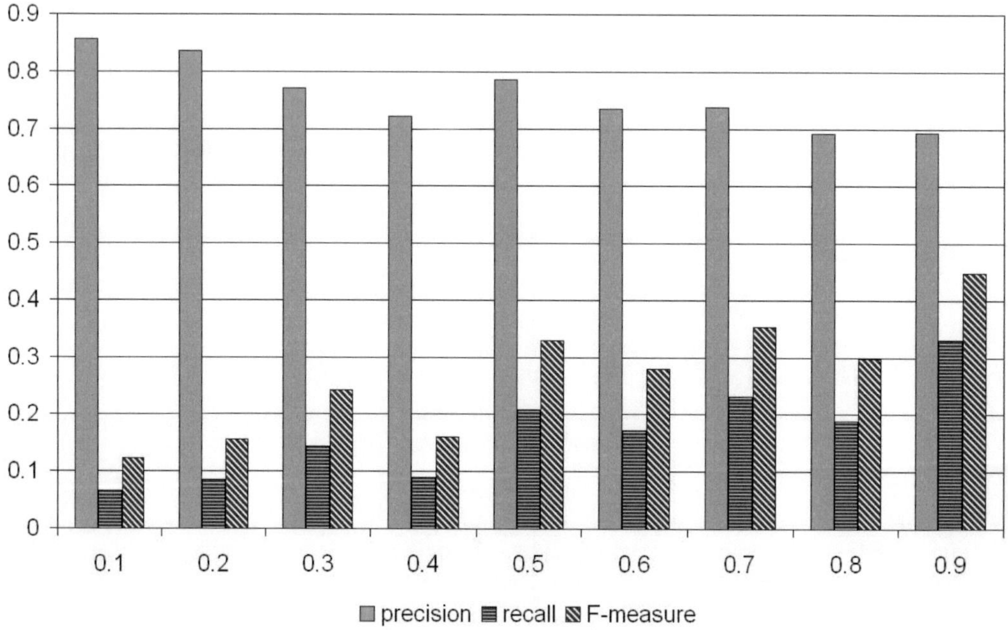

Figure 6.5: Precision, relative recall and F_1-measure over different choices of the $p_{filterInstances}$ filtering parameter for the *locatedIn* relation as extracted with the $score_{gold}$ filtering function.

6.3.2 Stability of Results over Iterations

When running the algorithm over many iterations, it is important to avoid as far as possible that the pattern precision decreases over the iterations due to the increasing amount of erroneous extractions. Hence, we need to show extraction quality decreases to such an extent that too much spurious results are introduced which render results of future iterations useless. Figure 6.6 shows precision values achieved with the individual filtering functions at each iteration averaged over all relations. As expected, the output generated by $score_{gold}$ remains stable in terms of precision as filtering is fully informed. $score_{support}$ is the most stable strategy loosing only 1.3 percentage points between iteration 2 and 5 (the average loss ex-

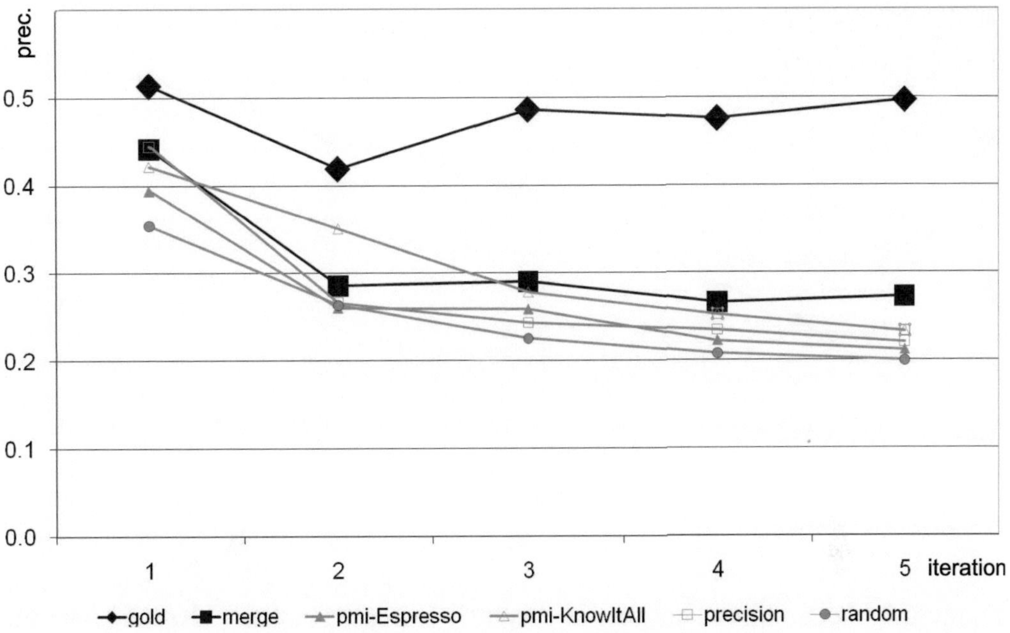

Figure 6.6: Precision of output over 5 iterations by filtering function averaged over all relations investigated. Results based on automatic evaluation. $score_{gold}$ and $score_{merge}$ are more stable than the others (grayed)

cluding $score_{gold}$ is 6.6). The scores of the other strategies are plotted with gray lines.

Furthermore one needs to show that the process does not converge to a small number of extracted instances after too few iterations. In order to show that this is not the case, we studied how the the number of correct extractions develops over time (cf. Figure 6.7). As it turns out, over the first 10 iteration the output increases steadily and lies around 40 to 50 instances per iteration.

6.3.3 Considerations on the Properties of Various Relations

Given the large quality differences reported above for the different relations, it is important to determine factors which influence the output quality of the learning algorithm depending on the relation. Table 6.3 shows the learned relations, sorted by the precision scores obtained with the most successful filtering function other than the gold standard. Along those precision scores and that of the extractions obtained with $score_{gold}$, five values are displayed that can be expected to have an influence on the "extractability" of the relations. The *web presence* value gives the average Google result count estimate for the 2000 relation instances most fre-

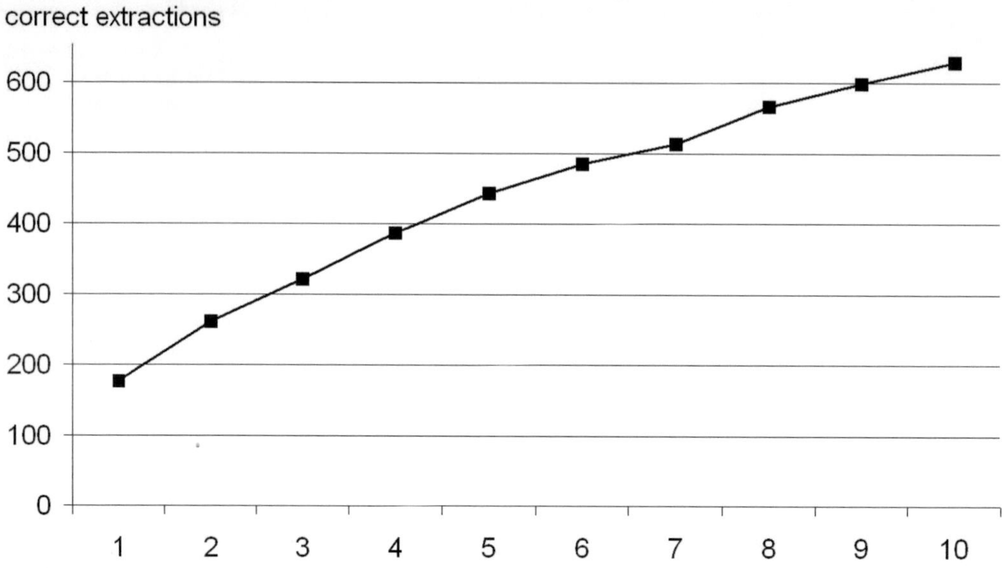

Figure 6.7: Accumulated number of correctly extracted instances learned over the number of iterations run averaged over all relations.

quently occurring on the Web. It is meant as an indicator of how frequently the most common instances appear on the Web. The *Arg 1/2 PNs* columns give the average percentage of proper nouns in the arguments[3]. *|Arg 1/2| length* are the respective average argument lengths.

While a much larger set of relations would be required to make conclusive statements, the data suggest that *locatedIn* and *productOf* owe their relatively high precision scores to the fact that the most prominent relation instances occur very frequently on the Web, which causes a high redundancy that can be exploited in the pattern induction process. In addition, good extraction performance seems to be correlated with the percentage of proper nouns in the argument positions. Proper nouns are likely to be more easily identified with patterns due to their special treatment in the English syntax.

6.4 Summary

We have investigated how the alternative approaches to pattern filtering affect the induction process. The conclusions of these experiments are in fact not only interesting for the Pronto pattern-learning systems, but for all bootstrapping-based systems in the sense that they shed light on the benefits and disadvantages of dif-

[3]Assessed with the IMS TreeTagger (`http://www.ims.uni-stuttgart.de/`) considering all tokens tagged NP and NPS proper nouns.

relation	size	P(gold)	best	P(best)	web presence
locatedIn	34047	0.75	Espresso	0.6	55820213
productOf	2650	0.72	KnowItAll	0.49	506697
albumBy	19852	0.56	support	0.33	10686457
bornInYear	172696	0.41	support	0.31	63756
currencyOf[2]	221	0.52	support	0.22	1916175
teamOf	8307	0.21	Espresso	0.09	1703556
headquarteredIn	14762	0.31	support	0.08	6908710

relation	Arg_1 PNs	Arg_2 PNs	$\|Arg_1\|$	$\|Arg_2\|$
locatedIn	0.93	0.94	1.23	1.31
productOf	0.79	0.96	2.33	1.08
albumBy	0.37	0.65	2.97	1.69
bornInYear	0.97	0	1.77	1
currencyOf	0.61	0.95	1.18	1.08
teamOf	0.85	0.3	1.34	2.12
headquarteredIn	0.84	0.99	1.98	1.37

Table 6.3: Relations with properties that may influence learnability, sorted by the result precision of the most successful non-gold filtering function.

ferent pattern evaluation strategies. In particular, we have shown the influence of pattern filtering on extraction quality by comparing random and fully informed filtering ($score_{random}$ and $score_{gold}$, respectively) to various filtering strategies based on evaluation functions presented in the literature. The results indicate that a relatively simple evaluation strategy, i.e. the simple support evaluation strategy overall yields better results than more elaborate measures such as PMI, which relies on web occurrence counts. In fact, the PMI-based scores were unable to outperform the random baseline in a statistically significant way, while the support strategy counting solely the number of distinct relation instances from which a pattern was generated does achieve statistical significance. This raises indeed doubts about the appropriateness of PMI and Web-based evaluation measures in general (compare also [Downey et al., 2005]). However, we have also shown that PMI yields a higher recall than the newly proposed support-based strategy, which is biased towards precision. Finally, the results also show that for each filtering function the applicability strongly varies depending on the specific relation considered and whether precision or recall is more important. As it turned out, precision and recall can also be controlled by the strictness of the filtering that is by varying the number of instances carried over into the next generation.

To conclude, pattern filtering (both the scoring function and the percentage filtered out) is an important design parameter in iterative pattern induction the choice of which strongly depends on the Information Extraction task. This chapter has discussed and compared various approaches. We classified them into syntactical, performance-based, inter pattern comparison, instance-pattern correlation and support-based measures. The informed upper bound that was used shows that pattern filtering (all other settings being equal) can double both precision and recall.

Chapter 7

The Influence of the Text Corpus on Extraction Dynamics

In Section 5.4 *Dependence on Redundancy* was identified as Challenge 4 to pattern based Information Extraction. By redundancy we mean that the same facts (i.e. relation instances) are mentioned several times in a corpus and that relation mentions share common features. The lack of redundancy particularly becomes a problem when Information Extraction is performed on corpora where redundancy is avoided on purpose. Specialized text corpora such as company intranets or collections of scientific papers are non-redundant by design because reading and writing the same information over and over again is costly. Yet they constitute a valuable source for Information Extraction as they are typically more reliable and focused than the general Web (cf. [Fagin et al., 2003] for an analysis of structure and content of corporate intranets).

After motivating and analyzing the dependence on redundancy further, we present in this chapter the empirical analysis of a newly developed approach to coping with this problem when performing Information Extraction on Wikipedia as an example of a hardly redundant corpus. The experiments show that the intentionally reduced redundancy in Wikipedia leads to the need of a larger amount of training data but that integrating Web extraction into the process leads to a significant reduction of required training data while maintaining the accuracy of Wikipedia. In particular we show that, though the use of the Web can have similar effects as produced by increasing the number of seed instances, it leads overall to better results. The approach thus allows us to combine advantages of two sources: The high reliability of a closed corpus and the high redundancy of the Web. Most of the results shown here were published at the ECML PKDD 2007 together with Philipp Cimiano [Blohm and Cimiano, 2007].

In the following, we will give an overview of related work before motivating the problem of low redundancy in more detail in Section 7.2. We then describe the approach taken in Section 7.3 which integrates Web extraction to improve instance quality which is subsequently evaluated experimentally (Section 7.4).

7.1 Related Work

In the computational linguistics community, it has been shown that the Web can in some cases be effectively used to overcome data sparseness problems (compare [Kilgariff and Grefenstette, 2003]).

In the present study, Wikipedia is used as a corpus. Wikipedia is currently widely used as a corpus for Information Extraction from text. One example is a study by Suchanek et al. [2008] who focus on high-precision ontology learning and population with methods specifically tailored to Wikipedia. Wikipedia's category system is exploited assuming typical naming patterns and composition of categories that allow the system to deduce semantic relations from category membership. In [Ruiz-Casado et al., 2005] Information Extraction from Wikipedia text is done using hyperlinks as indicators for relations just like in the present study. As opposed to the work presented here it relies on WordNet as a hand-crafted formal taxonomy and is thus limited to relations for which such sources exist. Precision of 61-69% is achieved on the hyponymy and holonymy relations which is comparable to the results presented here. Other related work makes use of information provided in Wikipedia-specific data structures called infoboxes [Wang et al., 2007; Auer and Lehmann, 2007; Wu and Weld, 2007]. Brin pioneered the use of Web search indices for this purpose [1999]. A recent successful system using Web data is KnowItAll which has been extended to automatic learning of patterns [Downey et al., 2004] as well as PANKOW [Cimiano et al., 2004]. Many studies have addressed IE based limited Web document collections of various sizes [Rosenfeld and Feldman, 2006; Banko et al., 2007; Tomita et al., 2006; Cafarella et al., 2005].

7.2 The Problem of Low Redundancy

In Section 5.4, the presence of redundant instances has been formulated as an assumption made when applying iterative pattern induction. Here, the intuition of this assumption is motivated further, before the lack of redundancy in the Wikipedia is investigated.

Take for example the relation *teamOf* which features soccer players and the national teams they were playing for. This information can quite reliably extracted

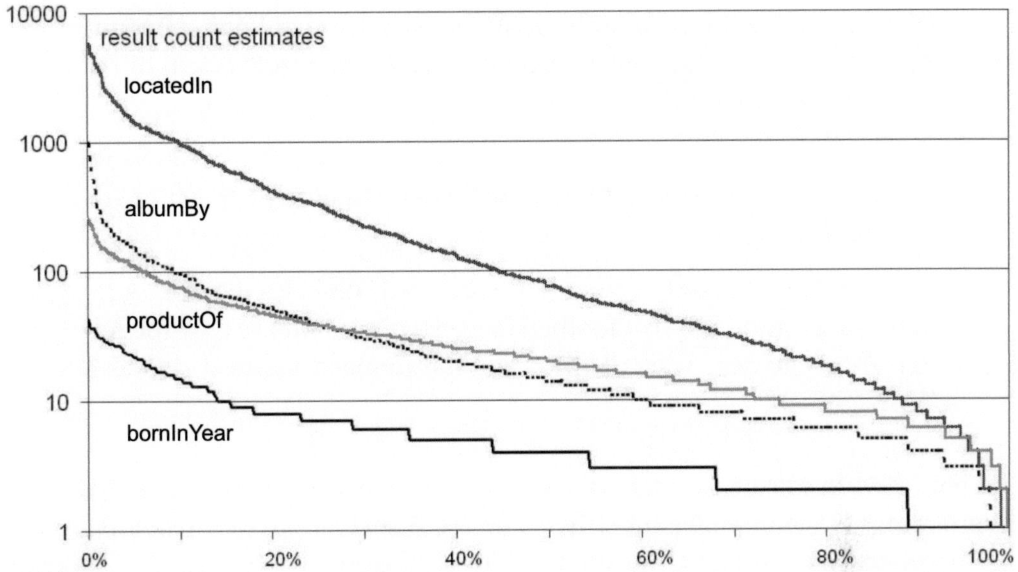

Figure 7.1: Page co-occurrences for instances of four of the test relations on Wikipedia. The counts are displayed on the Y-axis for individual instances ordered along the X-axis by decreasing co-occurrence counts.

from the first sentence of the Wikipedia article about each player as can be seen from the following examples taken from the English Wikipedia.[1]

> Henk Fräser (born July 7, 1966 in Paramaribo, Suriname) is a former football defender from The Netherlands.
>
> Gerald Glatzmayer (14 December 1968 - 11 January 2001) was an Austrian footballer who took part in the 1990 World Cup.
>
> Gabriel Jaime Gomez Jaramillo (born December 8, 1959 in Medellin) is a retired football midfielder who was capped 49 times and scored 2 international goals for Colombia between 1985 and 1995.
>
> Daniel Fonseca Garis (born 13 September 1969) is an Uruguayan former footballer, now a football player agent.
>
> Wilmer Cabrera Linares (born September 15, 1967 in Cartagena) is a retired football defender who was capped 48 times and scored 3 international goals for Colombia between 1989 and 1998.
>
> Guido Buchwald (born January 24, 1961) is a German former football defender and manager.

[1] The version of June 30th 2009

> Diego Armando Maradona (born 30 October 1960 in Lanus, Buenos Aires) is a former Argentine football player, and current coach of the Argentine national side.
>
> Edgardo Bauza (born 26 January, 1958 in Granadero Baigorria, Santa Fe) is a retired Argentine football defender and current coach of Al-Nasr in Saudi Arabia.
>
> Anthony Robert Dorigo (born 31 December 1965 in Melbourne, Australia) is a retired English football (soccer) player who played for Aston Villa, Chelsea, Leeds United and the England national side as a left-back.

However, in most cases, this is also the only sentence in which national team membership is mentioned explicitly.[2] There are several obvious patterns in this set of sentences involving the phrases "is a ... from ..."(1) "is a ... football player—defender"(2). If all instances occur only once in these first sentences and no seed is mentioned featuring a type (2) phrase, then also the patterns generated from the seeds will not contain a type (2) phrase. Consequently, none of their matches will be mentioned in a type (2) phrase which will prevent the phrase to be discovered as a reasonable pattern in the next iteration, too.

Data sparseness thus becomes a problem when trying to extract information from hardly redundant sources like corporate intranets, encyclopedic works or scientific databases (this is in line with observations mentioned by Wang et al. [2007]). In fact, Wikipedia authoring guidelines explicitly instruct authors to avoid redundancy by searching for existing or related articles about a given topic before inserting new information [Wikipedia Community, 2009].

To quantify this phenomenon, we discuss here the distribution of co-occurrences of relation instances in Wikipedia of four test relations taking the Google result count estimates for searches of individual relation instances limited to the Wikipedia site (Figure 7.1). The figure shows the counts on the Y-axis for individual instances ordered along the X-axis by decreasing co-occurrence counts. The labels on the X-axis give percentiles. One can see that most relation instances do not co-occur more than 100 times (median: 15) on a document level. When doing the same counts on the entire Web, hardly any instance occurs less than 100 times, the median lies at 48000. The effect increases when considering that page co-occurrence does not suffice for a relation instance to be extracted. Patterns only

[2] In the case of soccer players, Wikipedia provides a couple of lists or category pages that include this information. Yet, those are not generally accessible by window-based textual patterns as they are used here and they are not available for most other types of information. For work specialized in exploiting Wikipedia-specific information, refer to [Suchanek et al., 2008; Wu and Weld, 2007].

match a limited context. In the present case, Pronto matches 10 tokens around each link relating it to the document title. This reduces the number of times, a candidate relation instance occurs in the corpus dramatically to an average of 1.68 (derived by counting the number of times that the top 200 relation instances for each relation co-occur in one sentence in our Wikipedia dataset). Consequently, a large portion of relation instances does not occurr more than once which shows that sparseness is indeed an issue.

7.3 Approach

The approach presented here explores whether the Web can effectively help to overcome data sparseness as a supplementary data source for Information Extraction on limited corpora. Specifically, the Web is not used to extract additional information, but only to make up for a lack of redundancy in the small corpus. No information found on the Web goes into the result set without being verified on the small corpus as otherwise the benefits of the smaller corpus (higher quality, domain specificity, availability of further background knowledge) would be lost. The approach thus combines advantages of two sources: the high reliability of a closed corpus and the high redundancy of the Web.

Like in the previous chapter, Pronto (cf. Section 5.5) is configured to constitute a weakly-supervised pattern learning system in which patterns are induced on the basis of a few seed examples. In this study, matching takes place both on Wikipedia and the Web. Wikipedia is meant to be the primary source of information and the Web plays an auxiliary role. The idea for integration of the Web content in the Wikipedia extraction is as follows: given seed examples (e.g. $(Warsaw, Poland)$ and $(Paris, France)$) of a specific relation (e.g. *locatedIn*) to be extracted (appearing in the local corpus), Pronto can consult the Web for patterns in which these examples appear. The newly derived patterns, which in essence are a generalization of plain string occurrences of the instances, can then be matched on the Web in order to extract new examples which are taken into the next iteration as seeds. Then, Pronto can induce patterns from the Wikipedia corpus with an increased set of examples (coming from the Web), thus effectively leading to more patterns. Several variations of this approach are possible two of which are investigated below and compared to a Wikipedia-only baseline. Learning patterns separately on the Web and on Wikipedia and exchanging instances among the extraction processes of these sources is only one possible way of integration. In future work, it would be possible also to apply patterns induced on one source on the other source. Yet, we observed that very different patterns were learned in the different corpora so that it is not likely that exchanging patterns is beneficial. In particular, patterns generated on the Web specialize in prominent el-

WEB-WIKI PATTERN IND($Patterns\ P_{init-web}, Patterns\ P_{init-wiki}, Instances\ Inst'$)

$Inst \leftarrow Inst'$
$P_{pool-web} \leftarrow P_{init-web}$
$P_{pool-wiki} \leftarrow P_{init-wiki}$
while not DONE
do
    $M_i \leftarrow$ WEB-MATCH-INSTANCES($Inst$)
    $P_{pool-web} \leftarrow P_{pool-web} \cup$ LEARN-PATTERNS(M_i)
    $Eval_P \leftarrow$ EVALUATE-WEB-PATTERNS($P_{pool-web}$)
    $P_{pool-web} \leftarrow \{p \in P_{pool-web} \mid$ WEB-PATTERN-FILTER-COND($p, Eval_P$)$\}$
    $M_p \leftarrow$ WEB-MATCH-PATTERNS($P_{pool-web}$)
    $Inst \leftarrow Inst +$ EXTRACT-INSTANCES(M_p)
    $Inst \leftarrow \{i \in Inst \mid$ PRESENT-IN-WIKI(i)$\}$
    $Eval_I \leftarrow$ EVALUATE-WEB-INSTANCES($Inst$)
    $Inst \leftarrow \{i \in Inst \mid$ INSTANCE-FILTER-CONDITION($i, Eval_I$)$\}$
    $M_i \leftarrow$ WIKI-MATCH-INSTANCES($Inst$)
    $P_{pool-wiki} \leftarrow P_{pool-wiki} \cup$ LEARN-PATTERNS(M_i)
    $Eval_P \leftarrow$ EVALUATE-WIKI-PATTERNS($P_{pool-wiki}$)
    $P_{pool-wiki} \leftarrow \{p \in P_{pool-wiki} \mid$ WIKI-PATTERN-FILTER-COND($p, Eval_P$)$\}$
    $M_p \leftarrow$ WIKI-MATCH-PATTERNS($P_{pool-wiki}$)
    $Inst \leftarrow Inst +$ EXTRACT-INSTANCES(M_p)
    $Eval_I \leftarrow$ EVALUATE-WIKI-INSTANCES($Inst$)
    $Inst \leftarrow \{i \in Inst \mid$ INSTANCE-FILTER-CONDITION($i, Eval_I$)$\}$

Figure 7.2: Combined Web and wiki pattern induction algorithm starting with initial patterns $P_{init-web}$ and $P_{init-wiki}$ as well as instances $Inst'$ maintaining two pattern pools $P_{pool-web}$ and $P_{pool-wiki}$. The grayed instructions are not executed in the Wiki only condition and only once in the Web once condition.

ements that are typical of Web pages (e.g. the titles) and Wikipedia patterns focus on ways of mentioning facts that are specific to Wikipedia pages (e.g. listing birth years of peoples by year on specific pages).

Figure 7.2 describes the modification of the iterative pattern induction algorithm presented in Section 5.3. It basically consists of a subsequent application of the loop body on the Web and on Wikipedia. Web matching and Wikipedia matching contribute to the same evolving set of instances $Inst$ but maintain separate pattern pools $P_{pool-web}$ and $P_{pool-wiki}$. This separation is done to allow for different types of pattern representation for the different corpora (see below).

To assess the added value of Web extraction, the experiments discussed here compare three configurations of the algorithm in Figure 7.2.

Dual: Exactly as described in Figure 7.2, this condition iterates the bootstrapping performing both, Web and wiki extraction in every iteration.

Web once: The processing runs like in Figure 7.2 but the grayed lines are executed only in the first iteration. Thereby, the seed set is augmented once by a set of learned relation instances. After that, processing is left to Wikipedia extraction.

Wiki only: As a baseline condition, extraction is done on Wikipedia only. Thus the grayed lines in Figure 7.2 are omitted entirely.

An important novelty is checking each instance i derived from the Web calling PRESENT-IN-WIKI(i). This ensures that no knowledge that is actually not present in Wikipedia goes into the set of results. Otherwise, the extraction procedure would not be able to benefit from the higher quality in terms of precision that the wiki corpus can be assumed to present.

7.3.1 Extraction from Wikipedia

In the following, we will discuss how patterns are matched and relation instances are extracted from Wikipedia in the experiments presented here. We describe pattern structure and index creation before going into detail on the individual steps of the algorithm in Figure 7.2.

For pattern matching on Wikipedia, this study makes use of the encyclopedic nature of the corpus by focusing on pairs of hyperlinks and document titles. It is a common assumption when investigating the semantics in documents like Wikipedia (e.g. [Völkel et al., 2006]) that key information on the entity described on a article a lies within the set of links on that article $l(a)$ and in particular that it is likely that there is a salient semantic relation between a and $a' \in l(a)$. Link-title-pairs have been the focus in several studies on Information Extraction from Wikipedia [Culotta et al., 2006; Wang et al., 2007].

In this study, we therefore consider patterns consisting of the document title and a hyperlink within its context. The context of $2 * w$ tokens around the link is taken into account because we assume that this context is most indicative of the nature of the semantic relation expressed between the entity described in the article and the one linked by the hyperlink. In addition, a flag is set to indicate whether the first or the second argument of the relation occurs in the title. Each token can be required to be equal to a particular string or hold a wildcard character. For the experiments $w = 5$ was chosen. Increasing w further severely increased the induction algorithm's running time while bringing hardly any further payoff in terms of quality.

Henk Fräser

From Wikipedia, the free encyclopedia

Henk Fräser (born July 7, 1966 in Paramaribo, Suriname) is a former football defender from The Netherlands, who earned seven caps for the Netherlands national football team, in which he scored one goal. He was a

argInTitle	Title	t_{-5}	t_{-4}	t_{-3}	t_{-2}	t_{-1}	link	t_{+1}	t_{+2}	t_{+3}	t_{+4}	t_{+5}
1	Henk Fräser	a	former	football	defender	from	The Netherlands	,	who	earned	seven	caps
	ANY_{arg1}	*a*	*ANY*	*football*	*ANY*	*from*	ANY_{arg2}	*ANY*	*ANY*	*ANY*	*ANY*	*ANY*

Figure 7.3: Part of a Wikipedia article along with a record in the index database that reflects an instance of the *teamOf* relation and a pattern that matches this link-title pair.

To allow for efficient matching of patterns and instances we, created an index of all hyperlinks within Wikipedia. It consists of an accordingly indexed database table with one row for each title/link pair featuring one column for link, title and each context token position. Figure 7.3 depicts an excerpt from a Wikipedia article along with a record in the index database that reflects an instance of the *teamOf* relation. Below that, a pattern is shown that matches this link-title pair. The index was created using a Wikipedia database dump from December 17th 2006. The table has over 42 Million records. We omitted another 2.3 Million link-title-pairs for links lying within templates. This allows us to maintain generality as templates to not constitute free text and are a special syntactic feature of Wikipedia that may not transfer to similar corpora. Tokenization has been done based on white space. Hyperlinks are considered one token. Punctuation characters and common sequences of punctuation characters as well as HTML markup sequences are considered separate tokens even if not separated by white space. HTML comments and templates were omitted.

Instance Matching and Pattern Learning

For each of at most $num_{matchCandidates_{wiki}}$=200 instances, WIKI-MATCH-INSTANCES($Inst$) sends two queries to the index, one for each possibility to map argument 1 and 2 to title and link. Like in the Web case, there is a maximum limit for matches $num_{matchInstances_{wiki}} = 50$ but it is hardly ever enforced as virtually no instance is mentioned more than three times as a link-title pair. The same LEARN-PATTERNS(M_i) method is applied as in the study described in the previous chapter (Section 6.2.1). Like in the Web setting, EVALUATE-WIKI-PATTERNS($P_{pool-wiki}$) takes into account the number of distinct instances which participated in the creation of a pattern. Finally, WIKI-PATTERN-FILTER-COND(p) retains the top $pool_{wiki} = 50$ patterns for matching.

Pattern Matching and Instance Generation

WIKI-MATCH-PATTERNS(P) retrieves from the index a random sequence of $num_{matchPatterns_{wiki}}$ matches of the pattern by selecting those entries for which the non-wildcard context tokens of the patterns are present in the correct positions. EXTRACT-INSTANCES(M_p) then generates an instance for each distinct title/link pair occurring in the selected index entries. No filtering is done with EVALUATE-WIKI-INSTANCES($Inst$) and INSTANCE-FILTER-CONDITION(i) as initial experiments revealed that pattern matches of link-title pairs produce a relatively high precision. Nonetheless, these operations are mentioned in the algorithm formalization because filtering may become necessary for other relations or other corpora.

In the absence of a (application-dependant) stopping criterion, the termination condition DONE is currently implemented to terminate the processing after 10 iterations.

7.3.2 Extraction from the Web

Given a number of seeds at the start of each of the algorithm's iterations, mentions of these seed instances are searched on the Web. This is done as described in Section 5.5 and most settings have been chosen analogously to the experiments presented in Section 6.2.

For each instance in the current set of extracted instances $Inst$ a fixed number $num_{matchInstancesweb}$ of results is retrieved for a maximum of $num_{instanceLimit_{web}}$ instances. These mentions serve as input to pattern learning if the arguments are at most $max_{argDist}$ tokens apart. For the present experiments we set $max_{argDist} = 4$, $num_{matchCandidates_{web}} = 50$, and $num_{matchInstances_{web}} = 200$.

LEARN-PATTERNS generates more abstract versions of the patterns using the same setup as in Section 6.2.

EVALUATE-WEB-PATTERNS($P_{pool-web}$) is done using the $score_{support}$ evaluation strategy which was shown to be effective and fast at the same time. Essentially it is based on the number of different instances from which the pattern has been derived through merging. Evaluation is followed by filtering applying WEB-PATTERN-FILTER-COND(p) which ensures that the top $pool_{web} = 50$ patterns are kept. Note that like in Chapter 6, the patterns are kept over iterations but old patterns compete against newly derived ones in each iteration.

MATCH-WEB-PATTERNS is also done with the same settings as Web pattern matching in Chapter 6. For the present experiments $num_{matchPatterns_{web}} = 200$.

Parameter		Web	Wikipedia
Size of the seed set	$\|Inst'\|$	10,50,100	$10, 50, 100$
Size of pattern set	$\|P\|$	50	50
Number of instances matched	$num_{matchCandidates}$	50	50
Results retrieved for each instance	$num_{matchInstances}$	200	200
Maximum tokens between arguments	$max_{argDist}$	4	-
Windows around arguments	$t_{prefix} = t_{suffix}$	2	10
Minimum support for pattern	t_{merge}	2	2
Minimum number of constraints per pattern	min_{common}	2	2
Results retrieved for each pattern	$num_{matchPatterns}$	200	200
Instances kept after filtering	$p_{filterInstances}$	all in wiki	all
Number of iterations	$t_{iterations}$	10	10
Pattern filtering function	$score$	support and wiki presence	N/A

Table 7.1: Summary of parameter values for Web and Wikipedia extraction.

The above-mentioned PRESENT-IN-WIKI(i) check ensures that Web extractions for which no corresponding link-title pair is present in the Wikipedia are eliminated. This way, the high quality of content of Wikipedia is used to filter Web results and only those instances are kept that could in principle have been extracted from Wikipedia. Yet, the Web results increase the yield of the extraction process. Table 7.1 summarizes the parameter settings for Wikipedia and Web matching.

7.4 Experimental Evaluation

The goal of this study is to show how Information Extraction from the Web can be used to improve extraction results on a smaller corpus, i.e. how extraction on a precise, specialized corpus can benefit from a noisy but redundant source. We

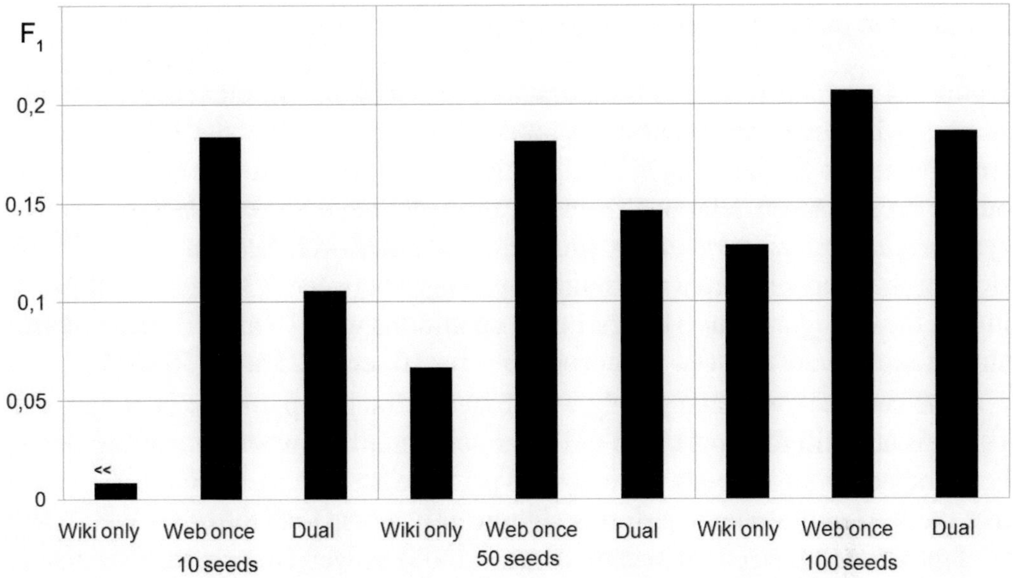

Figure 7.4: F-measure for results derived with different configurations and seed set sizes. The mark << is to indicate that output quality is statistically significantly worse than all other runs.

do so by running the system in two configurations employing Web extraction and an additional baseline condition. As the assumption is that Web extraction can make up for the lack of redundancy which is particularly important in the beginning of the bootstrapping process, we compare how the different configurations behave when provided with smaller and bigger amounts of seed examples. The experimental conditions have been described in Section 7.3. The *Dual* condition alternates Web and Wikipedia extraction. The *Web once* condition, performs Web extraction in the first iteration only and the *Wiki only* baseline restricts extraction to Wikipedia during the entire process. The evaluation looks at extraction results of the three configurations running for 10 iterations. The 10, 50 and 100 most prominent relation instances were used as as seed sets to test how the size of the seed set influences the ability of the various relations to bootstrap the extraction process.

7.4.1 Evaluation Measures

Like in the other chapters, we use precision and relative recall measures to evaluate system output. As described in Section 5.7.2. These measures compute the ratio of correctly found instances to overall instances extracted (precision) or all instances to be found (recall).

7.4.2 Impact of Web Extraction

Figure 7.4 presents results of the extraction runs with the different configurations starting with seed sets of different sizes. The figures show the F-measure after 9 iterations of the extraction algorithm. The scores are averaged over the output on the seven relations from the testbed (*albumBy*, *bornInYear*, *currencyOf,headquarteredIn,locatedIn*, *productOf*, *teamOf* – cf. Section 5.7.2). Precision for the Web-supported configurations ranges between 0.32 and 0.55 depending on the configuration. The wiki only conditions with 10 and 50 seeds returns almost exclusively the seed instances (95% for 10 seeds, 25% for 50 seeds).

One can observe that a purely wiki-based extraction performs very bad with 10 seeds and still far worse than the other configurations when comparing output bootstrapped from 50 seeds. A two-sided pairwise Student's t-test indicates in fact that the *Wiki only* strategy performs significantly worse than the other Web-based configurations at a seed set size of 10 ($\alpha = 0.05$) as well as for a seed set size of 50 ($\alpha = 0.1$). This clearly corroborates the claim that the integration of the Web improves results with respect to a Wiki-only strategy at 10 and 50 seeds.

In a more detailed account, extraction only from the wiki maintains only the seed set over the entire process when starting with 10 seeds and with 50 seeds only gains 113 instances on average between iteration 3 and 9 after extracting 320 in the first 3 iterations. In particular, with 10 seeds, the wiki only strategy does not find any useful patterns in the mentions of the seeds provided, while for 50 seeds this is the case for only two of the seven relations. Interestingly, the solely wiki-based extraction yields more correct results when starting with 100 seeds. This is due to one outlier, the *albumBy* relation, for which the wiki-based extraction with 100 seeds finds a set of patterns that extracts over 2500 correct instances in the first three iterations while none of the other configurations even reaches 2500 results in nine iterations. The reason is that the system learns that the prefix "debut album" or a preceding headline "discography" are very good indicators for an album name within an artist's Wikipedia document thus making use of the rare cases of redundancy of Wikipedia.

Figure 7.5 presents the same data in plots of precision and recall averaged over the three iterations. Like in the experiments from the previous chapter, the behavior of the various relations with regard to extraction quality varies strongly. Still, in almost all setups, the *dual* method and the *web once* clearly outperform the *wiki only* setup. For the 10 seed case, no additional instances at all were found in the *wiki only* setup. The ability to cope with so few seeds is clearly the advantage of working with a high-redundancy corpus like the web. For the *albumBy*, *locatedIn* and *bornInYear* relations it turns out that for the two methods that query the Web, going from 50 to 100 seeds actually reduces the quality (observe this by noticing that the circled datapoint is not highest and rightmost for the green variant). This

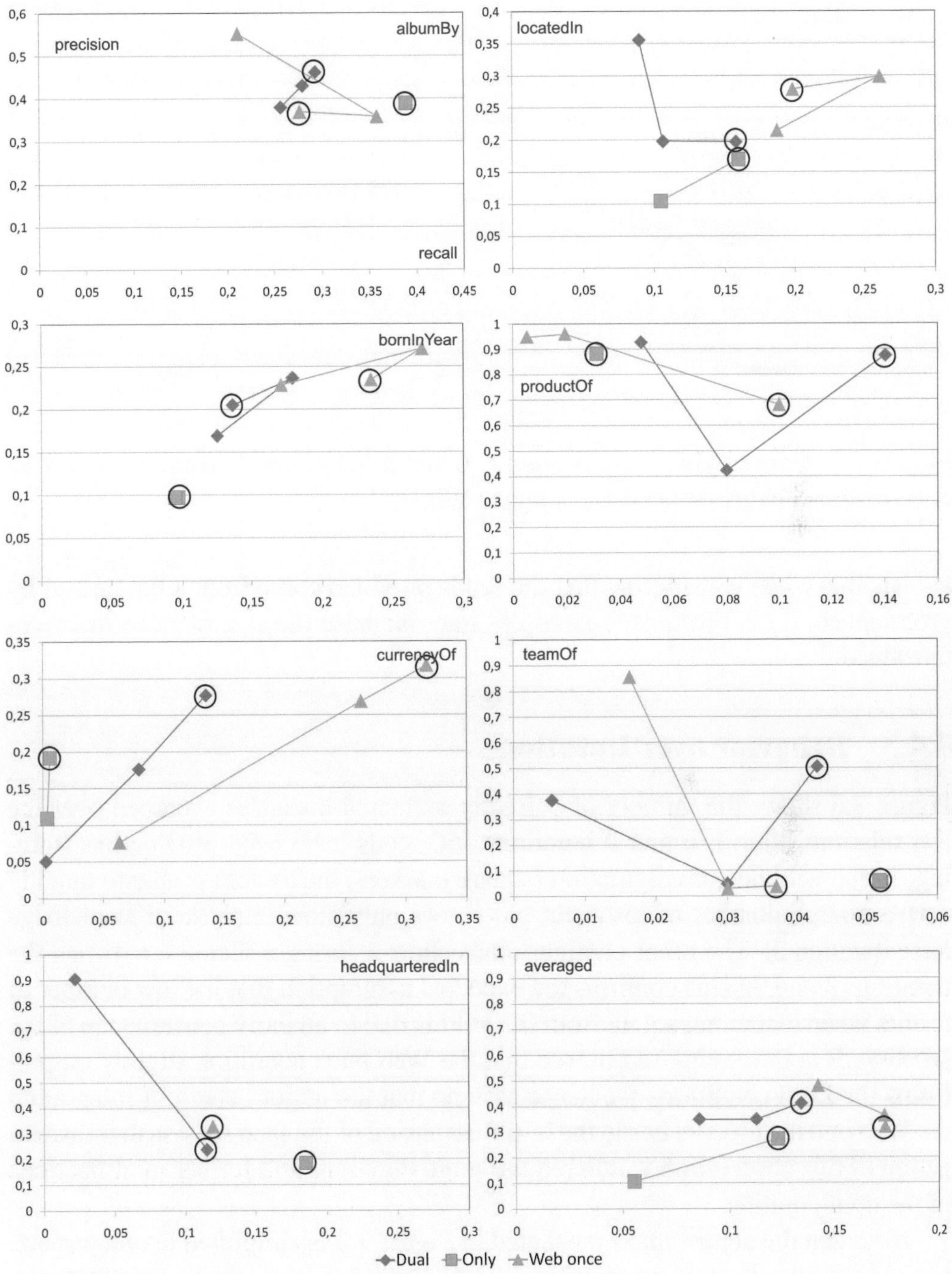

Figure 7.5: Precision and recall of extraction results after 9 iterations averaged over the relation starting with 10, 50 and 100 seeds. Results from the same configuation are connected by an arc for readabiliby reasons. The results for the 100 seed setup are circled.

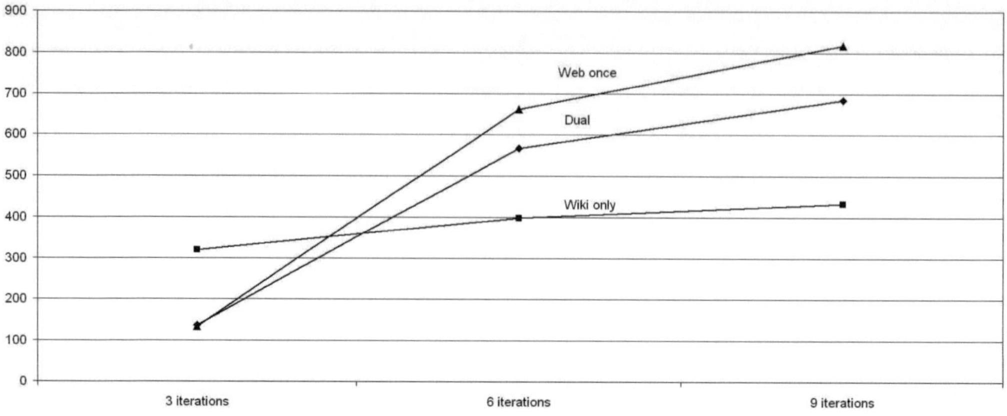

Figure 7.6: Correct yield counts after 3, 6 and 9 iterations. Triangles mark Web once results, diamonds Dual and squares Wiki only.

is plausible when considering that the seeds provided come from a list ranked by prominence. Less prominent examples may increase the risk of false instances introduced.

7.4.3 Behavior over Iterations

Figure 7.6 shows the number of correctly extracted instances averaged over the test relations after 3, 6 and 9 iterations. 50 seeds have been provided as training. In the wiki only configuration (square markers) the system is able to quickly derive a large number of instances but shows only slow increase of knowledge after iteration 3. The other configurations show a stronger increase between the iterations 3 and 9. This confirms the expected assumption that the low number of results when extracting solely from the wiki is due to an early convergence of the process. It is interesting to observe that the Web once condition slightly outperforms the Dual condition. We hence assume that the major benefit of integrating the Web into the process lies in the initial extension of the seed set. Further investigation of this observation would require more iterations and further modifications of the configuration.

Note that the algorithm as presented in Figure 7.2 is simplified in one respect. Initial tests revealed that performing the PRESENT-IN-WIKI(i) filter in every iteration was too strict so that bootstrapping was quenched. We therefore decided to apply the filter in every third iteration.[3] A considerable number of – not necessar-

[3] As the filter is always applied to all instances in $Inst$ this does not lead to the presence of non-wiki patterns in the final results. Yet, the non-wiki patterns seem to help bootstrapping before they are eliminated.

ily wrong – instances were filtered out when applying the filter. Consequently the figure only present results after iteration 3, 6 and 9 for comparability reasons.

Overall, we can conclude that in this setting using the Web as background knowledge allows us to produce more recall in hardly redundant corpora while maintaining the precision level. Our results show that the number of seeds required can be drastically reduced with the Web matching which reduces the amount of manual effort required.

7.5 Conclusion

The results indicate that Web-based information extraction can help improving extraction results even if the task at hand requires extraction from a closed, non-redundant corpus. In particular, it turned out that with extraction based on 10 seed examples and incorporating the Web as "background knowledge" better results can be achieved on average than using 100 seeds solely on Wikipedia. The potential of the approach lies in the fact that the additional information does not require formalization (like e.g. in WordNet) nor is it limited to a particular domain.

In practical applications, one can improve results by including additional techniques like part-of-speech tagging and named-entity tagging that have been omitted here to maintain generality of the study. In addition to the title-link pairs considered here, further indicators of relatedness can be considered to increase coverage.

The approach taken here may be particularly suited in domains like e-Science, corpora intranets or legal affairs because for these domains large non-redundant text collections are available.

Chapter 8

Efficient Pattern Induction with Data Mining Methods

A key step in the pattern induction framework is the generation of appropriate patterns (step 2 (*learn patterns*) in Figure 5.1). Various algorithms and implementations have been developed and applied in the literature. In this chapter, an efficient and versatile algorithm is presented. In order to motivate our work, we present here a set of design objectives that arise.

- **Objective 1: Quality of patterns.** Clearly, the induction process needs to produce patterns that are general enough to cover not only the training examples but as many correct potential extractions as possible while at the same time do not produce too many spurious examples.

- **Objective 2: Induction speed.** Furthermore, the time an induction algorithm takes to come up with patterns is an important factor. It determines the overall runtime of the system and may make the use of large amounts of data prohibitive. Fast, low-quality induction results may in some cases be favored over slower ones because there exist techniques that make use of bootstrapping mechanisms to compensate for low-quality induced patterns by means of several applications of the induction process [Riloff and Jones, 1999; McIntosh and Curran, 2009].

- **Objective 3: Feature richness.** Machine Learning models make use of the presence of information about the textual input in form of features. As outlined in Section 4.2.1, a wide range of features has been found applicable to IE. Yet, not all induction algorithms can incorporate a rich set of features.

- **Objective 4: Clear parameters of model.** An important challenge in IE is the adaptivity to new tasks (cf. Section 3.4). In order to make a model adaptable (regardless if this is done manually or automatically), it is of advantage to have a small, well understood set of parameters. Such parameters can be the pattern class, the minimum length of a pattern or other criteria that decide which patterns should be accepted. Some algorithms have less clear (implicit) parameters such as the order in which instances are processed.

In practical applications, the degree to which these objectives are fulfilled need to be traded against each other. For instance, a feature-rich model with clear parameters may be computationally expensive.

As outlined in Section 5.6.2, pattern induction can be viewed as the exploration of a space of potentially applicable patterns which is defined by the present textual examples. When operating in a semi-supervised Web-scale scenario, there is usually a large amount of text examples to incorporate into the mining process. Hence, the space of potential patterns becomes extremely huge which renders pattern induction computationally complex. The algorithm presented in this chapter addresses in particular the scalability aspect (Objective 2) by employing well-understood mining techniques. The presented solution also allows for the use of arbitrary token-based features (Objective 3) and resorts to a small set of parameters (Objective 4). The quality of patterns in a concrete scenario (Objective 1) is subject of the experimental evaluation (Section 8.2). We show that the optimized algorithm here is able to gain a significant amount of extraction speed without reducing the quality.

As identified in Section 5.6.2, there are several general approaches to pattern induction.

- Many algorithms are based on *organizing* mentions by some criterion and then performing a *generalization* step. For instance, Brin [1999] groups mentions by common infixes and URL prefixes and then generalizes by means of finding the longest common substring. The Snowball system [Agichtein and Gravano, 2000] groups mentions using vector space clustering and creates patterns by a median selection and bag-of-words vector aggregation.

- A frequently used technique is *pairwise generalization*. This approach is also referred to as *"bottom-up"* (cf. Section 2.3.1) because processing starts from concrete text sequences and abstracts from them towards more and more abstract patterns. There are several variants of these approaches some of which work exhaustively, generalizing over all possible pairs [Rosenfeld and Feldman, 2006], others produce different results depending on the order in which the mentions are processed [Ruiz-Casado et al., 2005] or on random choice [Pantel et al., 2004].

- Conversely, some implementations operate *top-down* starting with a very general pattern and refining it based on evidence. To reduce complexity, features can be added from one mention at a time [Ciravegna, 2001]. Ciravegna also excludes mentions used once from further processing which makes the algorithm's output depending on the order of processing.

- A further approach is to use a *summarizing data structure* to get an overview of the data and from that generate appropriate patterns. Ravichandran and Hovy [2001] do so by counting all mentions of all substrings in a suffix tree and Talukdar et al. [2006] induce an HMM for pattern generation.

- Finally, a trivial solution to come up with pattern is what we introduced in Section 4.2.2 as *underspecified representation*. All mentions are translated into patterns. The abstraction takes place only by not representing all aspects of the mentions. Such approaches leave it to other stages of the algorithm to cope with potential abundance [Snow et al., 2004; Xu et al., 2007; Yangarber, 2003].

The experiments in Chapters 6 and 7 perform exhaustive search for patterns which fulfill certain criteria (e.g. minimum support). We refer to this as its *standard* implementation. Thereby, the standard implementation relies on a bottom-up procedure. It allows using arbitrary token-based features and operates with a small set of parameters but at high expenses in terms of processing time. More specifically, the algorithm groups patterns if they share a minimum number min_{common} of words at the same positions and generalizes ("merges") over such groups by keeping all shared constraints and eliminating all others. To avoid too general patterns, a minimum number of non-wildcard tokens is enforced. To avoid too specific patterns, it is required that the merged mentions reflect at least t_{merge} different instances (support). In order to find patterns which can be merged, the mentions of relation instances are aligned by the instance argument positions. Then, an index data structure is created for each token. The indices are able to efficiently return for each token position p and each word w the set $g(p, w)$ of mentions that have w at position p. The merging algorithm explores combinations of p-w pairs for non-empty intersections which indicate mentions that can be merged. Exploration of these combinations is done in a breadth-first-search manner. Note that this abstraction step takes place for all mentions of all seed instances at a time. Thus, the generalization is effectively calculating the least general generalization (LGG) of patterns as typically done in bottom-up concept learning (cf. Section 2.3.1) or ILP approaches (compare [Muggleton and Feng, 1990]) and is closest to the bottom-up procedures discussed above.

This chapter experimentally compares the standard implementation to an improved implementation with regard to time efficiency while maintaining quality, the set of parameters and the ability to incorporate arbitrary (finite domain) token-based features. Most of the work presented in this chapter together has been published with Philipp Cimiano at the Ontology-Based Information Extraction Workshop at KI 2008 [Blohm and Cimiano, 2008]. The chapter is organized as follows. In the following section, the approach is outlined. In particular, the Apriori algorithm is introduced in Section 8.1.2 after reviewing related work. In Section 8.1.3, we describe how the induction of IE patterns can be viewed as a Frequent Itemset Mining problem that can be solved with Apriori. Before giving some concluding remarks, we present experimental results in Section 8.2 that indicate that modeling patterns as a collection of constraints which are selected by means of Frequent Itemset Mining increases the speed of pattern induction while maintaining the same level of quality.

8.1 Pattern Induction as Frequent Itemset Mining

The approach presented here is based on translating textual mentions of a specific relation into set representations and using the Apriori algorithm to find patterns in these mentions that exceed a certain minimum frequency (support). The task of finding frequent subsets within a collection of sets is typically called *Frequent Itemset Mining* (FIM). The approach presented here can thus be considered to consist of the creation of a *summarizing data structure* in combination with a *bottom-up* analysis of the data.

The mining for frequent itemsets is a subtask of Association Rule Mining and as such has been studied extensively with applications like market analysis in mind. Association rules are used to derive statements like "Customers who bought product X usually also bought product Y" from transaction databases. A transaction $t \in DB$ constitutes a shopping process with several items a from an alphabet of items A. DB is a multiset of subsets of A because transactions with the same items may re-appear. In the above example, A would correspond to a merchant's product line-up, each transaction t would correspond to one purchase of one or more products by a customer and DB would correspond to all transaction as they would be recorded by a cash register.

In a database DB of transactions the *frequent itemsets* $F \subset 2^A$ are defined as those sets that occur at least $freq_{min}$ times as subset of a transaction, i.e.

$$F = \{f \in 2^A || \{t \in DB | f \subseteq t\}| \geq freq_{min}\}$$

In the shopping example, the frequent itemsets at a minimum support of $freq_{min} = 4$ would be all the sets of items that have been purchased together at least four times regardless of what other items may have been purchased with them during these four or more transactions.

8.1.1 Related Work

While an overview of the related work in pattern-based IE is given in Chapter 4 and specific focus on various pattern induction algorithms is put in Section 5.6.2, this section focuses on related publications with regard to the use of Frequent Itemset Mining.

The field of Association Rule Mining goes back to seminal work by Rakesh Agrawal [1994] and his colleagues at IBM who also developed the Apriori algorithm. Extensions of this work have been developed in particular with respect to efficiency [Mueller, 1995] and the introduction of hierarchical background knowledge [Srikant and Agrawal, 1997]. A comprehensive overview of Association Rule Mining including further algorithms has been presented by Lars Schmidt-Thieme [2007] with a particular focus on mining complex structures studying application scenarios from the field of Web usage mining.

A similar approach to the one presented here is that of Jindal and Liu [2006]. They use Sequential Pattern Mining – a modification of Frequent Itemset Mining to derive textual patterns for classifying comparative sentences in product descriptions. Due to their way of encoding sequence information, their model is not able to account for several constraints per word. Additionally, the scalability aspect has not been focus of their study as mining has only be performed on a corpus of 2684 sentences with a very limited alphabet.

8.1.2 The Apriori Algorithm

Apriori [Agrawal and Srikant, 1994] is an algorithm for finding all frequent itemsets given a database and a frequency threshold. The algorithm identifies all frequent itemsets via breadth-first search in a graph representing all possible itemsets with connections among those that can be derived from each other by adding or removing one element. Apriori's optimization is based on the observation that an itemset f of size $|f| = n$ can only be frequent in DB if all its subsets are also frequent in DB (this is referred to as antimonotone property of support). Apriori thus significantly reduces the amount of itemsets that need to be explored by first deriving all frequent itemsets of size $n = 1$ and then progressively increasing n so that the above subset condition can be checked when generating the candidates for $n+1$ as all subsets of size n are known. Figure 8.1 formalizes the algorithm in pseudocode. It stores all frequent itemsets of size n in a set F_n (line 6) after verifying for each itemset that it occurs at least $freq_{min}$ times in DB (lines 5,6). The set of candidates C_1 for the first iteration is given by all elements of the alphabet (line 1). For the following iterations C_{n+1} is then generated by taking all elements of F_n and combining them if the condition $\text{MERGEABLE}(f, g)$ is fulfilled (line 7), which makes sure that f and g overlap in $n-1$ elements. $\text{PRUNE}(C_{n+1}, F_n)$

APRIORI($Alphabet\ A, Database\ DB \subset 2^A, Threshold\ freq_{min}$)
1 $C_1 \leftarrow \{\{a\}|a \in A\}$
2 $n \leftarrow 1$
3 **while** $C_n \neq \emptyset$
4 **do**
5     $\forall c \in C_n$: COUNTSUPPORT(c, DB)
6     $F_n \leftarrow \{c \in C_n|$SUPPORT$(c) >= freq_{min}\}$
7     $C_{n+1} \leftarrow \{f \cup g|f, g \in F_n \wedge$ MERGEABLE$(f, g)\}$
8     $C_{n+1} \leftarrow$ PRUNE(C_{n+1}, F_n)
9     $n \leftarrow n + 1$
10 **return** $F_1 \cup \ldots \cup F_n$

Figure 8.1: The Apriori algorithm.

removes all itemsets c from C_{n+1} (which all have length $n + 1$) for which one or more of all possible size n subsets of c are not contained in F_n which is the above-mentioned necessary condition for c to be frequent (line 8).

The performance of the Apriori algorithm depends on the efficient implementation of the operations COUNTSUPPORT(c, DB), MERGEABLE(f, g) and PRUNE(C, F_n). It is common to use a trie data structure (also called prefix tree) for this purpose. Given an arbitrary total order on A, one can represent the itemsets as ordered sequences with respect to that order. Tries are trees that represent sequences as paths in the tree along with their frequency counts. After constructing a trie from the DB, one can find and count non-continuous subsequences of DB entries very efficiently, which is the task of COUNTSUPPORT. Similarly, MERGEABLE and PRUNE can be implemented as traversal operations on the trie (as described in [Mueller, 1995] and [Schmidt-Thieme, 2007]).

Figure 8.2 shows a subset of the variable assignment during one execution of the algorithm along with a visualisation of the trie. Subscripts indicate frequency counts. Struck-out nodes have been generated by line 7 in iteration 2 but but they are not frequent enough to be kept. The grayed struck-out nodes (the ones below "a_2") and were directly pruned away in line 8 because the intersections of $\{a, b\}$ and $\{b, d\}$ were not frequent enough. Only the one invalid candidate (the struck-out"d_1" under "b'_2") was kept for the 3rd iteration and eliminated in line 6 because the counts to not exceed the minimum support.

8.1.3 Mining for Text Patterns with Apriori

The general idea of applying frequent itemset mining for text pattern induction is that a text pattern "`flights to *, *`" can be considered the frequent item-

$$
\begin{aligned}
DB &= \{\{a,b,c\},\{a,b,c,d\},\{c,d\}\} \\
freq_{min} &= 2 \\
F_1 &= \{\{a\},\{b\},\{c\}\} \\
F_2 &= \{\{a,b\},\{a,c\},\{b,c\},\{b,d\},\{c,d\}\} \\
F_3 &= \{\{a,b,c\}\} \\
C_3 &= \{\{a,b,c\},\{a,b,d\},\{a,c,d\},\{b,c,d\}\} \\
C_4 &= \{\}
\end{aligned}
$$

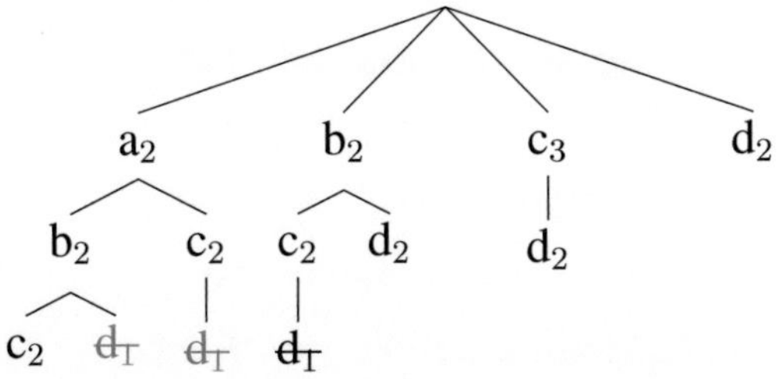

Figure 8.2: Example data for the execution of Apriori

set of the set of text mentions it has been generated from. We consider here an example with the following DB.

```
DB = { "We offer flights to London, England.",
       "I look for flights to Palo Alto, CA."}
```

We use a specific one-to-one mapping of text sequences to sets of integers that encodes each feature of the sequence as an integer item. Frequent itemsets among those sequence representations correspond to frequent patterns in the context of relevant instances. Some modeling of the nature of items is necessary to ensure that, in spite of the set nature of the itemsets, word order is preserved and to allow for additional constraints on words (e.g. part-of-speech). Specialized sequence mining algorithms have been developed (e.g. the one used by Jindal and Liu [2006]). Yet, in using them, it is not straightforward to encode multiple constraints per token. This is why we use in this chapter the more general model of itemsets and encode the position as described below.

We use the notion of constraints for describing the textual mentions and patterns. Each constraint has a type, a position and a value. A constraint is fulfilled for a given text segment if the value is present at the given position in a way described by the constraint type. The positions are the token numbers (aligned by the positions of the arguments). Feature types can be for example surface string, capitalization and part-of-speech with their respective sets of possible values. The textual mention "`We offer flights to *, *`" may be represented as the following set of constraints (subscripts of feature types denote positions):

$$\begin{aligned}
surface_2 &= we \\
capitalization_2 &= true \\
surface_3 &= offer \\
capitalization_3 &= false \\
surface_4 &= flights \\
capitalization_4 &= false \\
surface_5 &= to \\
capitalization_5 &= false \\
surface_6 &= , \\
capitalization_6 &= false
\end{aligned}$$

We then number the arguments as follows: 0 and 1 are reserved for the arguments. 2,3,4 are the tokens before the first argument (if t_prefix is 3) followed by the tokens from between the arguments. The last t_suffix numbers are reserved for the tokens coming after the last argument.

To make these attribute-value pairs accessible to FIM, we encode each constraint as a positive integer value using a function $encode : Type \times Position \times Value \rightarrow \mathbb{N}$ for which an inverse function $decode$ exists that decodes the encoded information.

One can think of this as the process of first "flattening" the structured information contained in the constraints to items like

$$\begin{aligned}
\{ \quad surface_2_we &, \; capitalization_2_true \,, \\
surface_3_offer &, \; capitalization_3_false \,, \\
surface_4_flights &, \; capitalization_4_false \,, \\
surface_5_to &, \; capitalization_5_false \,, \\
surface_6_COMMA &, \; capitalization_6_false \}
\end{aligned}$$

and subsequently translated to integer values:

$$\{987, 435, 656634, 4235, 234, 6453, 64, 242, 786, 89\}$$

More specifically, *encode* is defined as follows because this is a function for which given con and pos $value$ can be reconstructed from the result by simple arithmetics (see $decode_{value}$ below).

$$encode(con, pos, value) = \\ (value \cdot maxCon + (con - 1)) \cdot maxPos + pos$$

where con is the number of the constraint type, pos the position and $value$ is the value that the constraint takes. The remaining variables reflect the respective maximal values with respect to the given database. If for example we wanted to encode that at position 2 the constraint $surface$ has the value "offer", we would encode look up a dictionary id for "offer" (e.g. $value = 7$), and a constraint id for $surface$ (e.g. $con = 3$). With $maxCon = 8$ and $maxPos = 20$, one would encode:

$$encode(surface, 2, \text{“offer''}) = 7 * 8 * 20 + (2 + 20 * (3 - 1)) = 1162$$

Decoding a value at a given position and of a given constraint type would amount to computing:

$$decode_{value}(con, pos, code) = \frac{code}{maxCon * maxPos + (pos + maxPos * (con - 1))}$$

As shown in [Borgelt and Kruse, 2002] it leads to performance gains with respect to time and memory complexity if the items are numbered with decreasing frequency of occurrence and to process the item numbers with increasing natural order in the trie. Intuitively, this is due to the fact that the order changes the shape of the trie and consequently the order in which sets are eliminated from further exploration. When focussing on frequent words early-on, expensive alternatives, namely infrequent combinations of frequent items, are excluded earlier. To make use of these performance gains, we assume constraint type and position to be equally frequent while values (in particular words) strongly differ in frequency. Hence, we identify each word by its rank on a corpus word count list and design *encode* such that the magnitude of the output is particularly sensitive to the constraint value.

During the application of Apriori, only those subsets are retained that reflect a frequently occurring textual pattern:

$$\{6453, 64, 242, 786, 89\}$$

This set is smaller, because the codes for the non-frequently occurring constraints are eliminated. As an example the text fragment "we offer" may be less frequent and some of the capitalization constraints also. It is the assumption of this approach that the remaining (frequent) constraints are exactly those which reflect the text fragments that are typical of mentions of the target relation.

By means of $decode_{value}$, the textual representation of the pattern can be reconstructed from the remaining numbers:

```
"flights to *, *"
```

Apriori generates all patterns that exceed a given frequency threshold. Inevitably, this yields multiple patterns that are subsumed by each other (e.g. if `" * was born in * "` is frequent, then `" * was * in * "` is frequent as well). In order to avoid such too general patterns and at the same time avoiding too specific ones (e.g. `"Wolfgang Amadeus * was born in * "`), we introduce the following rule for removing more general patterns: if pattern a has all constraints also present in b and one more, b is removed unless $\text{SUPPORT}(b)$ is at least 20% higher than $\text{SUPPORT}(a)$. This rule is applied starting with the smallest patterns. Experiments showed that the threshold of 20% leads to a generally rather appropriate set of patterns. The remaining unwanted patterns are left to be eliminated by further filtering.

For the purpose of the experiments presented here, we used the following four types of constraints for *con*: The *surface* string of the words after a transformation to lower case. A Boolean constraint *capitalization* indicating if the first letter of the original surface string was a capital letter and the *number of tokens at the argument position* for both arguments.

8.1.4 Limitations of the approach

The above-described method is applicable whenever a pattern can be described with a limited set of constraints. The number of constraints grows rapidly as soon as features with a complex structure (e.g. parse-trees, annotations w.r.t. a formal ontology etc.) need to be taken into account. In general, the principle of Frequent Itemset Mining has been extended to complex structures like sequences of sets, sequences with wildcards of arbitrary length [Schmidt-Thieme, 2007] and items structured in a taxonomy [Srikant and Agrawal, 1997]. A more complex modeling with frequent itemset mining is applied in Chapter 9.

8.2 Experimental Evaluation

The goal of the experimental evaluation is to demonstrate the advantages of modeling the pattern abstraction subtask of iterative pattern induction as a frequent itemset mining (FIM) problem. We do so by comparing the performance achieved by the new itemset-based implementation with the abstraction algorithm we previously used (cf. Section 6.2.1). Most studies in Information Extraction do not report time efficiency of the employed pattern induction algorithms or even overall running times. This study thus takes an initial step to analyze the impact of the induction algorithm on runtime behavior in a large scale setting. Our study clearly shows that the modeling of pattern induction as a standard Data Mining problem is possible and beneficial. A more in-depth study of extraction performance would require a common evaluation dataset for large-scale Web relation extraction or at least a common basis of implementation.

8.2.1 Experimental Setup

The experiments were conducted on an Intel(R) Xeon ^{TM} dual processor system with Hyper-Threading technology running at 3.2 GHz. The system ran on a Java^{TM} 1.5 Virtual Machine with 2.6 GB RAM available.

To give an objective measure for temporal performance, we use the *Extraction Rate* that is the number of correctly extracted instances TP over the duration D of the extraction process in seconds:

$$Ex = \frac{TP}{D}$$

D was measured by logging start and end times of experimental runs in the file system.

8.2.2 Comparison with Previous Abstraction Algorithm

To assess the performance of the FIM version of Pronto, we compare precision, recall and F-measure with results of the standard configuration consisting in a bottom-up procedure for merging patterns described previously in Chapter 6.

Figure 8.3 shows precision, recall, F-Measure and the extraction rate for three configuration of the system: the *standard* configuration (using the best-

Parameter		standard and FIM-Pronto	FIM-Pronto tuned
Size of the seed set	$\|Inst'\|$	10	10
Size of pattern set	$\|P\|$	100	100
Results retrieved for each instance	$num_{matchInstances}$	200 – 20	**200**
Maximum tokens between arguments	$max_{argDist}$	4	4
Windows around arguments	$t_{prefix} = t_{suffix}$	2	2
Minimum support for pattern	t_{merge}	2	2
Minimum number of constraints per pattern	min_{common}	2	2
Results retrieved for each pattern	$num_{matchPatterns}$	200	200
Instances kept after filtering	$p_{filterInstances}$	top 50%	**top 50**
Number of iterations	$t_{iterations}$	5	5
Pattern filtering function	$score$	support or N/A.	N/A

Table 8.1: Parameter values as used in the experiments with Pronto for the comparison experiments.

performing setup from the study presented in Chapter 6), the *FIM-Pronto* configuration which uses the proposed modeling of the learning problem with all parameters unchanged and *FIM-Pronto tuned* for which the parameters have been optimized for the new learning algorithm. In particular, as FIM-Pronto is more efficient than the standard setup, the system can process a higher number of instances, such that we set the number of instance matched ($num_{matchInstances}$) to 200 (versus a decreasing number as indicated in Table 8.1 for the standard configuration) and accept the top 50 instances at each iteration instead of the top 50%. Overall, there is a small superiority of *FIM-Pronto* over the standard version in terms of precision and recall (0.33 vs. 0.29 and 0.15 vs. 0.11). Most importantly, there is a clear superiority in terms of extraction rate (0.19 vs. 0.05 instances/second). This difference is statistically significant according to a two-sided paired Student's t-test with an α-Level of 0.05. In addition to that, a performance gain can be achieved by optimizing the parameters of the overall system

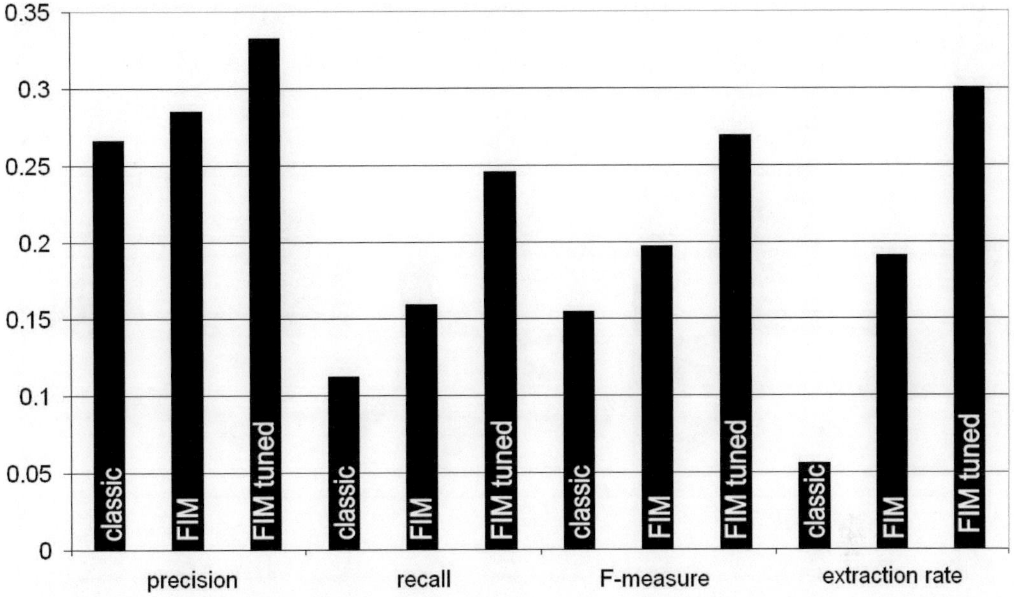

Figure 8.3: Precision, recall, F-measure and extraction rate for the individual configurations averaged over all relations.

to the properties of the new learning algorithm (*FIM-Pronto tuned*). The effect can be observed in Figure 8.4 where we compare the F-measure results of the FIM configurations with the classic configuration individually for the different relations.

It is important to note that in principle there are no reasons for any of the abstraction algorithms to extract instances of better quality because they both explore all possible frequently occurring patterns in a breadth-first-search manner. Differences are due to to three minor reasons: (1) There are minor differences in modeling (see below), (2) pattern filtering directly counts from Apriori's support counts and thus count the number of supporting mentions as opposed to supporting instances and (3) the fact that learning was cut off after one hour per iteration which was frequently the case with the standard induction algorithm.

One example of slight modeling differences which influenced performance is the treatment of multi-word instances. Pronto's pattern formalism allows it to generate queries in a way that differs in the representation of the argument wildcards when translated to search engine queries. The algorithm has to decide whether to insert one wildcard $*$ in an argument position (e.g. `"flights to *, *"`, nearly always matching exactly one word like in "flights to Seattle, Washington") or two (e.g. `"flights to * *, *"` allowing for two or more words like in "flights to San Jose, California"). The standard version keeps all mentions in memory during learning and takes the number of words in the argument of the

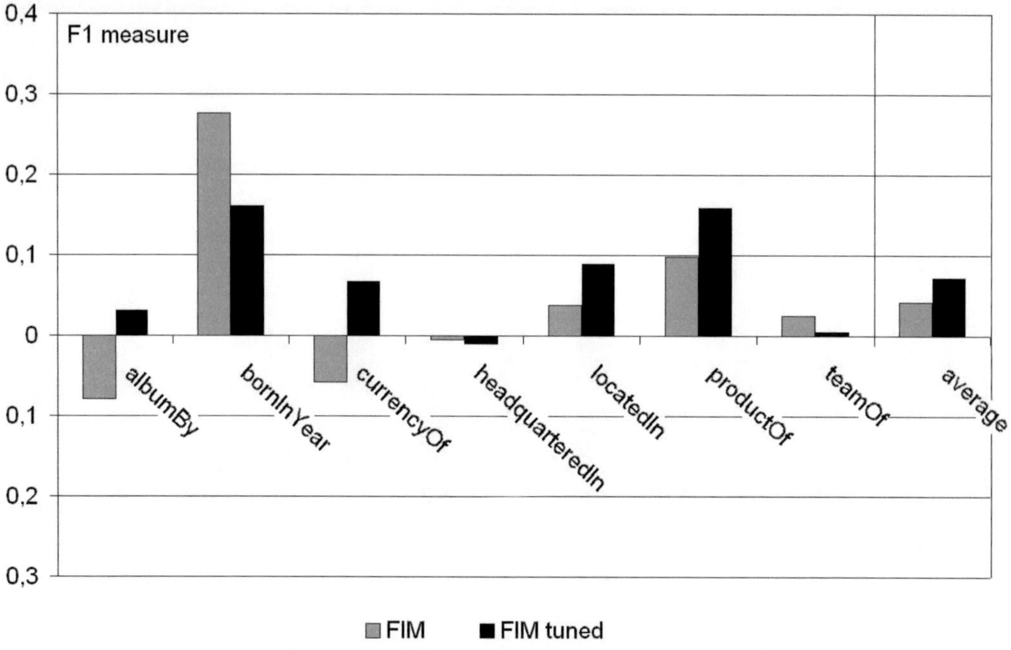

Figure 8.4: Relative differences in F-measure of extraction results with FIM for the individual relations compared to classic configuration.

first mention used for pattern creation as sample for the number of wildcards. The FIM version encodes the fact that an argument has more than one word as an additional constraint and consequently adds an item for it into the itemset. If this item is contained in a learned frequent itemset, a double wildcard is inserted. The strong differences in the *albumBy* and *bornInYear* relations can be explained in that way. The FIM version learns in the above way that person names have typically length 2 and birth years always have length 1 while the standard induction approach, which only takes individual sample instances into account, shows a greater variability here. That is the standard approach would be more likely to accept erroneously outputting multi-word expressions like “North Carolina” as birth years.

As indicated in Figure 8.5, the clear benefit of the FIM abstraction step lies in its runtime behavior. The duration of a pattern generation process is plotted over the number of sample instances to be generalized. To measure these times, both learning modules were provided with the same sets of mentions isolated from the rest of the induction procedure. The FIM shows a close to linear increase of processing duration for the given mention counts which reflect the range encountered in practice. Even though implemented with a number of optimizations, the standard induction approach clearly shows a more than proportional increase in computation time w.r.t. the number of input mentions.

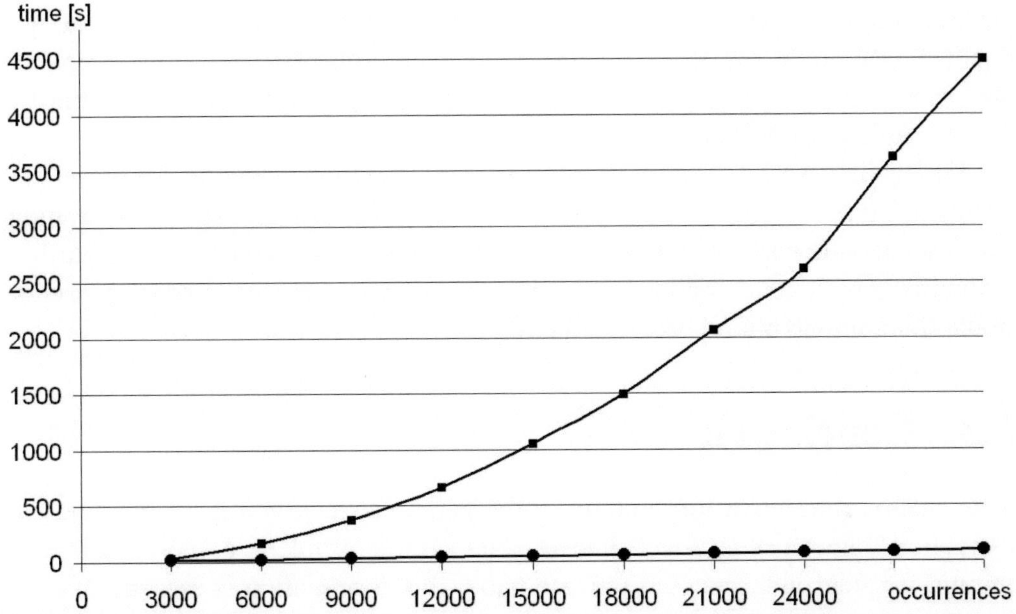

Figure 8.5: Time in seconds taken by a run of the classical induction algorithm (squares) and the FIM-based algorithm (circles) over the numbers of sample mentions provided for induction.

8.2.3 Discussion

The experiments show advantages of modeling textual mentions as itemsets and applying Apriori as an established Frequent Itemset Mining algorithm for this purpose. The key advantage lies in the fact that all individual constraints are independent from each other. Other summarizing data structures such as suffix trees as used in [Ravichandran and Hovy, 2001] or the automaton-based HMM model in [Talukdar et al., 2006] do not allow introducing a wildcard within a text sequence or keeping intact one piece of information (e.g. capitalization) and eliminating the surface string. This is due to the fact that both models are built on counting all sub-strings of the present text sequences. Counting all alternatives with wildcards at all positions would increase the computational complexity because there is an exponentially large amount of possible subsequences with wildcards added.

Modeling patterns as an aggregation of constraints which reflect small pieces of information also allows for high flexibility in pattern design. For example, in the new approach, argument length is implicitly learned by the algorithm as a further constraint on the positions. This way, the patterns for the *bornInYear* relation correctly reflect that the first argument (the name) is nearly always of length 2 while the the second argument (the year) is of length one. Like some of the other approaches discussed in Section 5.6.2 (in particular those based on Suffix-Trees,

HMMs and bag-of-words vectors), our approach takes corpus frequency into account. Based on the trie data structure, patterns and sub-patterns can be compared by mention counts and too general and too specific patterns can be ruled out by the above-described filtering rule.

Finally, the Apriori algorithm provides good runtime behavior. From the experiments, one can observe that in the present range of problem sizes, the running time increases linearly with the number of text mentions to abstract over. Further comparison with other approaches is difficult to achieve as most other approaches in the literature do not report on induction time.

8.3 Conclusion

This chapter presents a formulation of the pattern induction step of the iterative extraction framework as a well-known Data Mining problem, namely the one of mining frequent itemsets. On the one hand, this formulation is elegant and advantageous as it opens the opportunity to apply optimizations from the literature (compare for example [Han et al., 2004], [Zaki, 2000] and [Mannila et al., 1994]). On the other hand, we have shown that this formulation leads to a significant decrease in the running time. In particular, the empirical running time behavior decreases from polynomial to linear with the number of mentions to be generalized with respect to the non-optimized implementation of the induction step as presented in Chapter 6. Further, we have also shown that the quality of the generated instances increases slightly in terms of F-Measure with respect to our earlier approach.

The itemset-based formulation is also beneficial in this respect as it straightforwardly allows to incorporate additional knowledge in the form of constraints on the tokens. In the following chapter we present a study that uses a more sophisticated modeling based on FIM techniques to take into account taxonomic features which encode linguistic knowledge.

Reviewing the related work, we conclude that the setup presented here is at the state of the art with respect to extraction rate and extraction quality among those systems that are able to work at Web scale. However, the possibilities to compare our results with other works from the literature are limited because many researchers in this field have different types of applications and evaluation in mind. They thus work on different datasets and evaluate in many different ways.

Chapter 9

Pattern Expressivity

The goal of the experiments in this chapter is to investigate the impact of design choices with regard to what a pattern can express (the *pattern class*) on extraction quality. We introduced the notion of pattern classes in Section 5.2 and pointed out that most experiments in the field of IE have only been performed using one pattern class. Yet, one can expect that at least two aspects of pattern classes have a major impact on extraction performance. On the one hand, the pattern language elements that allow for underspecification (wildcard, skip, disjunction) and on the other hand the set of features that are taken into account during pattern matching. Figure 9.1 gives an example of a sentence that is indicative of an instance of

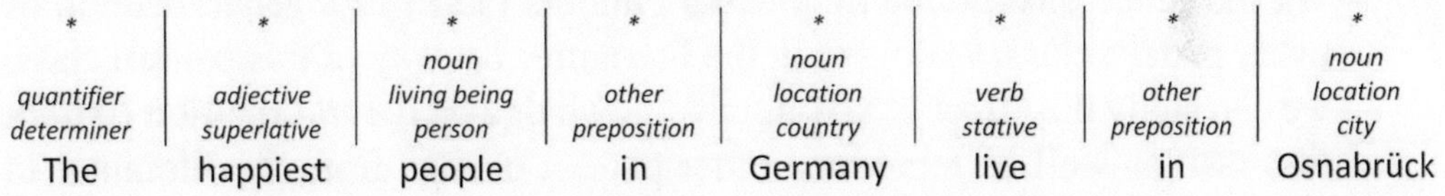

Figure 9.1: Example sentence with morpho-syntactic token features. The features for each token are ordered by generality. $*$ denotes the most general constraint, matching everything.

the *locatedIn* relation along with linguistic information that is available for each token. As discussed in Section 4.2.1, many approaches to IE have incorporated some sort of morpho-syntactic or semantic types into the pattern class in order to yield more general patterns (an overview of some pattern classes used in the literature is given in Section 9.2). The present work constitutes a generalization of these approaches allowing to integrate a taxonomy of morpho-syntactic and lexico-semantic features directly into the pattern mining process. The features for each token in Figure 9.1 are ordered by generality. That is, each column above the surface string of a token corresponds to the token's root path in a taxonomy.

The topmost row contains for each token the $*$ wildcard which is a feature that all tokens share. It constitutes the top concept of the taxonomy or, in a constraint-view, it is the constraint that does not exclude any token.

We present here a principled and uniform mining approach based on sound techniques from the area of knowledge discovery and in particular frequent sequence mining. We thereby extend the idea presented in Chapter 8 of using a FIM-based approach. Here however we use a sequence mining technique which allows us to generate a wide range of pattern classes. As a novelty, we allow for a special sort of wildcards that allow to identify for each token in the pattern the right level of detail at which a constraint is added to the pattern. In Figure 9.2 this is illustrated for the example sentence. The only the highlighted token information will be part of the pattern.

*	*	*	*****	*	*	*	*
		noun		*noun*			*noun*
quantifier	*adjective*	***living being***	*other*	*location*	*verb*	*other*	***location***
determiner	***superlative***	*person*	*preposition*	***country***	***stative***	*preposition*	*city*
The	happiest	people	in	Germany	live	**in**	Osnabrück

Figure 9.2: Possible choice of features for a pattern from the example sentence.

More specifically, this chapter makes the following contributions.

- We introduce Taxonomic Sequential Patterns (TSP) as a generalization of many pattern classes adopted in the literature. By way of this pattern class, we can study the effect of taxonomic knowledge on the Information Extraction task as well as reproduce other pattern classes from the literature to compare with. The question we want to answer here is whether TSPs are superior to other types of patterns in terms of precision and recall.

- We present a principled mining algorithm as an extension of the well-known Eclat algorithm [Han et al., 2004] that allows us to mine taxonomic sequential patterns and all the pattern classes that we directly compare with, e.g. the patterns used in the *URES* system [Rosenfeld and Feldman, 2006], as well as a few baseline pattern classes. Such comparisons of performance across different pattern classes do not exist, probably due to the fact that most mining algorithms are rather ad-hoc and cannot be straightforwardly extended to mine other types of patterns. The mining algorithm we present is principled in the sense that it is complete (i.e. it is guaranteed to find all patterns with a given frequency threshold of occurrence, called minimum support) and extensible by making minimal assumptions on the patterns (i.e. an order of specificity defined on them).

- We present results of experiments on 4 relations for 5 different pattern classes we consider, showing that TSPs perform generally better compared to URES pattern class and the other baseline pattern classes.

The chapter is structured as follows. In the following section, the role of pattern expressivity as a design choice of IE pattern induction is discussed and the work in this chapter is motivated. Some related work is discussed in Section 9.2 before the pattern classes and the mining algorithm are introduced (Sections 9.3 and 9.4). Then, in Section 9.5, we discuss our experimental results including a description of the experimental setup, the dataset and taxonomy used and the experimental setup before concluding.

The work presented here is joint work with Krisztian Buza, Philipp Cimiano, and Lars Schmidt-Thieme and has been submitted to Taylor and Francis as a chapter of the book "Applied Semantic Technologies: Using Semantics in Intelligent Information Processing." The focus of this chapter is the choice and evaluation of pattern classes as well as the application in the field of IE. A large portion of the work on the design and implementation of the algorithm for mining taxonomic patterns has been performed and published by Krisztian Buza and Lars Schmidt-Thieme [Buza and Schmidt-Thieme, 2008] who also performed the pattern induction part of the experiments presented here. The contribution of the author of this thesis lies in the development of an experimental framework for the purpose of Information Extraction and the conduction of the pattern class evaluation presented here.

9.1 The Role of Pattern Expressivity

The choice of the pattern class in which we can express patterns directly determines the search space for patterns and thus clearly has the potential of affecting performance. In this chapter, we explore one particular aspect of pattern expressivity by analyzing the impact of factoring taxonomic information into the pattern class. We do so by designing taxonomic sequential patterns as a generic pattern class which subsumes many of the pattern classes in the literature and allows us to explore the impact of taxonomic vs. non-taxonomic patterns. While many pattern-based approaches so far have incorporated type information (e.g. sense information, semantic or named entity tags etc.) into the patterns, the positive effect thereof has not been empirically demonstrated. For the sake of simplicity, we assume that all information can be encoded into one single hierarchy. This is a slight simplification as the hierarchy will then contain classes corresponding to different linguistic levels which are actually orthogonal. This assumption leads in some cases to rather ad-hoc modeling decisions such as putting the class of *person* under the part-of-speech *noun* in the hierarchy for instance. Nevertheless, this

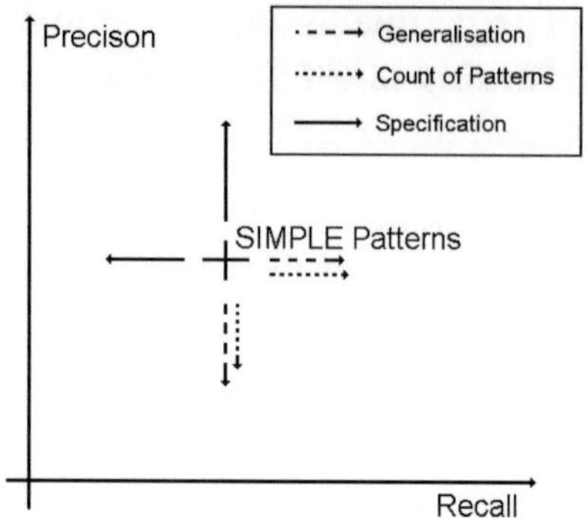

Figure 9.3: Quality-effects of the introduction of a taxonomy into a simple pattern class: concrete words in pattern may be generalised, the count of patterns increase, wildcard in patterns may be replaced by more specific taxonomical concepts.

assumption facilitates mining as because the use of one single taxonomy makes the hierarchical structure become part of the antimonotonicity of patterns. The antimonotonicity is the key to optimized pattern mining, in the case of taxonomic knowledge it can be used to conclude that if patterns with a *noun* at a given position are not frequent, patterns with specializations of noun (e.g. *person*) cannot be frequent either.

In most of the literature discussed in Section 5.2, the pattern classes have not been defined explicitly. Instead, the description of the pattern class itself is often mixed with the way the patterns are mined and matched. Such ad-hoc solutions make comparisons difficult. The absence of a common notion on syntax and (matching) semantics of patterns make the task of systematically analyzing the influence of the choice of a pattern class on the task of extracting information challenging. To address one point in this gap, we re-examine and substantiate with experimental evidence an assumption that many systems have made: that abstraction with respect to a type system or taxonomy can have a positive effect on extraction performance. This study is meant to clarify a foundational question which will help to take more informed decisions with respect to the design of the pattern class in future work on relation extraction.

While it sounds straightforward that additional information (e.g. part-of-speech or semantic tags) can improve extraction, an adverse effect is indeed possible (compare Figure 9.3). Suppose we are given a simple pattern class that only includes words and (untyped) wildcards (i.e. only featuring the topmost and the bottom line of features in Figure 9.1). The introduction of a taxonomy (i.e. as depicted in Figure 9.2 chose the pattern's constraints from the taxonomy root paths of the tokens) could have at least these three effects:

- *Generalisation effect*: The integration of type information (in form of taxonomic concepts) increases recall (and potentially decreases precision) as concrete tokens in the pattern might be replaced by more generic "types". This corresponds to selecting a feature at a higher level of abstraction in Figure 9.2 which may lead to matching more mentions each of which may be correct (increased recall) or incorrect (decreased precision).

- *Specification effect*: Gaps or untyped wildcards (tokens in patterns that match arbitrary input tokens) may be replaced by typed gaps or wildcards, thus restricting the sequences that the pattern matches and potentially increasing precision, but possibly at the expense of a decrease in recall. This corresponds to selecting a feature at a lower level of abstraction in Figure 9.2 which may lead to matching less mentions and thereby no longer matching correct (decreased recall) or incorrect (increased precision) instances.

- The *count of patterns* (frequent sequences) might change: there might be many new patterns containing the newly introduced taxonomic wildcards. Recall can increase at the cost of a possible decrease in precision. The reason why new patterns can occur is that shared features may not lie on the lowest level of abstraction but higher up in the taxonomy. Mining without taxonomy would miss out on these commonalities and not generate a pattern.

Figure 9.3 illustrates the generalization effect with dashed arrows, the specification effect with solid arrows and the altered pattern count with dotted arrows. While the three effects constitute classical precision/recall trade-offs, the crucial question is whether the three effects add up to yield an overall improvement. In particular, as all the three effects have some positive and negative side-effects it would be certainly desirable to balance these effects in such a way that both precision and recall increase. However, whether both precision and recall really improve is not obvious. In fact, this is the question we address in this work.

9.2 Related Work

There exist various types and formalisms for textual patterns. While all of them have in common that text fragments can be specified literally, they differ in the way they allow for variability in the text sequences they match. Before introducing the languages under investigation we review various pattern formalisms and their semantics in the literature which differ primarily along the lines of the following dimensions:

- *Abstraction over the surface string.* Some pattern formalisms allow for *wildcards* that match arbitrary single tokens (e.g. Pronto, ExDisco [Yangarber, 2003] or RAPIER [Califf and Mooney, 1997]), others allow for *skips* which ignore zero to many tokens at a time (e.g. URES, see below for a more detailed account).

- *Pattern length.* While some patterns match exactly one sentence (like URES, its sister system URIES [Rozenfeld and Feldman, 2006], KnowItNow [Cafarella et al., 2005] and work by Snow et al. [2004]), others focus on a window of a specific length (Pronto and DIPRE). A method of intelligently trimming patterns to an appropriate length has been described by Ravichandran and Hovy [2001].

- *Additional knowledge or structure.* Patterns are not bound to simply reflecting features of the surface string. Most systems incorporate further structural or linguistic features like Part-Of-Speech (e.g. URIES and RAPIER), Named-Entity-Tagging (URES, Snowball and Ravichandran and Hovy [2001]), word-sense disambiguation (ExDisco) and (shallow) parses [Snow et al., 2004; Cafarella et al., 2005]. The systems are usually limited to one kind of tags which is usually formalized by using typed wildcards. A method for employing a rich pattern structure with efficient Information Retrieval techniques is applied in KnowItNow.

- *Relevance of linear order.* While most patterns require tokens to occur in a particular linear order, exceptions are Snowball and LPPL [Tomita et al., 2006].

- *Argument identification.* Trivial as it may sound, identifying the actual relation instances within a pattern match can be done in different ways. While systems that build on NE-tagging can use this information, others usually employ a distinguished type of wildcard or skip or break apart the pattern into “prefix”, “infix” and “postfix” (cf. Section 4.2.2).

9.3 Taxonomic Sequential Patterns

We introduce Taxonomic Sequential Patterns as a generic pattern class allowing to integrate taxonomic knowledge into patterns. A pattern class in our sense consists of a repertoire of “pattern features” which can be used to express constraints on the set of sequences the pattern matches. TSPs are sequences consisting of standard tokens together with the following pattern features which have been introduced in Section 5.2:

- *Wildcards* ("ANY"): A token in the pattern that matches an arbitrary single token in the input sequence.

- *Typed wildcards* ("$ANY[type]$"): A token in the pattern that matches any single token of a certain type in the input sequence. Most systems use typed wildcards as a way to introduce additional external linguistic knowledge into the mining process, such as part-of-speech (POS) information, Named-Entity tags, word-sense information, as well as (shallow) parses. We use typed wildcards to factor in taxonomic information which can be used to constrain the tokens allowed at a certain position via these taxonomic types. As an example, the third column in Figure 9.2 corresponds to "$ANY[living\ being]$."

- *Gaps*: our patterns allow gaps while matching. Gaps are not specific to a certain position in patterns, but a global property which can be active or not. Gaps are implemented in our approach through "semi-continuous" patterns allowing to drop (leaving unmatched) tokens in the input sequence at arbitrary positions. We talk of (d, n)-semi-continuous patterns if at most n drop operations, each of them having a maximal length of d tokens, are allowed. In its $(3, 2)$-semi-continuous version, the pattern from Figure 9.2 would also match "The happiest people from Asia in Europe live in big cities like Paris." The two underlined sections would be dropped during matching. However it would neither be matched by the $(2, 2)$-semi-continuous version because it cannot drop the length 3 sequence "big cities like" nor by the $(3, 1)$-semi-continuous version because this one only allows to drop in one position.

- *Argument slots* ("$ANY[type]_{argn}$"): Many systems use special 'argument slots' to actually mark the position where the nth argument of the instance occurs. We allow in addition to restrict the argument slots to a specific taxonomic type as many other systems. In the example from Figure 9.2, the fifth column would translate to "$ANY[country]_{arg2}$"

Overall, the pattern intuitively illustrated in Figure 9.2 translates to the following notation:

"The $ANY[superlative]$ $ANY[living\ being]$ ANY $ANY[country]_{arg2}$ $ANY[stative]$ in $ANY[city]_{arg1}$"

The set of pattern classes we investigate experimentally is depicted in Figure 9.4. Our novel, *taxonomic sequential patterns* are tested in two variants TAX

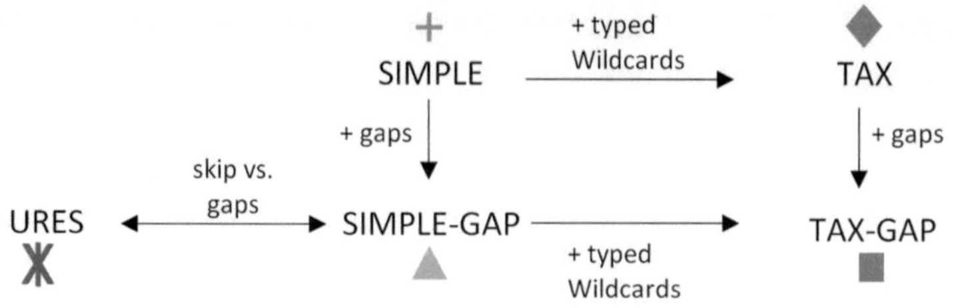

Figure 9.4: The pattern classes considered and in which features they differ.

and TAX-GAP. They both support *typed wildcards* and typed *argument slots*. While TAX-GAP allows semi-continuity (we report here results for $d = 1$ and $n = 2$ which despite the small numbers show a clear effect), TAX patterns are continuous in the sense that they do not allow for gaps (but nonetheless for typed wildcards). Apart from that, we investigate a SIMPLE pattern class as a baseline which only allows argument slots and untyped wildcards. We further use the above repertoire of pattern features to reproduce the URES pattern class[1].

While the pattern mining algorithm itself as described in the following section is exhaustive, we employ heuristics to reduce the number of patterns that are generated. The heuristics are as follows. (a) We disallow untyped wildcards in the taxonomic case. (b) We keep only the most specific frequent patterns with regard to typed wildcards. i.e. if patterns p_1 and p_2 are frequent and p_1 can be generated by exchanging the types of one or more typed wildcards in p_2 by their superconcepts, then only p_2 is kept. (c) Patterns are scored and all patterns below a given threshold are discarded. We vary the threshold as a parameter during the experiments. While each of these heuristics is optional, an evaluation of the pattern classes without these heuristics is computationally too complex. When mining exhaustively, the pattern sets generated are "stacked" in the sense that the TAX, TAX-GAP and SIMPLE-GAP patterns contain all SIMPLE patterns and that the TAX-GAP patterns will contain the SIMPLE-GAP and the TAX features. This is due to the fact, that all language elements these pattern classes add to the SIMPLE notion of patterns are optional. However, when the heuristics are applied, this stacked property is sacrificed to the goal of keeping the most promising patterns.

URES patterns feature (typed) *argument slots* and can contain *skips* which are marked in the pattern but differ from wildcards in the sense that they consume an arbitrary number of consecutive tokens.

[1]For the sake of generality we do not implement the very specific heuristics implemented in URES (e.g. providing a list of relation-specific and manually selected keywords which increase the probability that a text fragment considered already contains the relation in question) to ensure the generality of our results. We do thus implement the *patterns* used in URES but do not compare our results with the *URES system* as a whole with its very proprietary settings.

The taxonomy used for the TAX/-GAP class incorporates linguistic information at several levels of abstraction (syntactic and semantic). It comprises information on the *part-of-speech* level as well as on the *named-entity-tag* level and allows for sub-class relationships between entity tags (e.g. *city* is-a *location*). The taxonomy was constructed for the purpose of the study described here. The top-level consists of generic classes of part-of-speech tags (noun, verb etc.). Below that, more specific POS tags, WordNet supersense tags and WSJ tags (cf. Section 2.2.1)are included by way of manual alignment (see section 9.5.2 for more details.)

Taxonomic sequential patterns constitute a generalization over various approaches from the literature discussed in Section 9.2 (in particular RAPIER [Snow et al., 2004], ExDisco [Yangarber, 2003], Pronto (introduced in Section 5.5), KnowItNow [Cafarella et al., 2005], Espresso [Pantel and Pennacchiotti, 2006] and the patterns used by Ravichandran and Hovy [2001]) as it takes a more general approach to the integration of background knowledge by using a taxonomy. In this sense, the empirical investigation of TSPs re-examines the assumption in all of the above works that generalized patterns are useful and grounding it empirically.

9.4 Pattern Mining

The complete pattern mining algorithm we introduce here builds – like the one presented in Chapter 8 – on the basic idea of organizing the search in the space of potential patterns efficiently. This organization exploits the anti-monotonicity of patterns, i.e. on the basis of patterns already found to be non-frequent, one infers that all other patterns subsuming these are not frequent either which allows excluding them from further investigation and thus pruning the search space.

The differences between the algorithm presented in Chapter 8 and the one presented here lie in the way sequence and token-based features are encoded. On the one hand, we use here a sequence mining algorithm that is specialized on mining frequent subsequences (with wildcards), on the other hand, features are encoded differently by means of typed wildcards with types ordered in a taxonomy. Furthermore, the algorithm uses a different data model. This is due to the fact that the number of alternative frequent patterns is much larger when all alternative types for typed wildcards at all positions come into play. For example, if the pattern phrase "The happiest people in Germany live in Osnabrück" from Figure 9.1 is frequent, then all combinations in which one or more of the words are replaced by one of the concepts on the root path (i.e. the features displayed above the surface string, including the $*$ for the top concept) are frequent as well resulting in $4 \times 4 \times 5 \times 4 \times 5 \times 4 \times 4 \times 5 = 128000$ frequent patterns. Rather than in a breadth-first manner like in Apriori, the space of possible patterns is therefore explored in a depth-first manner using an extension of the Eclat algorithm [Han et al., 2004]. Eclat is based on using an auxiliary data structure, a set of so-called TID lists (for transaction identifier), which basically constitute an inverted index. Initially, a TID list exists for each token listing all sequences in the database in which the token occurs. During mining, TID-lists are generated for all frequent subsequences under investigation. Being an instance of depth-first search, the algorithm is most conveniently formalized in a recursive way as in Figure 9.5.

Input is given in form of a collection of textual sequences DB_s and a *minimum support threshold* $freq_{min}$ and a set of taxonomy root elements $Roots$. DB_s contains sequences of tokens from an alphabet A. Prior to the execution of the recursive algorithm in the figure, TID lists need to be computed so that GETTID(a) returns for each token a the set $\{s \in DB_s | s\ contains\ a\}$. For wildcard tokens, the interpretation of $contains$ depends on the definition of the wildcard. The function OCCURSAT evaluates to *true* if (a match of) the given pattern occurs in the sequence with the given id at least once and to *false* otherwise. To account for various pattern classes, OCCURSAT needs to be adapted depending on the various types of wildcards. DESCENDANTSOFLASTTOKEN(p) returns a set of tokens that are the immediate descendants of the last token of p in the taxonomy. REPLACELASTTOKEN(p, a) replaces the last token in sequence p by the token a. The algorithm starts with a maximally unspecific pattern and recursively specializes it in two ways:

- Extend the pattern in length by adding a (typed) wildcard as last token (line 4).
- Specialize the last token if it is a wildcard by replacing it with its immediate taxonomic descendants (line 8).

This way, all possible patterns that are potentially frequent are tested at some point during the execution of the algorithm. Further recursion only takes place for frequent patterns (RECURRIFFREQUENT). Note that a pattern p_2 that is a specialization of a pattern p_1 in one of the two above ways can only be frequent if p_1 is frequent. We thus exploit this anti-monotonicity by excluding specializations of infrequent patterns from further processing. The second type of extension is safely anti-monotone due to the definition of the taxonomy: A lower concept is only present if its superconcept is present as well. This is the reason why taxonomic features constitute an efficient way to mine patterns with a rich set of features.

ECLATRECURSION is called initially with $depth = 0$, $prefix =<>$ and tid containing the identifiers of all sequences in DB_s. In line 4, p is extended by all root tokens from the set of roots $Roots$. In line 8 the alternate specialization takes place by replacing the last token in p by a taxonomical subconcept. Both specialization steps are followed by the calling RECURRIFFREQUENT which computes the new TID list and, continues the recursion if the TID list indicates that the pattern is frequent. RECURRIFFREQUENT first computes a preliminary version of the new sequence's TID list by intersecting the old TID list with the TID list of the added or replaced token (line 1). At that point, tid_{new} contains all sequences from DB_s which contain p and a. In further processing, all those co-occurrences are excluded (line 7) in which a does not immediately follow p or respectively constitute the last token of p (line 6). This expensive check however is only done if the initial version of tid_{new} is large enough (line 2). OCCURRSAT is typically implemented by maintaining the position information of the occurrences within the TID lists as additional informatiln. If the final tid_{new} is large enough, the new pattern is recurred over for further extension (line 10).

Figure 9.6 shows an example database, an example taxonomy and the corresponding structure of recursive calls for the corresponding execution of the algorithm. We only show a part of the recursive structure graph which continues under the node labelled "…."

The version of Eclat used for these experiments enables mining of all the pattern classes presented in this chapter. Only the OCCURSAT method and the counting of the TID lists have to be adopted to enable the use of further language elements.

Note that like in the *URES* system, we use specificity as a criterion for pattern selection. If pattern p_1 can be derived from p_2 by removing a token or replacing a concrete token or wildcard by a more general one, p_1 will be removed, thus keeping only the most specific patterns. One should further note that as our aim is to fairly compare to the URES pattern class (described by its pattern features as in Section 9.3) and not to compare the naive pattern mining strategy in *URES* against complete mining we mine all pattern classes, including URES patterns, with a complete algorithm. In particular, the pairwise abstraction method of the *URES* system as described in Section 5.6.2 mines only a subset of the possible patterns of a given support (we give an example in Section 5.6.2). We ensure that all pairs are mined by using an Eclat miner to construct patterns of the URES pattern class.

9.5 Experiments

The goal of our experiments is to assess the performance of taxonomic patterns in comparison to patterns not incorporating taxonomic information. We perform our experiments on a large, publicly available corpus (thus making our results reproducible) and aim at extracting four non-taxonomic relations for which the full

```
ECLATRECURSION(Int depth, Sequence p, TIDList tid)
  Output ← Output ∪ p
  for a ∈ Roots
  do
      p_new ← CONCAT(p, a)
      RECURRIFFREQUENT(p_new, a, tid)
  for a ∈ DESCENDANTSOFLASTTOKEN(p)
  do
      REPLACELASTTOKEN(p, a)
      RECURRIFFREQUENT(p_spec, a, tid)

RECURRIFFREQUENT(Sequence p_new, Token newToken, TIDList tid)
  tid_new ← tid ∩ GETTID(newToken)
  if |tid_new| ≥ freq_min
    then
          for id ∈ tid_new
          do
              if notOCCURSAT(p_new, id)
                then tid_new ← tid_new \ {id}
          if |tid_new| ≥ freq_min
            then
                  ECLATRECURSION(depth + 1, p_new, tid_new)
```

Figure 9.5: The extended Eclat algorithm.

extension is assumed to be given for evaluation purposes ($freq_{min}$, Section 5.7). Furthermore, we isolate the task of relation extraction from lower-level preprocessing by using a corpus preprocessed with standard tagging tools (sentence splitting, tokenization, part-of-speech tagging, named entity tagging). We perform relation extraction with different pattern variants and compare the extraction quality.

9.5.1 Evaluation Protocol

With the goal in mind of investigating particularly the design of pattern languages and the use of taxonomic sequential patterns, we designed our experiments to maximize the generality of our results rather than optimizing the performance for a given setup. Towards this goal, it is important to avoid a large set of highly tuned parameters. We do so, in two different ways:

$$
\begin{aligned}
DB_s &= \{xzx, xyz, yzy\} \\
freq_{min} &= 2 \\
F_1 &= \{A, B, C, x, y, z\} \\
F_2 &= \{AA, AB, AC, Ay, Az, BA, BC, Bz, CA, CB, xA, yA, yC, yz\} \\
F_3 &= \{\{AAA, AAB, ABA, ACA, BAA, BAB, BCA, BCB, \\
&\quad BZA, BZB, xAA\}\}
\end{aligned}
$$

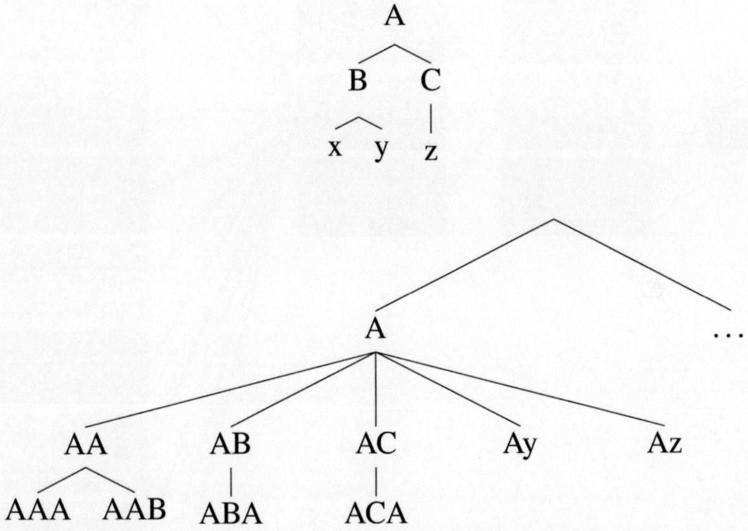

Figure 9.6: Example data for the execution of the Eclat taxonomy mining algorithm. The upper tree displays the taxonomy. The lower tree displays the nested recursive calls (only displaying the values for $prefix$)

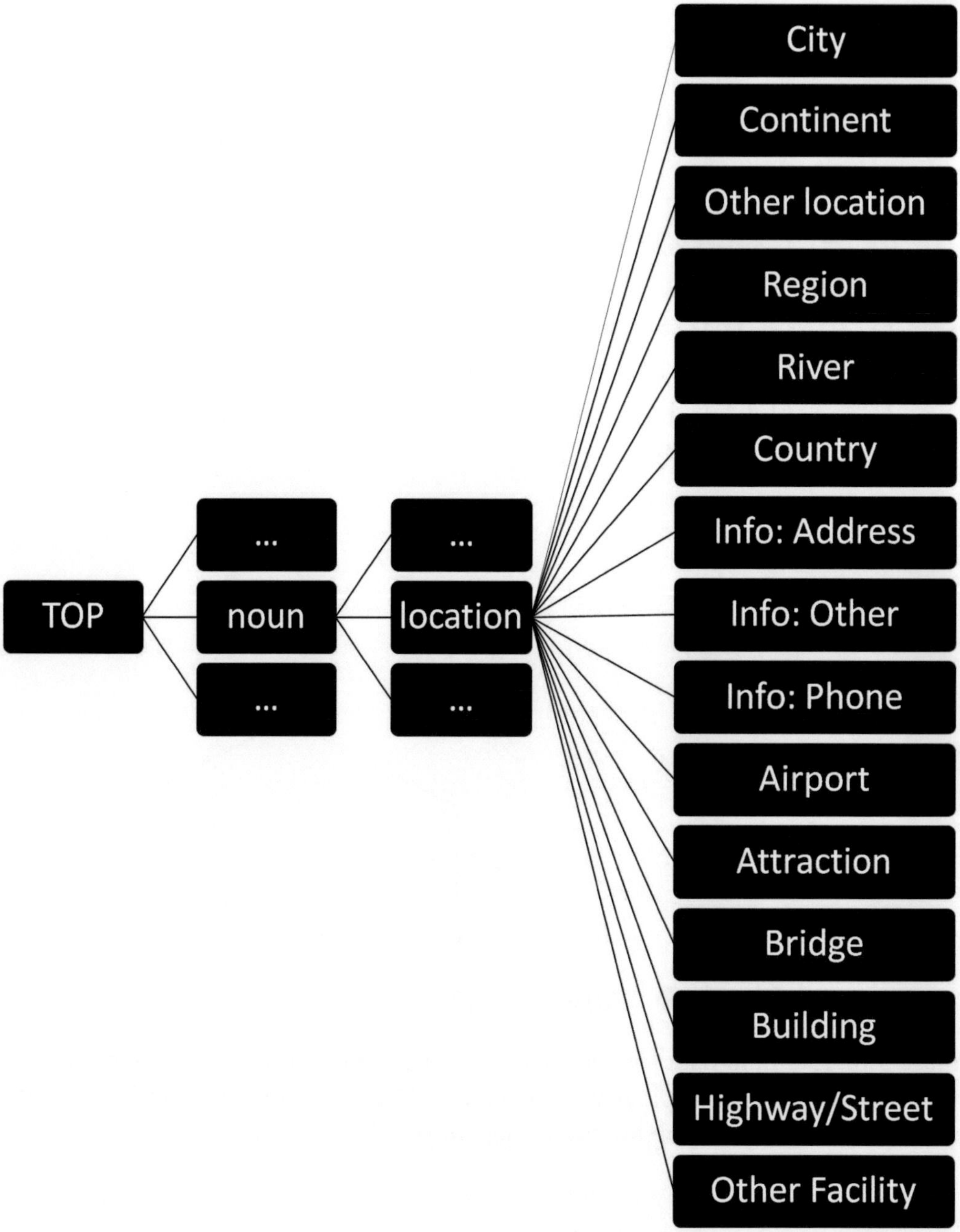

Figure 9.7: Excerpt from the taxonomy showing the noun subhierarchy for location along with its root path.

- As far as possible, parameters were avoided. The mining algorithm takes only one parameter (support $freq_{min}$), and a threshold t_{score} on the score of each pattern (see below). The values of these parameters were determined measuring the system performance on the training set as described below. This avoids tuning the parameters in an informed way. In particular, for each pattern language and each relation we determined the best parameter settings on the training data. We report results on test data using these parameter settings.

- For the parameters of the evaluation setup and the linguistic processing, parameters where chosen based on previous systems (see Section 9.5.2 for details).

The evaluation protocol has been designed following those employed with other recent Web-oriented relation extraction systems like the KnowItNow system [Cafarella et al., 2005], Espresso [Pantel and Pennacchiotti, 2006] and URES [Rosenfeld and Feldman, 2006]. Like in these studies, we identify a set of relations for which the extension of the relation is known. A small subset is taken as training data, while the remaining examples serve as test set against which the output is compared. The extracted instances are evaluated in terms of precision, recall and F-measure with respect to the gold standard.

Compared to the above mentioned systems we use a similar number of relations as test setup (KnowItNow uses 4, Espresso and URES 5). These studies however do not report recall numbers but resort to giving recall relative to previous systems (Espresso) or only absolute extraction counts (KnowItNow and URES). Clearly, a set of four relations does not allow a conclusive statement on the question whether taxonomic patterns are always or at least on average superior to other types of patterns. However, the set of four relations clearly suffices to show that using taxonomic information in the pattern language has the potential of increasing the performance of a pattern-based Information Extraction system, which has not been shown before.

We varied the minimum support $freq_{min}$ between 2, 5, 10, 15 and 20 and the cut-off percentile t_{score} for URES score of patterns from 0 to 100% in steps of 10%. After measuring precision and recall for each configuration *on the training data* we chose the best-performing support and pattern score cut-off values for each setup for evaluation on the test data.[2] The configurations are chosen based on the F_1 measure with respect to the training samples and the negative examples

[2]Due to the combinatoric number of possible frequent patterns that are possible through abstractions at different levels in the taxonomy, operating with a minimum support of 2 or 5 became computationally intractable for some relations so that these settings were skipped. However, in these cases, a good set of patterns were generated with higher minimum support due to the better ability to generalize that are enabled with taxonomic knowledge. Note that this limitation, if it has

generated from this. The strategy to generate negative examples from the provided seed set (including only positive examples) is explained in more detail below.

9.5.2 Dataset and Preprocessing

The textual dataset used for our experiments consists of the "Semantically Annotated Snapshot of the English Wikipedia", a publicly available dataset for hypertext mining provided by Hugo Zaragoza et al. [Zaragoza et al., 2007; Mika et al., 2008]. It contains all 1,490,688 articles of a December 2007 version of the English Wikipedia.

Our evaluation is performed on four semantic relations from different domains: 172,696 (61,476) famous persons and their year of birth, 14,762 (757) companies and the location of their headquarter, 34,047 (2,561) geographic entities and their location as well as 2,650 (406) products from the automotive domain together with their makers. The numbers in brackets indicate the actual co-occurrence counts of the complete extension within our chosen window size of 10 tokens in the corpus. We will refer to this as the *corpus-pruned extension* or *gold standard* for simplicity. This is a subset of the publicly available dataset introduced in Section 5.7 from which we excluded those relations for which no proper entity tagging was available in the corpus (albums and soccer teams) and which were too small for our setup (currencies).

The Wikipedia corpus is in turn restricted for each relation to those contexts containing entities of the appropriate type, i.e. $[Mozart]_{person}$ *was born in* $[1756]_{Year}$. would be retained as context for the *bornInYear* relation (as would also $[Mozart]_{person}$ *died in* $[1791]_{Year}$.) but not $[Mozart]_{person}$ *was born in* $[Salzburg]_{city}$ as it does not contain entities of the appropriate type. For this, we also simulate a perfect named-entity tagging by restricting ourselves to co-occurrences of entities that are mentioned in at least one instance in the gold standard of the target relation (obviously not necessarily in the same instance). It is important to note that the perfect tagging has been introduced to create a solid basis of comparison and does not favor any pattern language because these perfect tags are only taken into account during co-occurrence selection which is done in the same way for all pattern classes. We take into account mentions of the corpus for which the arguments of an instance are at most 10 tokens apart. Both during matching and evaluation we use WordNet and Wikipedia redirects as a source for (approximate) synonyms.

In order to incorporate taxonomic knowledge, we rely on the 'Semantically Annotated Wikipedia' snapshot, which has been pre-annotated with coarse se-

---

any impact at all, favors the baseline and the URES pattern language because for those all setups were available.

mantic categories including the word's part of speech (e.g. noun, infinite verb, pronoun or punctuation) and coarse semantic categories as well as named entity tags from the WSJ tagset. In total, there are 135 concepts in the taxonomy. An excerpt of the taxonomy corresponding to the location subhierarchy is displayed in Figure 9.7 (see [Zaragoza et al., 2007] for a documentation of the categories for verbs and nouns as well as of the tagset). We did not rely on WSJ tags for marking vehicle models because they were of very low precision for the respective classes.

The taxonomy of features was created manually by the authors. It integrates WSJ entity tags, part-of-speech tags and WordNet supersenses based on a set of assumptions mentioned below. The root concept constitutes a hypothetic universal "top" feature that is shared by all tokens. The level below that is formed by the generic linguistic concepts noun, adjective, adverb, pronoun, verb, other (e.g. preposition) and non-word. The generic assumptions to arrange WSJ tags, WordNet supersenses and POS tags below that are as follows: (a) WSJ have priority over supersenses which have in turn priority over POS-tags. (b) All named entities are assumed to be nouns. (c) A pragmatic approach is taken to treat punctuation, markup etc. They form general groups which together form the concept of non-word. (d) WSJ tags and supersense tags can be mapped under some common generic concepts (e.g. location) which may correspond to WordNet supersenses and in turn can be assigned under one POS tag. In sum, to create a taxonomy, two types of decisions have to be made:

- General linguistic: Which entity tag is a sub-concept of which POS tag. How are punctuation classified.
- Semantic: How to align different named-entity tag sets and other concept hierarchies.

The process of creating the taxonomy can be considered fairly generic: general linguistic decisions are done once and for all and the semantic decisions are done once per tagset. The design of the taxonomy is thus a parameter to the system like the choice of tagset itself.

The time required to mine taxonomic patterns of a given class at a given support strongly depends on the structure and size of the taxonomy. These differences are due to the fact that alternative candidate patterns are generated by trying out taxonomic specializations. While certain alternatives can be excluded relatively quickly in this way, the amount of possible specializations drastically increases with the size (in particular the depth) of the taxonomy. To investigate the impact of the taxonomy structure, we measured the time necessary for mining the patterns with three different taxonomies:

- **Tax1:** Taxonomy as described in Appendix A: two levels of hierarchy, three levels for nouns describing locations and organizations (groups) only. No

		Tax 1				Tax 2				Tax3
class	supp.	s	count	prec.	rec.	s	count	prec.	rec.	s
TAX	20	5	22	0.710	0.340	6	23	0.706	0.340	45477
TAX	15	7	32	0.721	0.380	5	35	0.722	0.383	413211
TAX	10	6	62	0.714	0.446	11	64	0.717	0.454	N/A
TAX	5	27	177	0.648	0.431	64	178	0.646	0.413	N/A
TAX-GAP	20	23	1344	0.553	0.475	48	2622	0.558	0.492	N/A
TAX-GAP	15	42	3420	0.528	0.493	86	7440	0.527	0.498	N/A
TAX-GAP	10	119	16312	0.528	0.495	260	42672	0.478	0.530	N/A
TAX-GAP	5	2319	474780	0.356	0.442	15073	2371008	0.420	0.560	N/A

Table 9.1: Mining time, counts, precision and recall for pattern sets for the *productOf* relation for TAX and TAX-GAP patterns of various support thresholds and the three taxonomies

untyped wildcard (top concept) allowed. This taxonomy was also the basis for the other experiments in this chapter.

- **Tax2:** Deeper taxonomy: three levels for more nouns, quantities, and punctuation. No untyped wildcard.
- **Tax3:** Consistent use of four taxonomic levels (including the top concept).

Table 9.1 shows mining times[3] for patterns of the *productOf* relation for the three different taxonomies. Mining times increase with lower support as more patterns are found. As expected, patterns with lower support are also less precise but produce more recall. The richer taxonomy, Tax 2, allows for the generation of a few more patterns at the expense of an increase of processing time. The taxonomy Tax3, which features a top concepts and a deeper structure, had to be excluded from the comparison. The number of possible candidates was so big that processing did only terminate for the strictest filtering conditions. Given the prohibitive mining times we did not apply the computationally even more costly post-filtering to determine counts and performance of the pattern sets. Overall, these results show that the approach of working with taxonomic patterns is very sensitive to the number of candidate patterns explored during induction. This number in turn depends on the structure of the taxonomy as well as on other parameters of the pattern class.

9.5.3 Experimental Setup

Our processing starts with a set of 100 most frequently mentioned sample relation instances for each relation. This number is larger than in most Web-oriented stud-

[3]Measured on a 2.4 GHz server-sized computing running a Java VM with 10GB of main memory allocated.

ies. We opted for this because, as shown in Chapter 7, Wikipedia pattern mining requires a larger seed set due to the low redundancy of the corpus.

We run all experiments over the five pattern languages described in Section 9.3. Overall, our setup is close to the one used by URES [Rosenfeld and Feldman, 2006], but we work on Wikipedia to have a closed corpus which is freely available and reproducible instead of the Web search results which are subject to continuous change. In addition, we do not require a set of additional "keywords" for each relation to be present in the contexts (as in the URES system) as we consider this condition too strict (with a bias towards precision) and would like to keep our settings fairly general.

The relevant parameters of our system are on the one hand the minimum support $freq_{min}$ as well as the threshold t_{score} on the scores of the patterns. For each target relation and each pattern class we varied $freq_{min}$ to be one out of $\{2, 5, 10, 15, 20\}$ and t_{score} to keep the best $10\%, 20\%, \ldots 100\%$ of the patterns according to the pattern score. As we are directly comparing to the URES system, we use the same score:

$$score_{URES}(p) \quad = \quad \frac{\sum_{i \in Inst \setminus N} c(p,i)}{\sum_{i \in N} c(p,i) + 1}$$

Thereby, $Inst$ is the set of extracted instances and $c(p,i)$ is 1 if pattern p extracts instance i and 0 otherwise. Refer to Section 5.6.3 for a more detailed discussion of this measure. This is a way of assessing the precision of the pattern. We differ slightly, however, in the strategy adopted to generate the negative examples N. Essentially, we consider all those mentions as negative which do not correspond to instances in the training set of the gold standard but which contain an instance which can be created by swapping arguments between different instances from the gold standard. For example, given that *Ankara* and *The Netherlands* appear in our gold standard as first and second argument of some instance (but not in the same), the instance $(Ankara, TheNetherlands)$ would constitute a negative example, such that every pattern matching the following sentence and extracting $(Ankara, TheNetherlands)$ should be penalized, e.g. *I met a blond girl from The Netherlands in Ankara.* Our method for generating negative examples is essentially the same as the one used in URES with two small deviations. On the one hand, we are able to generate more negative examples as we do not require a correct instance of the relation to be present in the negative sentence. On the other hand, we do not use positive examples of one relation as negative examples of another as in the URES system due to the fact that our relations have completely different type signatures and this would not generate

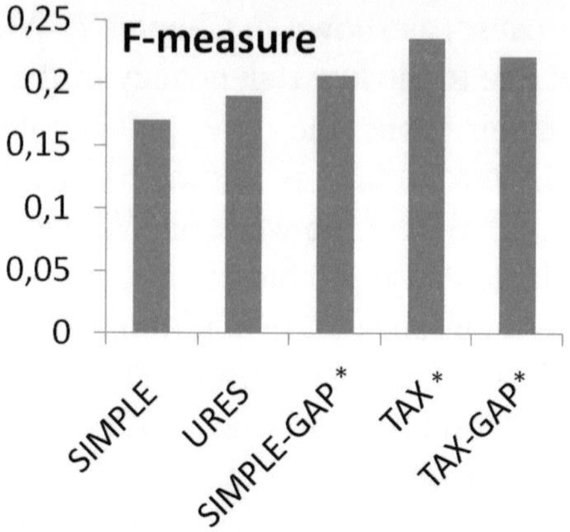

Figure 9.8: F-measure achieved with the different pattern languages averaged over the four relations. The strategies marked with $*$ perform statistically significantly better than the remaining ones.

any useful negative examples. Note that this method of generating negative examples does not require any additional negative training examples (i.e. non-instances of a relation). Instead, it is based on the assumption that for all entities mentioned in the training examples, the training set contains all relation instances they are part in (i.e. something a local closed-world assumption).

While we tried out various configurations with regard to minimum support $freq_{min}$ and pattern filtering threshold t_{score}, we use an automatic (and thus parameter free) method to determine the optimal setup:

- Based on the training data, the F-measure for each combination of $freq_{min}$ and t_{score} is computed. For this, only output corresponding to the 100 seeds is counted as correct and the set of negative examples N is generated only from these 100 examples.
- For further comparison, we select the combination that achieves the best F-measure based on the known top 100 dataset.
- For comparison, the F-measure computed based on the test data (full extension).

This corresponds to the best setup as chosen without knowing the full extension of the relation.

9.5.4 Experimental results

Figure 9.8 shows F_1-measure results for each pattern class averaged over all relations considered. Figure 9.9 shows precision over recall averaged over the four relations investigated and Figure 9.10 shows the results for the individual relations.

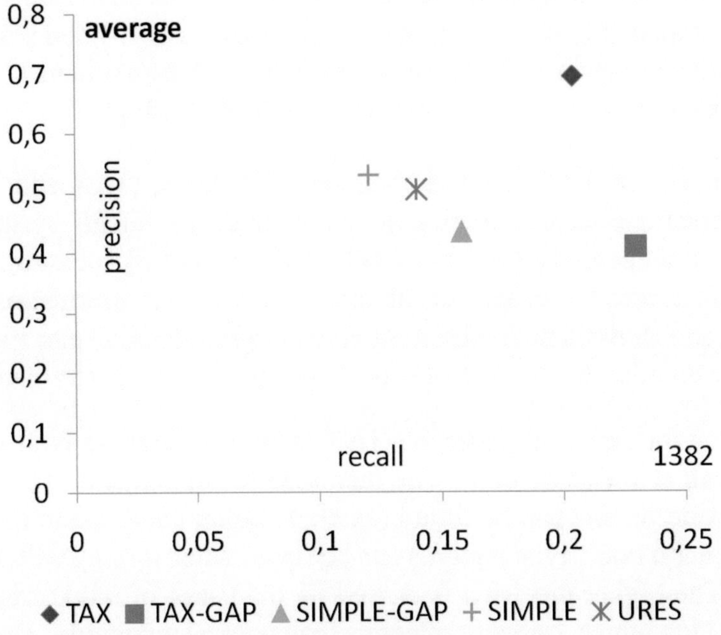

Figure 9.9: Precision over recall achieved with the different pattern languages averaged over all four relations. The scale on the X-axis also gives absolute result counts.

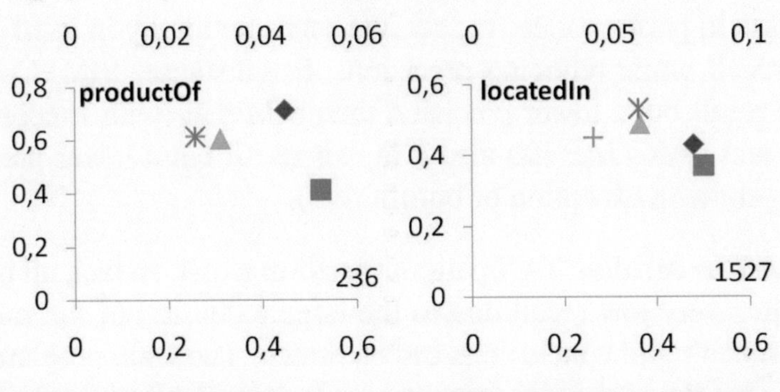

Figure 9.10: Precision over recall achieved with the different pattern languages for each of the four relations. The scale on the X-axis also gives absolute result counts.

Note that TAX, TAX-GAP and SIMPLE-GAP outperform our baselines URES and SIMPLE in a statistically significant manner (based on a two-sided pairwise Student's t-test with an α-level of 0.01) (shown in Figure 9.8 by a $*$ mark).

The conclusions to be drawn from our results are the following:

- As shown in Figure 9.8 Taxonomic Sequential Patterns, (TAX and TAX-GAP) outperform state-of-the-art patterns used in the URES system as well as simple sequential patterns (SIMPLE) in terms of F_1-measure. This clearly demonstrates the benefit of integrating taxonomic information into the patterns and shows that the different effects (generalization and specialization) play together in an positive way to increase overall performance.

- As Figure 9.9 indicates, in particular TAX is able to increase both precision and recall at the same time. The increased recall is due to the higher number of patterns that can be found (example below) and due to the fact that more general non-trivial patterns can be found when mining with typed wildcards. The higher precision is caused by the usage of wildcards with type information which are more selective than general wildcards. This can be seen in particular for the productOf, headquarteredIn and locatedIn relations, while on the bornInYear relation TAX seems to perform worst (see the comments on this below). On the averaged precision/recall diagram, one can clearly see that TAX increases both precision and recall compared to the other configurations we consider. TAX-GAP seems to increase recall at the expense of a reduction in precision, such that the introduction of gaps can be clearly considered as leading to over-generalization.

- The better performance of TAX-GAP does certainly not stem from the allowed GAPs only, as the comparison with SIMPLE-GAP shows, so that we can indeed claim that the taxonomic information is the main responsible for the increase in performance. In fact, the semi-continuity in itself seems to increase recall while reducing precision. For instance, SIMPLE-GAP has a higher recall but a lower precision than SIMPLE (with exception of bornInYear) and TAX-GAP has also a higher recall but a lower precision than TAX (again with exception of bornInYear).

- For the *bornInYear* relation, TAX patterns perform worst. In fact, all pattern classes produce very low recall due to the large extension of the relation, such that no meaningful conclusions can be drawn. The main problem with TAX here is that the parameter selection on training lead to a suboptimal configuration of the system. This also shows that more advanced strategies to determine the parameters are needed other than F-measure on the training data set.

Note that due to the stricter evaluation protocol, our scores cannot directly be compared with other results in the literature (see Section 9.2 for more details).

The reason why taxonomic patterns yield a higher recall is that they produce a higher number of patterns as well as more general ones. As an example, consider the example pattern from above:

"The $ANY[superlative]$ $ANY[living\ being]$ ANY $ANY[country]_{arg2}$ $ANY[stative]$ in $ANY[city]_{arg1}$"

where $ANY[stative]$ matches any state verb such as *live, stay* etc. This may be a reasonable pattern, which might not be found as a sequential pattern without taxonomic knowledge as each single state verb might occur too rarely individually. By referring to the class of state verbs rather than to single verbs, the pattern might suddenly become frequent. On the other hand, a system merely inserting an untyped wildcard for each typed wildcard used above would be likely to overgenerate.

This example illustrates nicely how the different effects that taxonomic generalization can produce play together, using taxonomic types to generalize patterns (i.e. using $ANY[creation\ verb]$ instead of specific verbs such as *build* for instance), increasing recall, at the same time making sure that no other verbs match the given position, thus ensuring precision.

9.6 Conclusion

In this chapter, we investigated a set of design alternatives in pattern languages. In particular, we investigated the aspects of abstraction over surface strings and of the use of additional knowledge and structure. To this end, we have introduced Taxonomic Sequential Patterns with optional semi-continuity for relation extraction together with an exhaustive mining algorithm that allows us to mine patterns across a variety of pattern classes. The algorithm is an extension of a sequence-mining version of Eclat which has been optimized for typed wildcards with types arranged in a taxonomy. We have shown that Taxonomic Sequential Patterns are generally superior to a non taxonomic baseline as well as to the state-of-the-art *URES* system with respect to both precision and recall.

The superiority of taxonomic patterns can be explained with the help of three effects discussed in Section 9.1: on the one hand, it is indeed the case that the taxonomic generalization yields more general patterns, effectively increasing recall (*generalization effect*), but at the same time increasing precision by replacing untyped wildcards by typed wildcards, thus adding stronger constraints (*specification effect*). On the other hand, by way of generalizing along a hierarchy, more patterns above the minimum support can be found, again increasing recall. The main contribution of our work is to show that the above effects nicely complement each other adding up to yield an overall improved performance with respect to approaches based on non-taxonomic patterns.

The impact of semi-continuity as an instance of abstraction over the pattern's surface string is ambivalent. We compared adding semi-continuity to two pattern classes. Irrespective of the pattern class and the relation extracted, the addition of semi-continuity leads to increased recall however almost invariantly at a more or less dramatic loss of precision. This reduction of precision indicates that the use of semi-continuity and possibly other forms of surface-string abstractions imply a *generalization effect*.

In general, our work shows that the choice of the pattern class provides an important set of design choices for pattern-based Information Extraction some of which have been investigated in more detail. The organization of several levels of background knowledge organized in a taxonomy has been shown to be beneficial.

Part III

Applications

Chapter 10

Web-wide Information Extraction for Market Analysis

In this chapter we present an application of the Pronto system and further IE approaches in an industrial application scenario in the automotive industry. The application is part of the X-Media integrated research project[1] which is concerned with Document and Knowledge Management in large enterprises in the field of mechanical engineering. The project focuses on extracting and representing knowledge that stems from various media types in a way that allows it to be aggregated, shared and reused.

This chapter first presents the task to which we apply IE from text before introducing the IE approaches taken (Section 10.2). Practical experiences that show the potential and limits of Web-based IE with textual patterns in this scenario are discussed in Section 10.3. The scenario and the application described here have been developed by many members of the X-Media project. Our focus has been, like in this chapter, the task of IE from text.

10.1 The Competitor Scenario Forecast Task

A crucial task in the development of products is to be aware of consumer needs and competitor actions in the market. Our use case partner maintains a department which has the goal to assist management and design decisions with information about the current and future product portfolio of competitors. The results of their market analysis are compiled into several reports, in particular a *release calendar*

[1] More information under `http://www.x-media-project.org`. The description of project results and use case setups in this chapter is kept on an abstract level in order to focus on generally applicable results and observations as well as to respect the project's privacy regulations.

is maintained that displays a time line of potential future product releases. Furthermore, *vehicle baskets* are collected that consist of vehicles that are related to specific management decisions. In order to combine these reports, a large variety of sources is gathered and reviewed periodically. The reports include memos from visitors to trade shows as well as news articles and blog posts. Individual items of information for market analysis are called *competitor scenarios* consisting of the information about one potential change in the market. Competitor scenarios include the acting competitor, the potential product's name and technical features as well as the point in time when the action is expected.

In a first step, we identified parts of the Competitor Scenario Forecast task that can be supported by automatic tools. The resulting tool setup consist of an integrated Web-based application that provides a view on relevant documents. It follows the idea of a Web portal in the sense that it aggregates and presents information from different sources. In particular, news and market reports from various providers which are enriched by meta-information that facilitates task-specific browsing. This meta information is either provided by the portal users or derived by text and image analysis components that process news articles. Furthermore, so-called *knowledge fusion* components integrate extraction results from multiple sources. The idea behind knowledge fusion is to derive global information from local annotations. The advantage of separating local extraction and integration into different components is to allow for the integration of extraction across documents, extraction approaches and modalities.

The portal provides three different views: The *news management page* which allows to search, browse, and annotate news articles. Articles can be grouped by various aspects of their topics (vehicle model, maker, market segment, technologies mentioned). Users can assign a status to each document to reflect, whether it has been read and whether it is accepted as a source for further processing. The *image management page* provides product images grouped by the depicted vehicle components and allows for image similarity search. Finally, the *calendar elaboration page* visualizes the assumed release dates of vehicles as extracted from the documents in a time line and arranged by market segments. It further allows to manually update release date information. The development and the evaluation of the portal are ongoing.

10.2 Information Extraction for Competitor Scenario Forecast

For IE from text, the following tasks are particularly relevant:

- **Identification of named entities:** The names of vehicle makers and models need to be recognized in the documents. While the set of makers is relatively fixed, new model names are constantly invented. The full complexity of named-entity detection has to be dealt with for model identification. When analyzing mentions of vehicle names, three peculiarities become obvious:

    1. Vehicle names frequently consist of common words of various parts of speech. Common nouns may be used ("Isuzu Axiom", "Volkswagen Rabbit") as well as verbs ("Toyota Wish"), adjectives ("Renault Rapid") and even named entities that commonly carry a different meaning ("Suzuki Verona") .
    2. Vehicle names are frequently combinations of letters and numbers. Some parts of the name are optional and it is not straight-forward to identify a generic name. Names may encode the size of the model (e.g. "Audi A2" vs. "Audi A8"), its body type (e.g. "Peugeot 406 Coupé"), its engine configuration (e.g. "Suzuki Swift GTi") or simply differ regionally (e.g. "Volkswagen Golf" is sold as "Volkswagen Rabbit" in the United States).
    3. The descriptions of vehicle models are rich in metaphors and frequently mentions are anthropomorphic. For example "The Otti is part of a new generation of minicars." or "The bigger Clio III arrived late last year, but its predecessor survives as the Clio Campus."

- **Identification of product features:** To allow for organizing and search vehicle models with regard to different product features, the textual descriptions of the vehicles need to be analyzed to identify the values for these features. We identified the following features as relevant: release date, top speed, consumption, engine power, length, width, height, body type (e.g. "hatch back" or "convertible"), and key technologies employed.

- **Product classification:** Both, release calendars and vehicle baskets are organized with regard to product classes. There are various systems to classify vehicles. We use here a classification into nine segments designed by the UK Society of Motor Manufacturers and Traders (SMMT) which is commonly used as a basis for legal cases on a European level [Commission of the European Communities, 1999]. We use product features, in particular the dimensions and the body type to perform this classification.

To address this task, we present in the following a setup of information extraction tools that essentially integrates three approaches:

- **Existing formalized knowledge**. Our use case partner maintains a high-quality list of previously released vehicle models along with their features. This information is used as a basis for annotations as it is more reliable than information that is automatically extracted.

- **Minimally-supervised text pattern induction on the Web**. The advantage of Web-based IE is that a large corpus of up-to-date information is provided. In particular new market developments are quickly reflected on the Web.

- **Supervised statistical Machine Learning**. Supervised extraction is beneficial when a larger amount of processing time can be invested into individual documents to compute relevant features. In these cases, statistical models are good at accounting for variability in the input.

The goal of this study is to use the most appropriate method for each part of the task, rather than comparing their performance among each other. The integration runs as follows: The portal system is aware of a set of websites which contain sufficiently reliable information on relevant market segments. These pages are crawled regularly. Annotation models that have been derived by supervised learning are used for identifying mentions of model and maker names in the crawled documents. Existing formal knowledge and output of minimally supervised Web IE are used to provide high-quality features for further extraction.

10.2.1 Pronto in the Competitor Scenario forecast application

We use the Pronto system for extracting relational information from the Web through a search engine. The Pronto setup used in the forecast application is closest to the one used in Chapter 6. One major difference comparted to the task in the previous chapters is that a larger seed set is used because many relation instances are already known and the goal is to find additional new instances that may reflect market changes. Pattern-based IE is most applicable when the text corpus is large and redundant (such as the Web). As opposed to extraction with statistical classifiers, this method avoids linear processing of the entire corpus when the model has been updated as we can directly use a search engine to query for the surface realization of a pattern. The patterns are induced in a bootstrapping manner (cf. Section 5.5) by abstracting over the mentions of previously found relation instances.

10.2.2 Supervised Information Extraction

In contrast to the Pronto approach, our CRF annotation does not aim at finding relation instances. It rather aims at identifying information of a specific type, thus performing entity extraction. This design choice is due to the way the annotated data is used in the portal. For supervised IE on Web documents two student assistants annotated at least 200 mentions of each type of vehicle feature and 300 mentions of models and makers in documents which are prototypic for portal content. More specifically, they annotated 150 documents completely for all target annotation types. For annotation types that were not mentioned 200 times in these documents, we additionally selected sequences that are likely to contain a target mention (e.g. all sequences containing numbers for numerical features). Note that both types of training data, the fully annotated documents and the additional sequences provide negative examples although only the former reflects the actual distribution of matches in the documents[2]. We trained a linear chain Conditional Random Field (CRF) to annotate such web documents. The training and application algorithms were taken from the Mallet toolkit [McCallum, 2002]. We provided a set of 19 token-based features which are listed in Figure 10.1. Some of the features (set in bold in the figure) require domain-specific knowledge. Knowledge of these types is available as pre-existing formalized knowledge and as extraction results from Pronto extraction.

10.3 Practical Experience

10.3.1 Assessment of Pronto performance

As a test collection, we chose four different datasets for three semantic relations from data provided by the use case partner:

- The *bodyType* relation relates vehicle models and the vehicle class they belong to. E.g. $(\mathrm{suzukiforenza}, \mathrm{sedan})$, $(\mathrm{hondapassport}, \mathrm{sportutility})$, $(\mathrm{gmcsafari}, \mathrm{minivan})$.
- The *modelForecastedRelease* relation captures the year in which a new version of the given model was or will (presumably) be released. We used two datasets for the sake of evaluation: $modelForecastedRelease_{DB}$ with data from the competitor database (which also includes past releases) and $modelForecastedRelease_{Cal}$ with data from the release calendar (future releases only).
- The *isManufacturerOf* relation assigns models to their maker.

[2]The pre-selection performed here is likely to increase precision at no expense of recall because all sentences not containing numbers almost certainly could only contribute false positives. However, for measuring the appropriateness of the method for the application at hand, the measured performance is still valid because the pre-selection can also be implemented in the target system.

feature	example matches
surface string	*all tokens*
model	*“3-series”, “Toledo”*
maker	*“BMW”, “Seat”*
year	*“2010”*
month or season	*“June”, “autumn”*
motorshow	*“IAA”, “Chicago”*
country	*“Belgium”, “Turkey”*
body type	*“SUV”, “supermini”*
price unit	*“EUR”, “$”*
speed unit	*“mph”,”km/h”*
consumption unit	*“mpg”, “g/100km”*
bracket	*“(“)*
punctuation	*“.”, “;”*
number < 1	*“0.45”*
number $\geq 1 < 100$	*“45”, “87.7”*
number $\geq 100 < 1000$	*“843.78”*
number ≥ 1000	*“439,843.43”*
integer	*“9’843”*
any number	*“439.843”*

Table 10.1: The feature set for CRF-based annotation. Features requiring up-to-date domain knowledge marked in bold.

- The *modelBelongsToSegment* relation assigns each model a market segment. E.g. *(honda passport, I)*, *(Smart, A)*, where segment *A* corresponds to “mini” cars and *I* to Sports Utility Vehicles (SUVs).

The seed selection has been limited to models that have been released in the last 10 years. Among those, random sampling has been applied. As an exception, the input for *bodyType* has been taken from DBPedia (which relies on Wikipedia as a source of knowledge) because the body type nomenclature in the competitor database was too technical to be found on the Web.

We assess for each condition the precision of the extraction results. When addressing extraction at a Web scale, recall assessment is difficult to make. In order to assess, how well the approach is able to generate many relation instances from a few examples we test extractions under two conditions. In the *10 to 100* condition, extraction starts with 10 examples and the extraction is stopped as soon as 100 examples have been found. In the *100 to 1000* extraction starts with 100 seeds and 1000 results are the stopping criterion.

Relation	10 to 100	100 to 1000
bodyType	0.97	0.95
modelForecastedRelease$_{DB}$	0.83	0.4
modelForecastedRelease$_{Cal}$	-	0.80*
isManufacturerOf	0.93	0.55*
modelBelongsToSegment	-	-

Table 10.2: Precision of extraction for the different relations in the 10 to 100 and the 100 to 1000 conditions. In cases marked with $*$ regular expression-based post filtering has been applied.

Table 10.2 shows precision scores for the different relations in the 10 to 100 and the 100 to 1000 conditions. *bodyType* extraction works very well under both conditions. For *modelForecastedRelease*$_{DB}$ and *isManufacturerOf* results are much better for the 10 to 100 condition than for 100 to 1000. This can be explained by the fact that success or failure of the extraction usually depends on very few patterns that are generated. The patterns in turn depend on very few instances that they initially occurred with. The more seeds there are, the more likely is it that a couple of seeds together generate a pattern that strongly overgenerates and introduces a lot of incorrect results.

Furthermore, an insufficient number of results is generated with the *modelForecastedRelease*$_{Cal}$ relation when starting with 10 seeds as well as with *modelBelongsToSegment* in both cases. This shows one important limit of the approach: While appropriate for relations that are mentioned frequently (e.g. in news coverage) it is not suitable for very technical or otherwise infrequently mentioned aspects. In particular, the seeds from *modelForecastedRelease*$_{Cal}$ as opposed to *modelForecastedRelease*$_{DB}$ come from the release calendar which only mentions future releases. Being rumors, those are not mentioned prominently enough on the web. Similarly, the market segments are not frequently mentioned along with the car as the letter code for market segments does not reflect the customer perspective on the product.

10.3.2 Supervised tagging performance

For the supervised annotation, we report precision and recall for the considered types of facts.[3] The numbers were obtained by means of 5-fold cross validation on the annotated data. As basis of precision and recall the counts for correctly and

[3]We excluded the dimension information *length*, *width* and *height* from further investigation because too few mentions ($< 10\%$) were found in the fully annotated documents. The same is true for market segment assignments which were not mentioned at in the example texts.

Entity type	Precision	Recall	F_1 measure
consumption	0.48	0.25	0.32
enginePower	0.89	0.77	0.81
price	0.77	0.64	0.64
releaseDate	0.56	0.46	0.48
model	0.83	0.66	0.73
topSpeed	0.81	0.73	0.73
maker	0.89	0.83	0.86
motorShow	0.78	0.56	0.61
bodyType	0.75	0.64	0.65
market	0.66	0.49	0.55

Table 10.3: Precision, recall and F-Measure of the supervised entity tagging with CRF

incorrectly assigned target information lables is taken.[4] The results presented in Table 10.3show that the supervised annotation performs at a state-of-the-art level of over 60% for most entities. However, one should not that some of the features provided are domain specific and very strong indicator for individual entity types (in particular units and gazetteer matches).

10.4 Summary

The goal of the study presented in this chapter is to employ IE technology to increase the efficiency of the work of market analysts. Thereby, IE plays a supporting role that allows the user to focus on relevant documents and suggests relevant target annotations. At the same time, all extracted information is subject to verification and possibly modification. Although the achieved precision values are in line with state-of-the-art IE systems, they are far from allowing for completely automatic compilation of strategically relevant documents like the release calendar and vehicle baskets.

The experiments show that not all relations can be extracted with the same quality. In particular, the bootstrapping-based Web extraction approach via a search engine only works if information is mentioned prominently. Supervised tagging by means of Conditional Random Fields works with higher precision and has a higher recall. It is therefore our method of choice for the annotation of the

[4]As opposed to also counting the absence of a tag additionally as a correct assignment of a label of class "none".

documents in the portal. Up-to-date background knowledge will be acquired by means of Web-scale Pronto extraction to ensure large coverage.

Chapter 11

Supporting Communities with Generating Structured Knowledge

This chapter presents an application of Information Extraction technology in an interactive scenario that allows online communities to formalize their knowledge while leaving repetitive annotation task to an automatic extraction system. More specifically, we set up Pronto to extract information from Wikipedia and learn a model for some interesting target relations. The learned model captures people's annotation behavior and is thus able to quickly extract new information to suggest corresponding annotations. We developed an extension to the Wikipedia's content management software MediaWiki that enables communities to validate IE output before it is integrated Wikipedia and at the same time give feedback to the extraction system in form of additional training examples. The goal of this work is thus to enable efficient creation of formalized relational information in which machines and human users play a part that bests suits their abilities.

While annotation tools exist, that aim at annotating Web pages, even the more prominent annotation frameworks such as CREAM [Handschuh and Staab, 2003], Annotea [Kahan and Koivunen, 2001] or the SHOE Knowledge Annotator [Luke et al., 1997] have had almost no practical impact at a larger scale. The main reasons for this lack of acceptance are that the creation of annotation is neither straightforward enough nor smoothly integrated into those environments where content is massively created. Thus, annotation still remains a significant hurdle for most casual users. Further, in the general case there are no clear incentives in terms of a return of investment for users to actually create annotations.

With the emergence of the so-called Web 2.0 [O'Reilly, 2009], a large number of communities with a strong will to provide content have emerged. Essentially, these are the communities behind social tagging and content creation software such as the bookmarking tool del.icio.us[1], the photo sharing platform Flickr[2], and Wikipedia. Thus, it seems that one way of obtaining massive amounts of annotated web content is to involve these communities in the endeavor and thus benefit from their enthusiasm and effort. This requires in essence two things: semantic annotation functionality seamlessly integrated into the standard software used by the community and, secondly, an incentive mechanism such that people can immediately benefit from the annotations created. This is for example the key idea behind projects such as Semantic MediaWiki [Krötzsch et al., 2007] and Bibsonomy [Hotho et al., 2006]. Direct incentives for creating semantic annotations in a Semantic MediaWiki are for example semantic browsing and querying functionality, but most importantly the fact that queries over structured knowledge can be used to automatically create views on data, e.g. in the form of tables.

In addition to the right provision of incentives, we need to use human resources economically, avoiding that people get bored by annotating obvious facts or the same things again and again. This is where standard Machine Learning techniques which detect regularities in data can help. However, any sort of learning algorithm will produce errors, either because they overgenerate or they overfit the training data. Thus, human verification is still needed. We show here by example that this verification can be provided by the community behind a certain project if the feedback is properly integrated into the tools they use anyway. This opens the possibility to turn information consumers into "passive annotators" which, in spite of not actively contributing content and annotations, can at least verify existing annotations if it is made easy enough. To realize this goal, we find the iterative framework for pattern induction as introduced in Section 5.3 particularly useful because it allows for flexible insertion of supervision in the filtering steps (Steps 3 and 6). Iterative processing can be paused and resumed upon availability of new instance data fitting the need of the wiki annotation.

The remainder of this chapter is organized as follows. In the next section we describe our approach to combining machine and human intelligence for semantic annotation in a wiki setting and describe how Semantic MediaWiki can be used for this purpose. We also derive requirements for such an integration and describe its corresponding architecture subsequently. We present an implementation based on the English Wikipedia (Section 11.2) and discuss practical experiences with a small group of community users (Section 11.3) before reviewing related work (Section 11.4) and concluding. A paper about the work presented in this chapter has been published at the workshop on Wikipedia and Artificial Intelligence at AAAI 2008 with Markus Krötzsch and Philipp Cimiano [Blohm et al., 2008].

---

[1] `http://del.icio.us`

[2] `http://www.flickr.com`

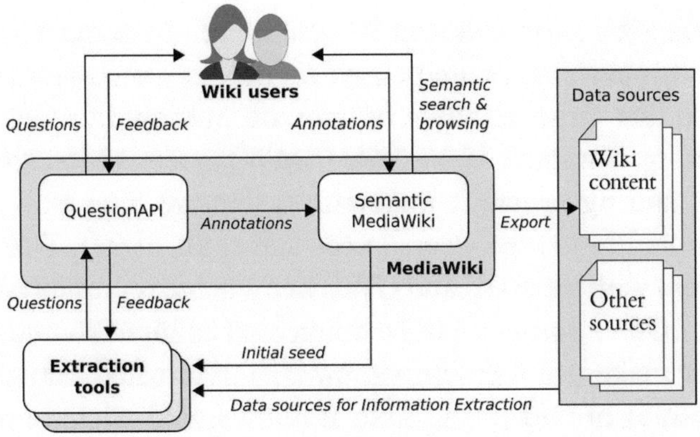

Figure 11.1: Integrating (semantic) wikis with Information Extraction tools – basic architecture.

11.1 Combining Human and Machine Intelligence

The crucial aspect of this application scenario is that community members and information extraction algorithms interact in such a way that they can benefit from each other. Humans benefit from the fact that information extraction systems can support them in the tedious work of manual annotation, and algorithms exploit human annotations to bootstrap and learn patterns to suggest new annotations. The workflow in our model is as follows:

1. Extraction tools use existing high-quality and community-validated human annotations to learn patterns in data, leading to the extraction of new annotations.

2. Users are requested to verify extracted data so as to confirm or reject it. This is done by presenting questions to users.

3. Confirmed extraction results are immediately incorporated into the wiki, if possible.

4. User replies are evaluated by extraction tools to improve future results (learning), and to gather feedback on extraction quality (evaluation), returning to (1) in a bootstrapping fashion.

The model thus is cyclic, but also asynchronous in nature, since learning, annotation, verification, and incorporation into the wiki interact with each other asynchronously. Assuming the model above, we present a concrete architecture and implementation. Figure 11.1 shows the relevant components – *(Semantic) MediaWiki*, the *extraction tools*, a novel *QuestionAPI* as well as their basic interactions. We have selected the wiki-engine MediaWiki as a basis for our work, since this system is widely used on publicly accessible sites (including Wikipedia), such that large amounts of data are available for annotation. Moreover, the free add-on *Semantic MediaWiki* (SMW) extends MediaWiki with means for creating and storing semantic annotations that are then exploited to provide additional functionality to wiki-users [Krötzsch et al., 2007]. Due to the fact that SMW is compliant with the RDF and OWL knowledge representation formalisms, a large variety of *Other sources* can be connected as input source for training examples and later make use the semi-automatically created knowledge. This infrastructure is useful in two ways: first, it allows wiki-users to make direct use of the freshly acquired annotations, and, second, it can support extraction tools by providing initial (user-generated) example annotations as seeds for learning algorithms.

As shown in Figure 11.1, our general architecture makes little assumptions about the type and number of the employed extraction tools, so that a wide range of existing tools should be usable with the system. We used the Pronto system for this purpose and configured it similar to the "wiki dual" setup described in Chapter 7.

11.1.1 Requirements on User Interaction

Successful wiki projects live from user communities that contribute and maintain content. Therefore our work makes the assumption that social processes and established interaction paradigms are crucial to the success of an annotation system. Likewise, any extended functionality that is to be integrated into existing wikis must also take into account the needs and interests of users and contributers. We therefore formulate a set of requirements that we identified to guide the design of the presented system:

(U1) Simplicity. Participating in the annotation process should be extremely simple for typical wiki users, and should ideally not require any prior instruction. The extension must match the given layout, language, and interface design.

(U2) Unobstructiveness and opt-out. In order to seriously support real-world sites an extension must not obscure the actual main functions of the wiki. Especially, it must be acknowledged that many users of a wiki are passive readers who do not wish to contribute to the collaborative annotation process. Registered users should be able to configure the behavior of the extension where possible.

(U3) User gratification. Wiki contributors typically are volunteers, such that it is only their personal motivation which determines the amount of time they are willing to spend for providing feedback. Users should thus be rewarded for contributions (e.g. by giving credit to active contributors), and they should understand how their contribution affects and improves the wiki.

```
The '''Peugeot 204''' is a [[class::compact car]] produced
by the [[French]] manufacturer [[manufacturer::Peugeot]]
between [[market entry::1965]] and [[1976]].
```

Figure 11.2: Annotated wiki source text.

(U4) Entertainment. Even if users understand the relevance of contributing feedback, measures must be taken to ensure that this task does not appear monotone or even stupid to them. Problems can arise if the majority of changes proposed by extraction tools are incorrect (and maybe even unintelligible to humans), or if only very narrow topic areas are subject to extraction.

(U5) "Social" control over extraction algorithms. Wiki users and contributors take responsibility for the quality of the wiki as a whole. Changes to wiki content are frequently discussed and reverted if deemed inappropriate. Credibility and authority play a crucial role here. Frequent inappropriate feedback requests and content modifications by information extraction systems may lead to frustration within the community. Therefore we propose to make the extraction tools identifiable by giving their name, methodology and author so that users can identify the origin of an annotation and contact responsible persons.

11.1.2 Semantic MediaWiki

Semantic MediaWiki (SMW) is an open source semantically enhanced wiki engine that enables users to annotate the wiki's contents with explicit, machine-readable information. This information is then used to offer typed search and browsing facilities within the wiki, as well as to export structured data in the standardised OWL/RDF format, thus supporting data reuse in other applications. A brief overview of both aspects is provided here – for further details and related work see [Krötzsch et al., 2007]. SMW's main annotation mechanism is the assignment of property-value-pairs to pages. Property values might be other pages (e.g. to express relations like "manufacturer"), or data values of a variety of specialised datatypes (e.g. for describing properties like "market entry"). Figure 11.2 provides a simple example of annotated wiki text, which is the basis for the HTML output of a wiki-page. Square brackets is the standard syntactic notation for hyperlinks, and in SMW these links can be annotated with properties separated by a double colon from the link-target. Based on such annotations, SMW can dynamically generate lists of query results, as e.g. the one shown in Figure 11.3.

Model	Manufacturer	Class
BMW M1	BMW	Super car
Dodge A100	Chrysler Corporation	
Ferrari F430	Ferrari	Sports car
Honda NSX	Honda Motor Company	Sports car
Porsche Cayman	Porsche	Sports car
Rover Metro	Austin Rover Group	Supermini car

Figure 11.3: Query result in Semantic MediaWiki: automobiles with mid-engine/rear-wheel drive, their manufacturers, and classes where specified.

11.2 System Design and Implementation

In this section we discuss the design and implementation of our approach, which realises the basic interactions shown in Figure 11.1. In order to enable easy integration of many extraction tools in asynchronous operation, all information exchange between wiki and extractors is realised via simple Web interfaces. This web API forms one major part of our *QuestionAPI* extension of MediaWiki developed in the context of the work described in this chapter. The other two main components of this module are its internal management of questions and answers, and its user interface extensions to the wiki. All three components will be described below, and it will be explained how the requirements identified are addressed by our particular design.

The main visible component of the QuestionAPI is its extension of the wiki user interface. The *QuestionAPI* extends MediaWiki with a simple web-based API that extraction tools can use to exchange information with the wiki. The QuestionAPI enables extraction systems to pose questions, to request gathered user feedback, and to remove questions from the system. Requests for feedback on extraction results are presented to the user as multiple-choice questions in a simple web-form, as shown at the bottom of Figure 11.4. Although we consider further answer formats, the current implementation supports only the answers “yes” and “no”, as well as a third option to defer a question. This last option allows users to skip questions without answering them, so that they can continue with other questions instead of accumulating questions that they are unable or unwilling to answer.

The architecture assumes that the information extractors implementing the question API will provide their questions in natural language. A corresponding question template for each relation can be formulated when setting up the extraction system for the use of the QuestionAPI.

All questions are associated with the extraction tool that requested the feedback, and this information is displayed with each question. A wiki page is main-

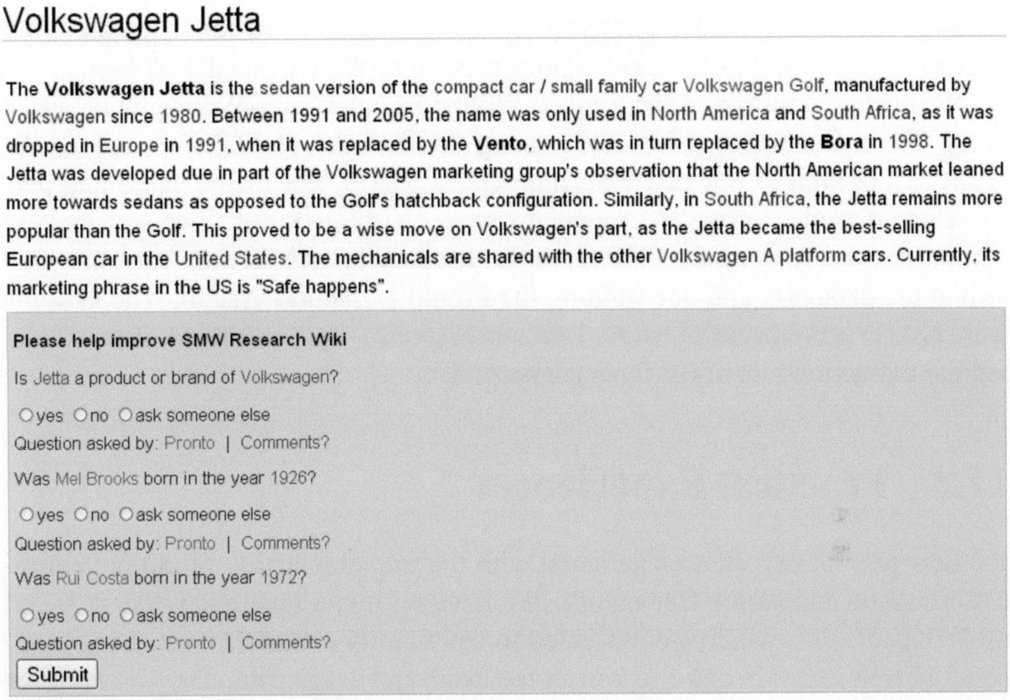

Volkswagen Jetta

The **Volkswagen Jetta** is the sedan version of the compact car / small family car Volkswagen Golf, manufactured by Volkswagen since 1980. Between 1991 and 2005, the name was only used in North America and South Africa, as it was dropped in Europe in 1991, when it was replaced by the **Vento**, which was in turn replaced by the **Bora** in 1998. The Jetta was developed due in part of the Volkswagen marketing group's observation that the North American market leaned more towards sedans as opposed to the Golf's hatchback configuration. Similarly, in South Africa, the Jetta remains more popular than the Golf. This proved to be a wise move on Volkswagen's part, as the Jetta became the best-selling European car in the United States. The mechanicals are shared with the other Volkswagen A platform cars. Currently, its marketing phrase in the US is "Safe happens".

Please help improve SMW Research Wiki

Is Jetta a product or brand of Volkswagen?

○yes ○no ○ask someone else

Question asked by: Pronto | Comments?

Was Mel Brooks born in the year 1926?

○yes ○no ○ask someone else

Question asked by: Pronto | Comments?

Was Rui Costa born in the year 1972?

○yes ○no ○ask someone else

Question asked by: Pronto | Comments?

Submit

Figure 11.4: Questions to users displayed at the bottom of wiki pages.

tained for each extraction tool, so that users can find additional information or provide comments (U5). Besides the general form of the request interface, an important question is *where* to display questions in the wiki. Following our requirement for unobstructiveness and opt-out (U2), the QuestionAPI can be configured to display a variable number of questions either at the bottom of all wiki pages, or only via a specific web interface ("special page") of the wiki.

After answering one or more questions, users are shown a summary of the submitted answers, as well as the option to answer further questions. The QuestionAPI supports *direct changes* based on answers to questions such that if a user has confirmed a certain semantic information, the QuestionAPI directly adds this fact as an annotation to the wiki. If this is enabled, changes will be done immediately when submitting an answer, and the answering user will get credit for the change just as if she would have edited the wiki manually. While this helps to increase user motivation (U3), it may also seem somewhat risky. But direct changes only *simplify* the editing process – the question whether or not a single user may modify a page still depends on the wiki's settings. The specification of direct changes currently works by specifying a string replacement *and* the page context of that replacement. The latter ensures that replacements happen only if the page still (locally) corresponds to the version inspected by the extraction tool. If other changes occurred, modifications need to be done manually by users.

We created a mirror of the English Wikipedia based on a Wikipedia database dump from December 17th 2006 using MediaWiki (1.12alpha) and SMW (1.0RC1), as well as our new extension QuestionAPI. For maintenance and performance reasons, software components were distributed over three server-sized computers: one running the PHP server for MediaWiki and its extension, one providing the database, and one running the Pronto extraction system. The systems were able to serve pages at below 1 second response time, and to run Pronto at its regular extraction rate of 0.3 facts per second.

11.3 Practical Experiences

We now present experiences gathered with the implementation of our collaborative semantic annotation framework. We have set up an integrated system based on Wikipedia data which we presented to community members on a publicly accessible web server in order to collect feedback and usage data. The observations discussed here are not meant to be a formal evaluation but rather to give an idea of the community uptake of the system as such, and the utility of the derived information.

Experienced wiki users and developers were asked to test the system via wiki-related mailing lists, and during a time of 5 days, 40 users (estimated from the number of distinct IPs) provided a total of 511 answers to the QuestionAPI. Of the 511 questions answered, 51% were answered with “no”, 34% were deferred, and the remaining 15% were answered with “yes” which in our setup led to automatic knowledge insertion. All users reacted positively to the interaction paradigm. The general purpose of the questions was quickly understood and appreciated, and no concerns were expressed with respect to obstructiveness or lack of simplicity. Several users mentioned that the questions reminded them of a quiz game, and suggested further uses of this extension beyond information extraction. We interpret this as positive effect with respect to the entertainment requirement (U4). In fact, game-like approaches to collaborative creation of knowledge exist [von Ahn and Dabbish, 2004; Siorpaes and Hepp, 2008].

During the experiment, the option for deferring a question had been labelled “don’t know” which was changed to “ask someone else” only later. This labelling is assumed to be responsible for the large portion of “don’t know” answers: users who considered the questions as a kind of quiz mentioned that they perceived it as “cheating” to look up an answer that they were not sure about, such that “don’t know” was considered more appropriate. This indicates that some introduction and/or clearer labelling is still needed to better convey the purpose of the questions. One consequence of this insight was the relabelling of "don't know" to "ask someone else" so as to communicate that personal knowledge is not to be tested, while still encouraging an answer by reminding the user that the task will otherwise be left to other users. Besides some bug reports about character encoding, the only actual complaints from users were related to the content of some types of questions, especially in cases where systematic errors occurred. This also produced some suggestions for filtering Wikipedia-specific extraction errors, e.g. caused by special kinds of frequent summary articles ("List of ...") that can normally not be involved in any relation.

In order to account for these observations, we formulate an extension of the *entertainment* requirement (U4): It is important to ensure that systematic errors in suggested relations are minimised beforehand, and excluded from verification through collaborative annotation. One interesting approach to do this automatically could be the use of unsupervised clustering methods that detect regularities, and to exclude questions belonging to large clusters for which only "no" answers have been provided so far. For this purpose, an additional answer option can be introduced to allow the users to mark individual relation instances as "unreasonable" suggestions.

11.4 Related Work

Annotation of web content has become popular in particular as *tagging* of various kinds of media resources. Marlow et al. [2006] give an overview of tagging systems, and discuss dimensions in which they can differ. While not a tagging system in the stricter sense, the setup presented here would thereby be classified as a *free-for-all set model* system with high *resource connectivity* and a special form of *tag support*. The paper discusses various forms of incentives ranging from future retrieval to opinion expression. As Wikipedia already has a vivid community, we did not consider incentives for this study, and assume that our architecture helps to involve a larger user community by providing a low-entry threshold for contribution. An innovative approach with respect to incentives and human-machine collaboration in tagging is the ESP game [von Ahn and Dabbish, 2004] which asks pairs of users to come up with common tags for images by guessing what the other user might tag or OntoGame [Siorpaes and Hepp, 2008] which asks quiz-like questions to users. Further related work is done in the field of assisted semantic annotation of websites (e.g. [Dzbor et al., 2003]). While our approach is largely tailored to semantifying sources like Wikipedia, other projects have studied the interaction between human input of facts and Data Mining technology. The Open Mind initiative studies the interaction of Web users and knowledge bases. Their Common Sense [Pentney et al., 2007] system prompts users for natural language statements on a given entity. In a similar way, the Knowledge Base of the True Knowledge^{TM} question answering system can be extended by users (`http://www.trueknowledge.com/`).

Unlike in classical tagging, annotations in Semantic MediaWiki are structured statements that establish relationships between entities, or describe properties of these. This is possible because each page is assumed to describe an ontological element, and links are assumed to express relations between them. As described above, annotations in SMW have a formal semantics suitable for exchanging them via the Web. Some tagging systems are also working towards a more formal interpretability of tags. Flickr introduced "machine tags" which allow unambiguous expression of facts about the annotated media. Bibsonomy [Hotho et al., 2006] provides the possibility to organize tags by asserting relations among them. The Spock person search engine (`http://www.spock.com`) provides the possibility to mark existing tags as correct and incorrect. Wikipedia as a data source is described in Section 4.1.1 For related work on IE with Wikipedia refer to Section 7.1.

While in our implementation we use IE from text to automatically derive suggested annotations of Wikipedia hyperlinks, our architecture is not limited to that setting. As reviewed and discussed in by Hendler and Goldbeck [2008], much potential lies in the links and network structure as well as in social connections between users. The authors argue that the social interactions enabled by annotation constitute an important incentive for producing them.

11.5 Summary

In this chapter we present a new approach for facilitating semantic annotation of wikis by means of community-supervised information extraction, and we have presented a concrete practical realisation of this idea based on Semantic MediaWiki and an extraction system. Our robust and flexible design enables the loose, web-based integration of a wide range of extraction tools into existing community portals – thus tapping a large application field for information extraction on the one hand, and new content-creation solutions for community platforms on the other. Our contribution removes the major barrier between two important fields of research and application, and thus opens up a range of new opportunities for both areas. The first step certainly is to apply and evaluate information extraction tools on real-world community platforms. Our approach has been designed to be completely open, such that existing extraction tools can use our system with very little effort. The study shows that Web-scale pattern-based techniques as presented in this thesis can be used for generating formal knowledge from large unstructured sources such as Wikipedia.

Part IV

Conclusion

Chapter 12

Synopsis of Results

The focus of this thesis is on providing methods for Information Extraction on the Web and thus in particular addressing the scale and the heterogeneous and redundant nature of Web content. We described and analyzed various approaches from the literature in a common framework (Chapter 5) and identified five key challenges in iterative pattern induction (Section 5.4). Those are the *cost of supervision* (1), the computational *complexity of generalization* (2), the *pattern quality prediction dilemma* (3), the *dependence on redundancy* (4) and *error proliferation*~(5).

The contribution of this thesis consists in presenting methods to address these challenges. The methods have been implemented in systems that perform at state-of-the-art levels and have been published and discussed at international conferences and workshops. We give an overview of the novelties and contributions in the following sections.

12.1 Controlling Quality of Iterative Pattern Induction

In a comparative study presented in Chapter 6 we investigated how to best overcome the pattern quality prediction dilemma (Challenge 3). This dilemma is due to the fact that extraction systems need to guide their choice of patterns by estimating the quality of their matches. An ultimate decision on the correctness of a match can not be met without knowing the intended output. We compared pattern quality measures that heuristically operate in the absence of such knowledge. In particular, we compared measures extrapolating pattern quality from training examples, measures modelling pattern-instance correlation, and a measure based on support (frequency). Furthermore the study includes a naive lower baseline and a fully informed upper baseline. We demonstrated that in our Web extraction scenario, only the support-based measure statistically significantly outperforms the random baseline with regard to precision, while all evaluation scores stay clearly below the informed upper baseline. We further showed that the strictness of pattern filtering allows to trade precision for recall and thereby to reduce error proliferation (Challenge 5).

12.2 Supervision and Redundancy

Like many other researchers in the field we made use of the richness of Wikipedia as a source for Information Extraction. In the study in Chapter 7 we show that despite its vast coverage, IE from Wikipedia cannot be addressed with the same extraction methods that are appropriate for the Web. We argued that this is due to the fact that information is covered in a far less redundant manner. Our results show that facts extracted from the Web can be used as additional supervision for Wikipedia extraction allowing to produce with 10 seed examples better extraction results than on Wikipedia alone with 100 seed examples. These results indicate that the dependence on redundancy (Challenge 4) and the amount of required supervision (Challenge 1) in fact interact and that a more redundant corpus allows to reduce supervision.

12.3 Rich Patterns and Scalable Induction

The study presented in Chapter 8 shows that the formulation as a Frequent Itemset Mining problem is a beneficial new way of guiding the search for the most salient patterns. It strongly diminishes the generalization complexity (Challenge 2). The induction process thereby relies on established and well-optimized Data Mining techniques. We demonstrated a strong increase of the extraction rate at the same level of quality as opposed to bottom-up exploration.

We identified in Section 5.2 a variety of ways in which patterns are formulated in the literature. Pattern elements allow to define pattern classes which determine the type of constraints that can be imposed on matching sequences. While in the studies in the literature the choice of pattern class is not discussed or justified, we showed empirically that it constitutes an important parameter to the mining process. For our experiments in Chapter 9 we identified several possible effects that the introduction of pattern elements can have on extraction quality. To analyze the effects, we developed an algorithm that enables mining various pattern classes so that we can isolate the effect of individual pattern elements. We demonstrated that the introduction of typed wildcards increases the F_1 measure for most target relations. This effect reflects that the introduction of additional knowledge in the model increases extraction quality. Furthermore, the introduction of semi-continuity, a way of allowing more variability in content during mining and matching, allows to trade precision for recall.

12.4 Applications

The Pronto information extraction system has been applied in two practical scenarios: The extraction of information for market analysis in the automotive industry and the support of the generation of a structured knowledge source in an online community. The precision of the results achieved in the automotive scenario is comparable to state-of-the-art extraction systems. The strength of Web IE is that it provides an overview of developments of the whole Web. For the annotation of a smaller number of individual Web pages the annotation by means of Conditional Random Fields (CRF) proved more applicable. For the interactive use in the Wikipedia community application, the iterative nature of the pattern induction algorithm proved particularly useful. Taking community feedback between iterations of the pattern induction algorithm is a way to control error proliferation (Challenge 5).

Chapter 13

Outlook

To conclude this thesis, this chapter gives an outlook on potential uses of the methods presented as well as on possible further developments of the methods. We start out by describing three exemplary usage scenarios. We then suggest, based on observations we made and results we obtained, future work on Information Extraction.

13.1 Application Scenarios

Automatically extracted information can be applied wherever automatic interpretation of textual information is beneficial. Many kinds of information systems make use of IE as well as applications where large text collections need to be processed. For the sake of illustration these scenarios are described concretely. Nevertheless, they stand for general areas of application in which many usages are possible.

Scenario A: Keeping Track of Web User Opinions. Understanding the market situation by analyzing customer behavior has been the key motivation behind the development of Data Mining techniques such a s the Apriori algorithm [Agrawal and Srikant, 1994]. The increasing presence of product reviews in blogs and specialized portals and the large volume of product-related news articles has given rise to research on the analysis of textual sources for market analysis. One popular instance is the task of *sentiment analysis* that aims at assessing the authors' attitude towards individual aspects of a product. Sentiment analysis is typically done by means of text classification with a specialized choice of text sources and features [Pang et al., 2002]. Monitoring the entire Web by these means however is not possible. Almost everybody interested in the market standing of a given product will today take an approach like the one suggested by Jarvis: querying Google for `"ABC sucks"` when interested in the situation of the product "ABC" [Jarvis, 2009]. Jarvis argues for the economic importance of constantly monitoring customer opinions on the Web. The techniques presented in this thesis allow to automate such an analysis in two ways: Not only can the querying and interpretation of query results be automated, pattern induction can also be used to generate the most salient queries for the task at hand.

Scenario B: Missing Links in Linked Data. The Linked Data initiative [Bizer et al., 2009] recently bundles efforts of many parties to publish data of various kinds so that it can easily be combined for new tasks. Key ingredients of linked data are an interoperable data format and unique identification of entities of discourse. As an example a travel information system which is based on linked data may provide its users with information about their destination which was integrated from various sources. Existing repositories provide the geographic location (e.g. GeoNames), nearby attractions and famous residents (e.g. DBPedia) web services such as those from Yahoo! Inc. provide weather and news events. However, other information such as leisure activities and local events may only be available in textual form on various web pages. To integrate them, the system can resort to textual patterns that have been induced during portal setup and are posed after having been augmented by the information provided in the linked data repository. The system thus makes use of the explicit nature of textual patterns by using them to retrieve on-demand information on a specific entity.

Scenario C: Collective Authoring. The application described in Chapter 11 can serve as an example for a further range of applications in which human users and IE systems develop a structured knowledge resource. When applied to Wikipedia, such structured knowledge can be used to facilitate both editing and browsing. In terms of browsing, faceted search and search by means of natural language questions would be beneficial extensions. Editing could be improved by consistency checks and additional possibilities to integrate knowledge from other pages into a new page (cf. [Krötzsch et al., 2007]). By the methods presented in Chapter 11, Wikipedia can be extended in an unobstructive manner. Users would annotate hyperlinks freely within the usual wiki setup. The IE system aggregates tags and acts in the background when sufficient information becomes available. Feedback and further annotations can be collected as users answer questions or edit wiki pages. With the help of additional ML methods, the recognition of relevant relations and the mapping of tags to relations can partially be automated.

13.2 Advancing IE Methods

The results presented in Chapter 9 show that patterns that capture additional information about the matched text sequences (types of wildcard in our study) improve both precision and recall. Future research in IE has to ensure that as much relevant information about mentions of target relation instances as possible is captured. Many different *structural aspects of textual mentions* contribute to conveying meaning. In addition to the text's surface form, various forms of grammatical structures can play a role as well as terminological knowledge which can be formalized by arranging terms in structures (e.g. ontologies). Finally non-textual structures like page layout (e.g. adjacency in tables) and document organization (e.g. hyperlinks and category systems) convey meaning. Although approaches in which selected aspects are integrated exist (e.g. document structure [Wu and Weld, 2007] and ontologies [Culotta et al., 2006]), the integration of arbitrary structured features constitutes still an open issue. Such research would require the identification of appropriate representation structures as well as the adaptation of Machine Learning and Data Mining methods to the corresponding structure.

A further line of research is the *elimination of the borders between pattern-based and statistical methods* in IE. There have been few works in which pattern matches have been treated as features [Etzioni et al., 2005; Snow et al., 2004]. In these studies, instances were described by the set of patterns that were matched in order to obtain them. Following this idea, the steps of pattern and instance evaluation can be viewed as a classification or regression problem to which pattern-instance co-occurrences serve as features. Patterns are more salient than typical classification (e.g. word presence) and can be obtained efficiently. Statistical classification could overcome the limitations of their usual interpretation as conjunction of Boolean constraints.

Finally, we expect a – once again – increasing amount of interaction of IE research with research on *linguistic formalisms* as well as *formal logics*. Most recent research on Information Extraction has focused on scalable processing of large text corpora and therefore omitted cost-intensive in-depth analysis of the textual input. Although there exist automatic methods for the translation of natural language text into rich linguistic formalisms as well as inferencing tools which operate on formalized knowledge, their application at a large scale has not yet been possible. However, recent promising studies used techniques from uncertain logical inferencing for IE [Suchanek et al., 2009] and transferred large amounts of text into rich abstract linguistic descriptions [Curran et al., 2007].

Appendix

Appendix A: Taxonomy used in Chapter 9

The reduced taxonomy as used in the experiments in Chapter 9. Concepts with prefix "E." are defined by WSJ tags, a "POS." prefix indicates definition by part-of-speech all other concepts stem from WordNet supersenses.

- noun
  - noun.artifact
  - noun.body
  - noun.food
  - noun.substance
  - noun.object
  - noun.act
  - noun.cognition
  - noun.communication
  - noun.event
  - noun.process
  - noun.quantity
  - noun.time
  - noun.attribute
  - noun.feeling
  - noun.motive
  - noun.phenomenon
  - noun.relation
  - noun.shape
  - noun.state
  - noun.animal
  - noun.person
  - noun.plant
  - E.PRODUCT.OTHER
  - E.PRODUCT.DRUG
  - E.PRODUCT.FOOD
  - E.PRODUCT.OTHER
  - E.PRODUCT.VEHICLE
  - E.PRODUCT.WEAPON
  - E.PRODUCT.DESC.OTHER
  - E.PRODUCT.DESC.VEHICLE
  - E.PRODUCT.DESC.WEAPON
  - noun.group
    - E.ORG.CITY
    - E.ORG.CORPORATION
    - E.ORG.EDUCATIONAL
    - E.ORG.GOVERNMENT
    - E.ORG.HOSPITAL
    - E.ORG.HOTEL
    - E.ORG.MUSEUM
    - E.ORG.OTHER
    - E.ORG.POLITICAL
    - E.ORG.RELIGIOUS
    - E.ORG.STATE.PROVINCE
    - E.ORG.DESC.CORPORATION
    - E.ORG.DESC.EDUCATIONAL
    - E.ORG.DESC.GOVERNMENT
    - E.ORG.DESC.HOSPITAL
    - E.ORG.DESC.HOTEL
    - E.ORG.DESC.MUSEUM
    - E.ORG.DESC.OTHER
    - E.ORG.DESC.POLITICAL
  - noun.location
    - E.LOCATION.BORDER
    - E.LOCATION.CITY

E.LOCATION.CONTINENT
E.LOCATION.OTHER
E.LOCATION.REGION
E.LOCATION.RIVER
E.GPE.COUNTRY
E.CONTACT.INFO.ADDRESS
E.CONTACT.INFO.OTHER
E.CONTACT.INFO.PHONE
E.FAC.AIRPORT
E.FAC.ATTRACTION
E.FAC.BRIDGE
E.FAC.BUILDING
E.FAC.HIGHWAY.STREET
E.FAC.OTHER
E.FAC.DESC.AIRPORT
E.FAC.DESC.ATTRACTION
E.FAC.DESC.BRIDGE
E.FAC.DESC.BUILDING
E.FAC.DESC.OTHER
E.FAC.DESC.HIGHWAY
E.GAME
E.LANGUAGE
E.LAW
E.EVENT.HURRICANE
E.EVENT.OTHER
E.EVENT.WAR
E.DISEASE
E.WORK.OF.ART.BOOK
E.WORK.OF.ART.OTHER
E.WORK.OF.ART.PAINTING
E.WORK.OF.ART.PLAY
E.WORK.OF.ART.SONG
verb
verb.consumption
verb.possession
verb.weather
verb.body
verb.competition
verb.contact
verb.social
verb.cognition
verb.communication
verb.emotion
verb.perception
verb.change
verb.creation
verb.motion
verb.stative
POS.MD
adjective
adj.all
POS.JJR
POS.JJS
E.NORP.NATIONALITY
E.NORP.OTHER
E.NORP.POLITICAL
E.NORP.RELIGION
adverb
POS.WRB
POS.RB
POS.RBR
POS.RBS
pronoun
POS.WP
POS.WPD
POS.PRP
other
POS.POS
POS.RP
POS.CC
POS.TO
POS.UH
POS.EX
POS.FW
POS.IN
nonword
NT.sentence.delimiter
NT.quote
POS.CLOSEBRACK
POS.
POS.OPENBRACK
POS..

POS.DOLLAR
POS.SYM
POS.LS

Bibliography

Agichtein E, Gravano L (2000) Snowball: extracting relations from large plain-text collections In *DL '00: Proceedings of the fifth ACM Conference on Digital libraries*, pp. 85–94, New York, NY, USA. ACM.

Agrawal R, Srikant R (1994) Fast algorithms for mining association rules In *Proceedings of the 20th International Conference on Very Large Data Bases (VLDB)*, pp. 487–499. Morgan Kaufmann.

Agrawal R, Srikant R (1995) Mining sequential patterns In *Proceedings of the Eleventh International Conference on Data Engineering*, pp. 3–14.

Akamajian A, Deemers RA, Farmer AK, Harnish RM (1995) *Linguistics. An introduction to Langauge and Communication* MIT Press.

Alfonseca E, Ruiz-Casado M, Okumura M, Castells P (2006) Towards large-scale non-taxonomic relation extraction: Estimating the precision of rote extractors In *Proceedings of the 2nd Workshop on Ontology Learning and Population: Bridging the Gap between Text and Knowledge*. Association for Computational Linguistics.

Ashburner M, Ball CA, Blake JA, Botstein D, Butler H, Cherry JM, Davis AP, Dolinski K, Dwight SS, Eppig JT, Harris MA, Hill DP, Issel-Tarver L, Kasarskis A, Lewis S, Matese JC, Richardson JE, Ringwald M, Sherlock GMRG (2000) Gene ontology: tool for the unification of biology. *Nature Genetics* 25:25–29.

Auer S, Bizer C, Lehmann J, Kobilarov G, Cyganiak R, Ives Z (2007) Dbpedia: A nucleus for a web of open data In *Proceedings of the 6th International Semantic Web Conference (ISWC)*.

Auer S, Lehmann J (2007) What have innsbruck and leipzig in common? extracting semantics from wiki content In *Proceedings of the 4th European Conference on The Semantic Web (ESWC)*, pp. 503–517, Berlin, Heidelberg. Springer.

Baeza-Yates RA, Ribeiro-Neto BA (1999) *Modern Information Retrieval* ACM Press / Addison-Wesley.

Banko M, Cafarella MJ, Soderland S, Broadhead M, Etzioni O (2007) Open information extraction from the web. In Veloso MM, editor, *Proceedings of International Joint Conference on Artificial Intelligence (IJCAI)*, pp. 2670–2676. Morgan Kaufmann.

Banko M, Etzioni O (2008) The tradeoffs between open and traditional relation extraction In *Proceedings of the 46th Annual Meeting of the Association for Computational Linguistics: Human Language Technologies*, pp. 28–36, Columbus, Ohio. Association for Computational Linguistics.

Berners-Lee T, Hendler J, Lassila O (2001) The Semantic Web. *Scientific American* 284:34–43.

Bizer C, Heath T, Berners-Lee T (2009) Linked data – the story so far. *International Journal On Semantic Web and Information Systems* Special Issue on Linked Data.

Bloehdorn S (2008) Kernel Methods for Knowledge Structures Ph.D. diss., Universität Karlsruhe (TH), Institut AIFB, D-76128 Karlsruhe.

Bloehdorn S, Blohm S (2006) A self organizing map for relation extraction from wikipedia using structured data representations International Workshop on Intelligent Information Access (IIIA-2006), Helsinki, Finland, July 6-8, 2006.

Blohm S, Cimiano P (2007) Using the web to reduce data sparseness in pattern-based informatin extraction In *Proceedings of the 11th European Conference on Principles and Practice of Knowledge Discovery in Databases (PKDD)*, pp. 18–29. Springer.

Blohm S, Cimiano P, Stemle E (2007) Harvesting relations from the web - quantifiying the impact of filtering functions In *Proceedings of the 22nd Conference on Artificial Intelligence (AAAI)*, pp. 1316–1323. AAAI Press.

Blohm S (2005) Exploiting organizational information in enterprise text search Master's thesis, Universität des Saarlandes, Universität des Saarlandes, Postfach 151150, D-66041 Saarbrücken.

Blohm S, Brefeld U, Jungermann F, Yangarber R, editors (2008) *Proceedings of the ECML PKDD Workshop on High-level Information Extraction.*

Blohm S, Cimiano P (2007) A human evaluation of filtering functions for pattern-based extraction of arbitrary relations from the web In *Building and Exploring Web Corpora. Proceedings of the 3rd Web as Corpus Workshop*, pp. 17–32. Presses Universitaires de Louvain.

Blohm S, Cimiano P (2008) Scaling up pattern induction for web relation extraction through frequent itemset mining In Adrian B, Neumann G, Troussov A, Popov B, editors, *Proceedings of the KI 2008 Workshop on Ontology-Based Information Extraction Systems.*

Blohm S, Krötzsch M, Cimiano P (2008) The fast and the numerous – combining machine and community intelligence In *Proceedings of the AAAI 2008 Workshop on Wikipedia and Artifical Intelligence*, Vol. Technical Report WS-08-15. AAAI Press.

Borgelt C, Kruse R (2002) Induction of association rules: A priori implementation In *Proceedings of the 15th Conference on Computational Statistics*, pp. 395–400. Physica Verlag.

Boser BE, Guyon IM, Vapnik VN (1992) A training algorithm for optimal margin classifiers In Haussler D, editor, *Proceedings of the 5th Annual Workshop on Computational Learning Theory (COLT '92), July 27-29, 1992, Pittsburgh, PA, USA*, pp. 144–152. ACM Press, New York, NY, USA.

Brin S (1999) Extracting patterns and relations from the world wide web In *Selected papers from the International Workshop on The World Wide Web and Databases (WebDB)*, pp. 172–183, Londonand UK. Springer-Verlag.

Bunescu R, Mooney R (2006) Subsequence kernels for relation extraction In *Advances in Neural Information Processing Systems 18*, pp. 171–178.

Buza K, Schmidt-Thieme L (2008) Motif-based classification of time series with bayesian networks and SVMs In *Proceedings of the Annual Conference of the Gesellschaft für Klassifikation (GfKl)*. Springer.

Cafarella MJ, Downey D, Soderland S, Etzioni O (2005) Knowitnow: Fast, scalable information extraction from the web In *Proceedings of the Human Language Technology Conference and Conference on Empirical Methods in Natural Language Processing*, pp. 563–570, Morristown, NJ, USA. Association for Computational Linguistics.

Califf M, Mooney R (1997) Relational learning of pattern match rules for information extraction In *Proceedings of the ACL Workshop on Natural Language Learning*, pp. 9–15. Association for Computational Linguistics.

Cardie C, Isabelle P, editors (2006) *ACL 2006, 21st International Conference on Computational Linguistics and 44th Annual Meeting of the Association for Computational Linguistics, Proceedings of the Conference, Sydney, Australia, 17-21 July 2006*. Association for Computer Linguistics.

Carroll J, Zaenen A, van den Bosch A, editors (2007) *ACL 2007, Proceedings of the 45th Annual Meeting of the Association for Computational Linguistics, June 23-30, 2007, Prague, Czech Republic*. Association for Computer Linguistics.

Chakrabarti S (2002) *Mining the Web: Discovering Knowledge from Hypertext Data* Morgan-Kauffman.

Chen J, Ji D, Tan CL, Niu Z (2006) Relation extraction using label propagation based semi-supervised learning In *Proceedings of the 21st International Conference on Computational Linguistics (COLING) and the 44th Annual Meeting of the Association for Computational Linguistics (ACL)*, pp. 129–136. Association for Computational Linguistics.

Ciaramita M, Altun Y (2006) Broad-coverage sense disambiguation and information extraction with a supersense sequence tagger. In *Proceedings of the 2006 Conference on Empirical Methods in Natural Language Processing (EMNLP)*, pp. 594–602, Morristown, NJ, USA. Association for Computational Linguistics.

Cimiano P (2006) Ontology Learning and Population from Text Ph.D. diss., Universität Karlsruhe (TH), Institut AIFB, D-76128 Karlsruhe.

Cimiano P, Handschuh S, Staab S (2004) Towards the self-annotating web In *Proceedings of the 13th International Conference on World Wide Web (WWW)*, pp. 462–471. ACM, New York.

Cimiano P, Staab S (2004) Learning by googling. *SIGKDD Explorations Newsletter* 6:24–33.

Ciravegna F (2001) Adaptive information extraction from text by rule induction and generalisation. In Nebel B, editor, *Proceedings of the International Joint Conference on Artificial Intelligence (IJCAI)*, pp. 1251–1256. Morgan Kaufmann.

Commission of the European Communities (1999) Regulation (EEC) no 4064/89 merger procedure Case No COMP/M.1406 -HYUNDAI / KIA http://ec.europa.eu/competition/mergers/cases/decisions/m1406_en.pdf.

Converse T, Kaplan R, Pell B, Revost S, Thione L, Walters C (2008) Demo: A natural language search engine for wikipedia In *Proceedings of the AAAI 2008 Workshop on Wikipedia and Artifical Intelligence*, Vol. Technical Report WS-08-15. AAAI Press.

Culotta A, Sorensen J (2004) Dependency tree kernels for relation extraction In *Proceedings of the 42nd Meeting of the Association for Computational Linguistics (ACL)*, pp. 423–429.

Culotta A, McCallum A, Betz J (2006) Integrating probabilistic extraction models and data mining to discover relations and patterns in text. In Moore RC, Bilmes JA, Chu-Carroll J, Sanderson M, editors, *Proceedings of the Main Conference on Human Language Technology Conference of the North American Chapter of the Association of Computational Linguistics*, pp. 296–303. The Association for Computational Linguistics.

Cunningham H (2005) Information Extraction, Automatic. *Encyclopedia of Language and Linguistics, 2nd Edition* .

Cunningham H, Maynard D, Bontcheva K, Tablan V (2002) GATE: A framework and graphical development environment for robust NLP tools and applications In *Proceedings of the 40th Anniversary Meeting of the Association for Computational Linguistics*.

Curran JR, Clark S, Bos J (2007) Linguistically motivated large-scale NLP with C&C and boxer In *Proceedings of the 45th Annual Meeting of the ACL on Interactive Poster and Demonstration Sessions (ACL)*, pp. 33–36, Morristown, NJ, USA. Association for Computational Linguistics.

Dadzie AS, Bhagdev R, Chakravarthy A, Chapman S, Iria J, Lanfranchi V, Magalhaes J, Petrelli D, Ciravegna F (2008) Applying semantic web technologies to knowledge sharing in aerospace engineering. *Journal of Intelligent Manufacturing* pp. 611–623.

Davidov D, Rappoport A, Koppel M (2007) Fully unsupervised discovery of concept-specific relationships by web mining In *Proceedings of the 45th Annual Meeting of the Association for Computational Linguistics*, pp. 232–239. Association for Computational Linguistics.

Dean J, Ghemawat S (2008) Mapreduce: simplified data processing on large clusters. *Communications of the ACM* 51:107–113.

Downey D, Etzioni O, Soderland S, Weld D (2004) Learning text patterns for web information extraction and assessment In *Proceedings of the AAAI Workshop on Adaptive Text Extraction and Mining*. AAAI Press.

Downey D, Etzioni O (2008) Look ma, no hands: Analyzing the monotonic feature abstraction for text classification. In Koller D, Schuurmans D, Bengio Y, Bottou L, editors, *Twenty-Second Annual Conference on Neural Information Processing Systems (NIPS)*, pp. 393–400. MIT Press.

Downey D, Etzioni O, Soderland S (2005) A probabilistic model of redundancy in information extraction In *Proceedings of the International Joint Conference on Artificial Intelligence (IJCAI)*, pp. 1034–1042. Morgan Kaufmann.

Duda RO, Hart PE, Stork DG (2001) *Pattern Classification* John Wiley & Sons, Inc.

Dzbor M, Domingue J, Motta E (2003) Magpie – towards a semantic web browser In *Proceedings of the 2nd International Semantic Web Conference (ISWC)*, Vol. 2870 of *Lecture notes in computer science*, pp. 690–705, Sanibel Island (FL US). Springer.

Embley D, Campbell D, Smith R, Liddle S (1998) Ontology-based extraction and structuring of information from data-rich unstructured documents In *Proceedings of the 7th International Conference on Information and Knowledge Management*, pp. 52 – 59, Bethesda, MD. ACM.

Etzioni O, Cafarella M, Downey D, Popescu AM, Shaked T, Soderland S, Weld D, Yates A (2005) Unsupervised named-entity extraction from the web: an experimental study. *Artificial Intelligence* 165:91–134.

Fagin R, Kumar R, McCurley KS, Novak J, Sivakumar D, Tomlin JA, Williamson DP (2003) Searching the workplace web In *Proceedings of the 12th International Conference on World Wide Web (WWW)*, pp. 366–375. ACM Press.

Ferrucci D, Lally A (2004) UIMA: An Architectural Approach Unstructured Information Processing in the Corporate Research Environment. *Journal of Natural Language Engineering* 10:327–348.

Freitag D (1998) Machine Learning for Information Extraction in Informal Domains Ph.D. diss., Carnegie Mellon University.

Giles CL, Bollacker KD, Lawrence S (1998) Citeseer: an automatic citation indexing system In *DL '98: Proceedings of the third ACM Conference on Digital libraries*, pp. 89–98, New York, NY, USA. ACM.

Giuliano C, Lavelli A, Romano L (2007) Relation extraction and the influence of automatic named-entity recognition. *ACM Transactions on Speech and Language Processing* 5:2:1–2:26.

Grishman R, Sundheim B (1996) Message understanding conference - 6: A brief history In *The 16th International Conference on Computational Linguistics*. Association for Computational Linguistics.

Hahn U, Buyko E, Tomanek K, Piao S, McNaught J, Tsuruoka Y, Ananiadou S (2007) An annotation type system for a data-driven NLP pipeline In *Proceedings of the Linguistic Annotation Workshop*, pp. 33–40, Prague, Czech Republic. Association for Computational Linguistics.

Han J, J.Pei, Yin Y, Mao R (2004) Mining frequent patterns without candidate generation. *Data Mining and Knowledge Discovery* 8:53–87.

Handschuh S, Staab S (2003) CREAM - creating metadata for the semantic web. *Computer Networks* pp. 579–598.

Hearst MA (1992) Automatic acquisition of hyponyms from large text corpora In *Proceedings of the 14th Conference on Computational Linguistics-Volume 2*. Association for Computational Linguistics.

Hendler J, Golbeck J (2008) metcalfe's law applies to web 2.0 and the semantic web. *Journal of Web Semantics* .

Hirschman L, Colosimo M, Morgan A, Yeh A (2005) Overview of BioCreAtIvE task 1B: normalized gene lists. *BMC Bioinformatics.* 6:S11.

Hitzler P, Krötzsch M, Rudolph S (2009) *Foundations of Semantic Web Technologies* Chapman & Hall/CRC.

Hofmann-Apitius M, Fluck J, Furlong L, Fornes O, Kolark C, Hanser S, Boeker M, Schulz S, Sanz F, Klinger R, Mevissen T, Gattermayer T, Oliva B, Friedrich CM (2008) Knowledge environments representing molecular entities for the virtual physiological human. *Philosophical Transactions of the Royal Society* 366:3091–3110.

Hotho A, Jäschke R, Schmitz C, Stumme G (2006) BibSonomy: A social bookmark and publication sharing system In *Proceedings of the Conceptual Structures Tool Interoperability Workshop at the 14th International Conference on Conceptual Structures*, pp. 87–102. Aalborg University Press.

Iria J, Brewster C, Ciravegna F, Wilks Y (2006) An incremental tri-partite approach to ontology learning In *Proceedings of the 5th edition of the International Conference on Language Resources and Evaluation (LREC)*, pp. 197–202. European Language Resources Association (ELRA).

Iria J, Uren V, Lavelli A, Blohm S, Dadzie AS, Franz T, Kompatsiaris Y, Magalhaes J, Nikolopoulos S, Preisach C, Slavazza P (2007) Enhancing enterprise knowledge processes via cross-media extraction In *Proceedings of the Fourth International Conference on Knowledge Capture Poster Session (K-CAP)*, pp. 175–176. ACM.

Iria J, Xia L, Lavelli A, Romano L, Giuliano C, Blohm S (2009) Report on the final library of ie from text technologies. deliverable 5.7 Technical report, X-Media Consortium. The University of Sheffield.

Jarvis J (2009) *What Would Google Do?* HarperBusiness, New York.

Jindal N, Liu B (2006) Mining comparative sentences and relations In *Proceedings of the 21st Conference on Artificial Intelligence (AAAI-06)*. AAAI Press.

Jurafsky D, Martin J (2000) *Speech and Language Processing: An Introduction to Natural Language Processing, Computational Linguistics and Speech* Prentice-Hall, NJ, USA.

Kahan J, Koivunen MR (2001) Annotea: an open RDF infrastructure for shared web annotations In *Proceedings of the 10th International World Wide Web Conference*, pp. 623–632. ACM Press.

Kaufman L, Rousseeuw P (1990) *Finding Groups in Data An Introduction to Cluster Analysis* John Wiley and & Sons, Inc., New York.

Kilgariff A, Grefenstette G, editors (2003) *Special Issue on the Web as a Corpus*, Vol. 29 of *Journal of Computational Linguistics* MIT Press.

Klimt B, Yang Y (2004) The enron corpus: A new dataset for email classification research. In *Proceedings of the European Conference on Machine Learning (ECML) and the 8th European Conference on Principles and Practice of Knowledge Discovery in Databases (PKDD)*, pp. 217–226.

Kobilarov G, Scott T, Raimond Y, Oliver S, Sizemore C, Smethurst M, Bizer C, Lee R (2009) Media meets semantic web - how the BBC uses dbpedia and linked data to make connections. In Aroyo L, Traverso P, Ciravegna F, Cimiano P, Heath T, Hyvönen E, Mizoguchi R, Oren E, Sabou M, Simperl EPB, editors, *Proceedings of the 6th European Conference on The Semantic Web (ESWC)*, Vol. 5554 of *Lecture Notes in Computer Science*, pp. 723–737. Springer.

Kohonen T, editor (1997) *Self-organizing maps* Springer-Verlag New York, Inc., Secaucus, NJ, USA.

Kohonen T, Kaski S, Lagus K, Salojarvi J, Paatero V, Saarela A (2000) Self organization of a massive document collection. *IEEE Transactions on Neural Networks* 11:574–585.

Kok JN, Koronacki J, de Mántaras RL, Matwin S, Mladenic D, Skowron A, editors (2007) *Knowledge Discovery in Databases: PKDD 2007, 11th European*

Conference on Principles and Practice of Knowledge Discovery in Databases, Warsaw, Poland, September 17-21, 2007, Proceedings, Vol. 4702 of *Lecture Notes in Computer Science*. Springer.

Kononenko IK M (2007) *Machine learning and data mining : Introduction to principles and algorithms* Horwood Publ., Chichester, 1. publ. edition.

Krötzsch M, Vrandecic D, Völkel M, Haller H, Studer R (2007) Semantic wikipedia. *Journal of Web Semantics* 5:251–261.

Lafferty J, McCallum A, Pereira F (2001) Conditional random fields: Probabilistic models for segmenting and labeling sequence data In *Proceedings of the 18th International Conference on Machine Learning (ICML)*, pp. 282–289. Morgan Kaufmann.

Lavelli A, Califf ME, Ciravegna F, Freitag D, Giuliano C, Kuschmerick N, Romano L, Ireson N (2008) Evaluation of machine learning-based information extraction algorithms: criticisms and recommendations. *Language Resources & Evaluation* 42:361–393.

Li Y, Liu B, Sarawagi S, editors (2008) *Proceedings of the 14th ACM SIGKDD International Conference on Knowledge Discovery and Data Mining, Las Vegas, Nevada, USA, August 24-27, 2008*. ACM.

Li Y, Krishnamurthy R, Raghavan S, Vaithyanathan S, Jagadish HV (2008) Regular expression learning for information extraction. In *2008 Conference on Empirical Methods in Natural Language Processing, EMNLP 2008, Proceedings of the Conference*, pp. 21–30. Association for Computational Linguistics.

Liu B (2007) *Web Data Mining* Springer-Verlag Berlin Heidelberg.

Luke S, Spector L, Rager D, Handler J (1997) Ontology-based web agents In *Proceedings of the First International Conference on Autonomous Agents (Agents'97)*, pp. 59–68. ACM Press.

Mädche A, Staab S (2004) Ontology learning In Staab S, Studer R, editors, *Handbook on Ontologies*, International Handbooks on Information Systems, pp. 173–190. Springer.

Mannila H, Toivonen H, Verkamo A (1994) Efficient algorithms for discovering association rules In *AAAI Workshop on Knowledge Discovery in Databases (KDD-94)*, pp. 181–192. AAAI Press.

Manning CD, Schütze H (1999) *Foundations of Statistical Natural Language Processing* MIT Press, Cambridge, MA.

Marcus M, Marcinkiewicz M, Santorini B (1993) Building a large annotated corpus of english: the penn treebank. *Computational Linguistics* 19:313–330.

Marlow C, Naaman M, Boyd D, Davis M (2006) Ht06, tagging paper, taxonomy, Flickr, academic article, to read In *Proceedings of the seventeenth Conference on Hypertext and Hypermedia (HYPERTEXT'06)*, pp. 31–40, New York, NY, USA. ACM.

McCallum A, Li W (2003) Early results for named entity recognition with conditional random fields, feature induction and web-enhanced lexicons In *Proceedings of the Seventh Conference on Natural Language Learning at HLT-NAACL 2003*, pp. 188–191, Morristown, NJ, USA. Association for Computational Linguistics.

McCallum AK (2002) MALLET: a machine learning for language toolkit http://mallet.cs.umass.edu.

McDowell LK, Cafarella M (2008) Ontology-driven, unsupervised instance population. *Journal of Web Semantics* 6:218–236.

McIntosh T, Curran JR (2009) Reducing semantic drift with bagging and distributional similarity In *Proceedings of the Joint Conference of the 47th Annual Meeting of the Association for Computational Linguistics and the 4th International Joint Conference on Natural Language Processing of the Asian Federation of Natural Language Processing*, pp. 396–404. Association for Computational Linguistics.

Mika P, Ciaramita M, Zaragoza H, Atserias J (2008) Learning to tag and tagging to learn: A case studiy on wikipedia In *IEEE Intelligent Systems*, Vol. 23, pp. 26–33. IEEE.

Miller G (1995) Wordnet: A lexical database for english. *Communications of the ACM* 38:39–41.

Mitchell TM (1997) *Machine learning* McGraw-Hill Series in Computer ScienceMcGraw-Hill international editions. McGraw-Hill, New York [u.a.], internat. ed. edition.

Moench E, Ullrich M, Schnurr HP, Angele J (2003) Semanticminer — ontology-based knowledge retrieval. *Journal of Universal Computer Science* 9:682–696.

Mooney RJ, Brew C, Chien LF, Kirchhoff K, editors (2005) *HLT/EMNLP 2005, Human Language Technology Conference and Conference on Empirical Methods in Natural Language Processing, Proceedings of the Conference, 6-8 Octo-*

ber 2005, Vancouver, British Columbia, Canada. Association for Computational Linguistics.

Mueller A (1995) Fast sequential and parallel algorithms for association rule mining: a comparison Technical report, University of Maryland at College Park, College Park, MD, USA.

Muggleton S, Feng C (1990) Efficient induction of logic programs In *Proceedings of the 1st Conference on Algorithmic Learning Theory*, pp. 368–381. Ohmsma, Tokyo, Japan.

Nadeau D, Sekine S (2007) A survey of named entity recognition and classification. *Linguisticae Investigationes* 30:3—26.

Netzel R, Perez-Iratxeta C, Bork P, Andrade MA (2003) The way we write. *EMBO Reports* 4:446–451.

NIST (2008) Automatic content extraction 2008 evaluation plan (ACE08) http://www.itl.nist.gov/iad/mig//tests/ace/2008/doc/ace08-evalplan.v1.2d.pdf.

Normand E, Grant K, Ioup E, Sample J (2009) Proceedings of the 21st international conference on scientific and statistical database management (ssdbm) In Winslett M, editor, *SSDBM*, Vol. 5566 of *Lecture Notes in Computer Science*, pp. 553–561. Springer.

Ogden CK, Richards IA (1923) *The Meaning of Meaning: A Study of the Influence of Language upon Thought and of the Science of Symbolism* Magdalene College, University of Cambridge.

O'Reilly T (2009) What is web 2.0 – design patterns and business models for the next generation of software O'Reilly Media, Inc. http://oreilly.com/pub/a/web2/archive/what-is-web-20.html.

Page L, Brin S, Motwani R, Winograd T (1998) The pagerank citation ranking: Bringing order to the web Technical report, Stanford Digital Library Technologies Project.

Pang B, Lee L, Vaithyanathan S (2002) Thumbs up? Sentiment classification using machine learning techniques In *Proceedings of the 2002 Conference on Empirical Methods in Natural Language Processing (EMNLP)*, pp. 79–86. Association for Computational Linguistics.

Pantel P, Ravichandran D, Hovy EH (2004) Towards terascale knowledge acquisition In *Proceedings of the 20th International Conference on Computational Linguistics (COLING)*, pp. 771–777. Association for Computational Linguistics.

Pantel P, Pennacchiotti M (2006) Espresso: Leveraging generic patterns for automatically harvesting semantic relations In *Proceedings of the 21st International Conference on Computational Linguistics (COLING) and the 44th Annual Meeting of the Association for Computational Linguistics (ACL)*, pp. 113–120, Sydney, Australia. Association for Computational Linguistics.

Paşca M, Lin D, Bigham J, Lifchits A, Jain A (2006) Names and similarities on the Web: Fact extraction in the fast lane In *Proceedings of the 21st International Conference on Computational Linguistics and 44th Annual Meeting of the ACL*, pp. 809–816, Sydney, Australia. Association for Computational Linguistics.

Pentney W, Philipose M, Bilmes JA, Kautz HA (2007) Learning large scale common sense models of everyday life In *Proceedings of the Twenty-Second AAAI Conference on Artificial Intelligence (AAAI)*, pp. 465–470.

Rau LF (1991) Extracting company names from text. In *Proceedings of the Conference on Artificial Intelligence*. IEEE.

Ravichandran D (2005) Terascale Knowledge Acquisition Ph.D. diss., University of Southern California.

Ravichandran D, Hovy E (2001) Learning surface text patterns for a question answering system In *Proceedings of the 40th Annual Meeting of the Association for Computational Linguistics (ACL)*, pp. 41–47, Morristown, NJ, USA. Association for Computational Linguistics.

Reiss F, Raghavan S, Krishnamurthy R, Zhu H, Vaithyanathan S (2008) An algebraic approach to rule-based information extraction. In *Proceedings of the 24th IEEE International Conference on Data Engineering (ICDE)*, pp. 933–942. IEEE.

Riloff E, Jones R (1999) Learning dictionaries for information extraction by multi-level bootstrapping In *AAAI '99/IAAI '99: Proceedings of the Sixteenth National Conference on Artificial Intelligence and the Eleventh Innovative Applications of Artificial Intelligence Conference innovative applications of artificial intelligence*, pp. 474–479, Menlo Park, CA, USA. American Association for Artificial Intelligence.

Rosenfeld B, Feldman R (2006) URES : an unsupervised web relation extraction system. In *Proceedings of the COLING/ACL 2006 Main Conference Poster Sessions*, Morristown, NJ, USA. Association for Computational Linguistics.

Rozenfeld B, Feldman R (2006) High-performance unsupervised relation extraction from large corpora In *Proceedings of the Sixth IEEE International Conference on Data Mining (ICDM)*, pp. 1032–1037.

Rozenfeld B, Feldman R (2008) Self-supervised relation extraction from the web. *Knowledge and Information Systems* 17:17–33.

Ruiz-Casado M, Alfonseca E, Castells P (2005) Automatic extraction of semantic relationships for wordnet by means of pattern learning from wikipedia In *Proceedings of the 10th International Conference on Applications of Natural Language to Information Systems (NLDB)*, pp. 67–79. Springer, Berlin / Heidelberg.

Sarawagi S (2008) Information extraction. *Foundations and Trends in Databases* 1:261–377.

Saric J, Jensen L, Ouzounova R, Rojas I, Bork P (2004) Extraction of regulatory gene expression networks from PubMed In *Proceedings of the Annual Meeting of the Association for Computational Linguistics (ACL)*, pp. 191–198. Association for Computational Linguistics.

Schmidt-Thieme L (2007) Assoziationsregel-Algorithmen für Daten mit komplexer Struktur Ph.D. diss., Universität Karlsruhe (TH), D-76128 Karlsruhe.

Siorpaes K, Hepp M (2008) Games with a purpose for the semantic web. *IEEE Intelligent Systems* 23:50–60.

Smith B, Ashburner M, Rosse C, Bard J, Bug W, Ceusters W, Goldberg LJ, Eilbeck K, Ireland A, Mungall CJ, Leontis N, Rocca-Serra P, Ruttenberg A, Sansone SA, Scheuermann RH, Shah N, Whetzel PL, Lewis S (2007) The OBO foundry: coordinated evolution of ontologies to support biomedical data integration. *Nature Biotech* 25:1251–1255.

Snow R, Jurafsky D, Ng AY (2004) Learning syntactic patterns for automatic hypernym discovery In Saul LK, Weiss Y, Bottou L, editors, *Advances in Neural Information Processing Systems NIPS 17*, pp. 1297–1304, Cambridge, MA. MIT Press.

Soderland S, Cardie C, Mooney R (1999) Learning information extraction rules for semi-structured and free text. *Machine Learning* 34:233–272.

Sowa J (2000) *Knowledge Representation: Logical, Philosophical and Computational Foundations* Brooks/Cole.

Srikant R, Agrawal R (1997) Mining generalized association rules. *Future Generation Computer Systems* 13:161–180.

Steinbach M, Karypis G, Kumar V (2000) A comparison of document clustering techniques In *KDD Workshop on Text Mining*.

Strickert M, Hammer B, Blohm S (2005) Unsupervised recursive sequence processing. *Neurocomputing* 63:69–97.

Studer R, Benjamins R, Fensel D (1998) Knowledge engineering: Principles and methods. *Data and Knowledge Engineering* 25:161–198.

Suchanek FM, Ifrim G, Weikum G (2006) LEILA: Learning to extract information by linguistic analysis In *Proceedings of the 2nd Workshop on Ontology Learning and Population: Bridging the Gap between Text and Knowledge*, pp. 18–25, Sydney, Australia. Association for Computational Linguistics.

Suchanek FM, Kasneci G, Weikum G (2007) Yago: A Core of Semantic Knowledge In *Proceedings of the 16th International Conference on World Wide Web (WWW)*, pp. 697 – 706. ACM Press.

Suchanek FM, Kasneci G, Weikum G (2008) YAGO: A Large Ontology from Wikipedia and WordNet. *Elsevier Journal of Web Semantics* .

Suchanek FM, Sozio M, Weikum G (2009) SOFIE: a self-organizing framework for information extraction. In Quemada J, León G, Maarek YS, Nejdl W, editors, *Proceedings of the 18th International Conference on World Wide Web (WWW)*, pp. 631–640. ACM.

Sutton C, Mccallum A (2006) *Introduction to Conditional Random Fields for Relational Learning* MIT Press.

Talukdar PP, Brants T, Liberman M, Pereira F (2006) A context pattern induction method for named entity extraction In *Proceedings of the Tenth Conference on Computational Natural Language Learning (CoNLL-X)*, pp. 141–148. Association for Computational Linguistics.

Thompson C, Califf M, Mooney R (1999) Active learning for natural language parsing and information extraction In *Proc. 16th International Conf. on Machine Learning*, San Francisco, CA. Morgan Kaufmann.

Tomita J, Soderland S, Etzioni O (2006) Expanding the recall of relation extraction by bootstrapping In *Proceedings of the Workshop on Adaptive Text Extraction and Mining (ATEM 2006)*, pp. 56–63. Association for Computational Linguistics.

Umbrich J, Blohm S (2008) Exploring the knowledge in semi structured data sets with rich queries In *Proceedings of the SemSearch08 Workshop on Semantic Search at the ESWC 2008*, pp. 89–101, Teneriffa, Spain.

Vapnik VN (1995) *The Nature of Statistical Learning Theory* Springer New York Inc., New York, NY, USA.

Völkel M, Krötzsch M, Vrandecic D, Haller H, Studer R (2006) Semantic wikipedia In *Proceedings of the 15th International Conference on World Wide Web (WWW)*, pp. 585–594. ACM Press.

Völker J (2008) Learning Expressive Ontologies Ph.D. diss., Universität Karlsruhe (TH), Institut AIFB, D-76128 Karlsruhe.

von Ahn L, Dabbish L (2004) Labeling images with a computer game In *CHI '04: Proceedings of the SIGCHI Conference on Human factors in computing systems*, pp. 319–326, New York, NY, USA. ACM Press.

Wang G, Yu Y, Zhu H (2007) PORE: Positive-only relation extraction from wikipedia text In Aberer K, Choi KS, Noy N, Allemang D, Lee KI, Nixon LJB, Golbeck J, Mika P, Maynard D, Schreiber G, Mauroux PC, editors, *Proceedings of the 6th International Semantic Web Conference and 2nd Asian Semantic Web Conference (ISWC/ASWC2007), Busan, South Korea*, Vol. 4825 of *LNCS*, pp. 575–588, Berlin, Heidelberg. Springer Verlag.

Wikipedia Community (2009) Wikipedia: The perfect article http://en.wikipedia.org /w/index.php?title=Wikipedia:The_perfect_article&oldid=298222338.

Winston PH (1975) Learning structural descriptions from examples In Winston PH, editor, *The Psychology of Computer Vision*, New York. McGraw-Hill.

Wu F, Weld DS (2007) Autonomously semantifying wikipedia In *Proceedings of the Sixteeth International Conference on Information and Knowledge Management (CIKM)*, pp. 41–50. ACM Press.

Xu F, Uszkoreit H, Li H (2007) A seed-driven bottom-up machine learning framework for extracting relations of various complexity In *Proceedings of the 45th Annual Meeting of the Association for Computational Linguistics (ACL)*, pp. 584–591. Association for Computer Linguistics.

Yangarber R (2003) Acquisition of domain knowledge In *Lecture Notes in Computer Science*, Vol. 2700, pp. 1–28. Springer-Verlag Berlin.

Zaki M (2000) Scalable algorithms for association mining. *Knowledge and Data Engineering* 12:372–390.

Zaragoza H, Atserias J, Ciaramita M, Attardi G (2007) Semantically annotated snapshot of the english wikipedia v.1 http://www.yr-bcn.es/semanticWikipedia.

Zelenko D, Aone C, Richardella A (2003) Kernel methods for relation extraction. *Journal of Machine Learning Research* 3:1083–1106.